AN INTRODUCTION
TO THE
NEAR
EAST

AN INTRODUCTION TO THE

NEAR EAST

**Donald Magnetti, Ph.D.
and Mary Ann Sigler**

OUR SUNDAY VISITOR, INC.
Noll Plaza, Huntington, Indiana 46750

ISBN: 0-87973-851-0

Library of Congress Catalog Card Number: 73-86930

Cover design by James E. McIlrath

Photo credits: UNRWA, Myrtle Winter 65/ Arab Information Center 84/ Jobal Joufeh 106 and 107/ Kuwait Museum 115. Maps: New York Times 57 and 76.

Published, printed and bound in the U.S.A. by Our Sunday Visitor, Inc., Huntington, Indiana 46750

851

Contents

Introduction

The world of the twentieth century is what it is because of the peoples of the Near East. The course of development of Western thought, religion, and culture has been altered again and again by Near Eastern events and personalities. All too often, however, Westerners know little about the modern Near East and its problems. Erroneously, they think it is only a place of sand, oil, camels, and occasional armed conflicts. The pyramids of Egypt, the life of Jesus, and the efforts of the Crusaders are to many the only known events of the area's history. Frequently forgotten are the facts that we have our system of writing from the ancient Phoenicians, our religious heritage from the early Israelites, and much of our philosophy, medicine, and astronomy from the medieval Arabs. Few people know the background of the present Arab-Israeli conflict or of the relatively recent birth of Arab and Israeli nationalism. It is only a rare modern history textbook which includes more than very basic facts and references.

It is hoped that this study-guide will serve as a resource supplement to modern history courses. Naturally, space prevents complete details in many areas. The first chapter cursorily examines the ancient and medieval history of the Holy Land as an introduction to a more detailed consideration of the Arab-Israeli conflict. It is necessary to be acquainted with the background of this problem in order to appreciate the United Nations debates, the armed clashes, the incidents of terrorism, and all the charges and counter-charges. The historical survey is followed by profiles of the various Near Eastern countries. It should be noted that only the countries of the Near East proper have been considered in this chapter. Absent are profiles of the North African Arab nations of Algeria, Morocco, and Tunisia, as well as the non-Semitic countries of Iran and Turkey. To understand the Near East today, one must consider the development of the three monotheistic religions of the area: Judaism, Christianity, and Islam. Thus, the third chapter is devoted to this subject. Because most Western students know more about Christians and Jews than about Muslims, the life and times of the prophet Muhammad have been examined in depth. Muslim religious practices, theological controversies, and further developments have not been studied in this survey. For those interested, the bibliography offers more specific books in this area.

The authors wish to thank the following for information and help: the Arab Information Center, the Consulate General of Israel, the *New York Times* Map Department, and the Pontifical Mission for Palestine.

Donald L. Magnetti, Ph.D.

New York
August 15, 1973

CHAPTER I

Part 1

A Short History
of the Near East

Ancient Times to 1914

The Great Civilizations of the Ancient Middle East

Students of history will recognize the familiar references to the Middle East as the "Cradle of Civilization" and the "birthplace" of the three great monotheistic religions of man. Indeed, this area of the world has the longest known span of recorded history. Two of the greatest civilizations of ancient times emerged in the Middle East almost simultaneously: in Mesopotamia, the land region lying between the Tigris and Euphrates rivers, and in Egypt, along the Nile River valley, where records show a united kingdom existing as early as 3100 B.C. The legacies which these two great civilizations left to mankind are manifold.

The first people to figure prominently in the Mesopotamian civilization were the Sumerians who settled in the southern or lower Mesopotamian land area nearly three thousand years before the birth of Christ. It is not known from where the Sumerians originally came, but they are believed to have been a non-Semitic people who migrated to the area. They settled in the region north of the site of the present city of Basra, Iraq, and began to farm the rich alluvial soil brought to the area by the flooding of the Euphrates and Tigris rivers, which at that time probably met here and then continued as one until emptying into the Persian Gulf.

Though the area where the Sumerians settled had rich soil, it was marshy. These early settlers, therefore, developed an elaborate irrigation system of canals which was used both to drain the marshes and to store water for irrigation to be used during the dry winter months. The canals also helped control the flooding of the two rivers.

It is evident that in order to develop this complex system of irrigation, there had to be cooperation among the many small farming communities which had sprung up along the rivers. This cooperation formed the basis for some of the earliest governmental structures developed by the Mesopotamian civilization. Gradually, these agrarian communities grew and prospered, and by about 3000 B.C., they had been transformed into small city-states.

With this urbanization came the demand for consumer goods, and soon trading became a dominant part of the Sumerian way of life. And, as trading increased among the city-states, the need for a uniform method of record-keeping grew. Gradually, a pictorial system of writing developed which later evolved into what we now call cuneiform script. Out of this trade there also grew a simple yet effective system of mathematics based on the unit six. Our present use of the sixty second minute, twenty four hour day, and 360 degree circle all come from the ancient Sumerians.

While the Sumerian civilization was developing in Lower Mesopotamia, tribesmen of Semitic origin had migrated from the western arc of the Fertile Crescent to Upper and Central Mesopotamia. Though less advanced than the Sumerians, these nomadic peoples gradually settled into city-states similar to those in Lower Mesopotamia. In approximately 2400 B.C., one of the Semitic leaders, later known as Sargon I, managed to unite the city-states of Upper Mesopotamia. He then advanced into Lower Mesopotamia, conquered the Sumerians, and forced them to submit to his rule. There followed the gradual assimilation of the Sumerian and Semitic peoples.

Out of this conquest emerged the first unification of Mesopotamia which is now referred to as the Akkadian Empire. The Semites ruled the region for two centuries and then, in turn, were conquered by another Semitic tribe known as the Amorites who had been living in the region now known as Syria. The empire which developed under their rule was known as the Babylonian Empire, and it extended out of Mesopotamia northward into the area known as Assyria.

One of the most notable achievements of the Babylonian Empire was the codification of existing laws by the king, Hammurabi. As is the case where any governmental structures exist, laws had been established in the various city-states of Mesopotamia. About the middle of the seventeenth century B.C., Hammurabi, drawing on the various existing law codes, formulated one uniform legal code to be used throughout the Babylonian Empire. While many of the laws appear unjust by modern standards because of the harsh measures taken to punish lawbreakers, the Code of Hammurabi was an important step forward in man's development.

*   *   *

Unlike the Mesopotamian culture, which developed around city-states, the Egyptian civilization grew, almost from the very beginning, along the lines of a unified monarchical form of government. Because the land lying outside the Nile River valley is mostly uninhabitable desert, the Egyptians settled along the fertile banks of the Nile itself. About 3100 B.C., records show that a Southerner, Menes, managed to unify the many small kingdoms in the Nile Valley, and thus became the first king. He then built the city of Memphis, which for many centuries served as capital of the Egyptian Empire.

Under Menes and his successors, the Egyptians created a society which excelled in architecture as can be seen in the awesome pyramids dating back to 2900 B.C. The Egyptians also engaged in academic pursuits, and there is evidence that their interests ranged from science and technology to medicine and the fine arts. Like the Sumerians, they also developed a pictorial method of writing known as hieroglyphics which can be seen today on the remaining walls of their tombs and temples.

The Lesser Civilizations of the Ancient Middle East

In the region lying between the two great valley civilizations which now encompasses the modern states of Jordan, Israel, Lebanon, and Syria, there lived many semi-nomadic tribes. They engaged in almost continual warfare in an effort to acquire land upon which to graze their herds and raise crops. Egypt and Mesopotamia influenced the development of the area through military expansion and trade contacts.

To the north, in the area which is today known as Asia Minor, lived the powerful Hittites who dominated Anatolia and Syria from 1900 B.C. to 1200 B.C. They also defeated the first Babylonian Empire around 1600 B.C. and retained power there for some time.

Along the northeastern coast of the Mediterranean, in the area which is today Lebanon, lived the Phoenicians. They were a seafaring people who engaged in trading enterprises which carried them throughout the Mediterranean. The Phoenicians too developed a form of writing, and it is their alphabet which later served as the base upon which the Hebrew, Greek, and Roman alphabets were built.

Other tribes living in the region between the two major civilizations included the Canaanites who settled in the area known as Palestine, the Philistines who lived in the area of Gaza, the Ammonites who had settled to the east of the Jordan River, the Jebusites and Moabites who lived to the west and the east of the Dead Sea, respectively, and the Arameans who settled near the city of Damascus. The language of these last peoples, Aramaic, eventually became the everyday speech of Syria and Palestine.

The Hebrews were one of the most well-known of the smaller tribes of ancient times. Some of them had migrated to Egypt from the northern part of the Fertile Crescent. In the thirteenth century B.C., under their leader, Moses, they fled from Egypt after being subjected to the *courvet* or forced labor, imposed by Pharaoh Ramses II on all able-bodied males living in the Egyptian kingdom.

For months the Hebrews wandered in the Sinai Desert until at last they encamped at the foot of Mount Sinai. Here Moses experienced a supernatural revelation from their God who was to become known to them as Yahweh. Through Moses, a covenant, or agreement, was made between Yahweh and the Hebrews. The people would refrain from the worship of multiple gods and would respect with absolute fidelity a code of law given them by Yahweh. The Hebrews believed that their "Promised Land" lay along the Jordan River, so they migrated northward to that region to unite with their kinsmen who had settled there previously. The new arrivals brought with them the first monotheistic religion known to man: the cult of Yahweh.

Under the leadership of Moses' successor, Joshua, the people settled throughout ancient Palestine and engaged in warfare with various other tribes already living there. One by one the Hebrews defeated these peoples and then settled down to farm their newly acquired lands. For two hundred years, however, the twelve tribes were united only loosely under a type of tribal confederacy around a religious center, the town of Shechem. This disorganization left the Hebrew tribes exposed to almost constant attacks from enemies, and in approximately 1000 B.C., the twelve tribes agreed to unite as a kingdom.

The first Hebrew king was Saul, but it was under his successor, David, that true unification of the tribes took place. David united the tribes militarily and with his newly formed army managed to defeat the Philistines and to capture much of their land. The new kingdom needed a capital, which was outside any one tribe's territory, so David led his army against the Jebusites and captured one of their fort-like strongholds, Jerusalem. This city was surrounded by a thick wall and was situated on a

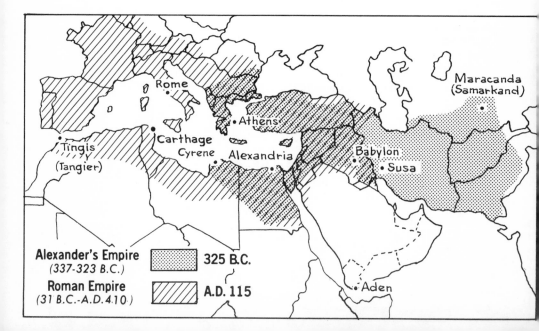

Alexander's Empire (337-323 B.C.)   [dotted] 325 B.C.
Roman Empire (31 B.C.-A.D. 410)   [hatched] A.D. 115

series of hills overlooking the countryside, thus making it easily defensible.

Under David's son, Solomon, a palace and the first Hebrew temple were built in Jerusalem. Solomon was not so capable an administrator as his father and was far more interested in living a life of luxury than in maintaining the security of the Hebrew kingdom. This, in part, is the reason the country remained unified for only one hundred years. Following Solomon's death, it was split by petty rivalry, and the ten tribes which had settled in northern Palestine banded together to form the kingdom of Israel, which had the city of Bethel as its capital. The two remaining Hebrew tribes united to form the kingdom of Judah and retained Jerusalem as their capital.

The Period of Empires

During the eighth century B.C., the entire Middle East came under attack by the Assyrians, who had settled originally in Upper Mesopotamia. They had borrowed heavily from the culture of the Sumerians and their successors, the Babylonians, and when they swept southward through the Middle East to Egypt, they had already reached an advanced degree of civilization. One of the many victims of the Assyrian assault was the Hebrew kingdom of Israel which was destroyed in 721 B.C. The ten tribes living there were dispersed throughout the Assyrian Empire.

The Assyrians were, in turn, defeated towards the end of the seventh century B.C. by a combination of forces which included the Babylonians of Lower Mesopotamia and the Medes and Persians who lived in the area now known as Iran. The Medes and Persians created what was known as the Median Empire, while the Babylonians took control of the area lying between the Mediterranean Sea and the Tigris River. It was the Babylo-

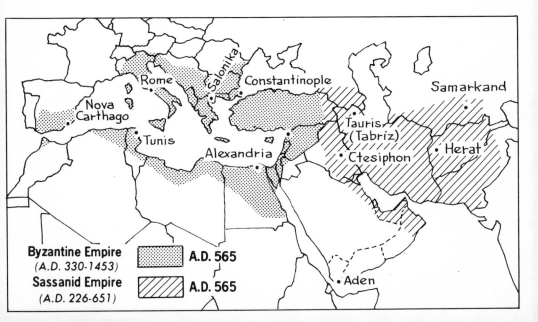

Byzantine Empire
(A.D. 330-1453)   A.D. 565

Sassanid Empire
(A.D. 226-651)   A.D. 565

nian king, Nebuchadnezzar, who captured the Hebrew kingdom of
Judah and destroyed both the city of Jerusalem and the first Hebrew temple in 586 B.C. He then took the leaders of Judah into exile in Babylonia.
During this period of exile and after it the Hebrews became known for
the first time as Jews, a word derived from the Hebrew *Yehudi,* "man
from Judah."

In 538 B.C., Cyrus the Great of Persia defeated the Babylonians and
went on to build the greatest empire the area had known to that time. The
empire extended into Asia Minor, Egypt, and what is now Pakistan and
Afghanistan. The conquest of the Middle East by the Persians, who were
not of Semitic origin, brought a new dimension in cultural enrichment to
the area. It also focused the attention of the growing Western power,
Greece, on the Middle East as a land bridge to the wealthy Persian Empire. For two hundred years the Persians dominated the area until at last
in 332 B.C., Alexander the Great attacked the area and conquered it for
the Greeks.

The influence of the Persians on the Middle East had been felt primarily in governmental administration, language, and religion. The
Greeks now brought to the area their interest in art, poetry, and philosophy. The period during which they controlled the Middle East is often
referred to as the age of Hellenization.

Another Western empire was to leave its mark on the Middle East,
for in 63 B.C. the Romans defeated the Greeks. The Romans wished to
superimpose their way of life on the Semitic peoples of the area also. This
was particularly true in the realm of religion, but they were generally tol-
erant of Judaism. During the Roman occupation of the Middle East, the
second major monotheistic religion known to man, Christianity, was
born in the area of Palestine.

As a result of an outbreak of Jewish nationalism and a subsequent
revolt against Rome in 70 A.D., the Romans destroyed what remained of
the kingdom of Judah by sowing the fields around Jerusalem with salt
and banishing all Jews from the city forever.

The Middle East from the Mediterranean to the Euphrates remained
under Rome's rule for the next four hundred years. During this time the
followers of Christ struggled to spread his teachings. They moved northward to Damascus, then west to Antioch and finally through Greece to
Rome. Because polytheism was the state religion of the Empire, religious
persecution against the Christians increased. Then suddenly in 330 A.D.,
the Roman Emperor Constantine granted all Christians religious freedom and a few years later, he issued an edict announcing that Christianity was to become the official religion of the Roman Empire.

Constantine was aware that the paganism of Rome might seriously
jeopardize Christianity's development. He, therefore, decided to build a
second capital for the Roman Empire where Christianity would be the
sole religion. The city of Constantinople on the Straits of Bosphorus

became the capital of the Eastern Empire. A rift between the two Empires began to develop, and Rome and Constantinople became rivals especially over the land lying at the eastern end of the Mediterranean. In 476 A.D., the Eastern, or Byzantine, Empire wrested control of the area from Rome and established its supremacy in the region.

The next 150 years witnessed a further struggle over the area between the Byzantine Empire and the still powerful Persian Empire. Both claimed supremacy over the land, but neither power was able to gain effective continual control of the territory.

The Conquest of Islam

In the middle of the seventh century A.D., there arose in the Arabian Peninsula a force which was to shape the future of the entire Middle East. Strangely enough, it was not initially a military force. Rather, it was the third major monotheistic religion to arise in the Middle East — Islam. The religion took its strength and shape from a man known as Muhammad, the Prophet. In the beginning his converts were few in an area where strong polytheistic religious practices still prevailed, alongside Christian and Jewish sects. In less than two decades, however, Muhammad and his followers through religious conversions and military means had brought most of the Arabian Peninsula under Islamic control.

Within ten years after the death of Muhammad in 632, his successors Abu Bakr and 'Uthman had conquered the entire Middle East from Syria to Egypt. Inspired by this success, the followers of Islam, known as Muslims, moved westward across North Africa, and in 715, they gained control of Spain. Muslims advanced eastward into Afghanistan, Pakistan, and India, and by the middle of the eighth century, the Islamic Empire girdled almost a fifth of the globe. One proof of the far-reaching in-

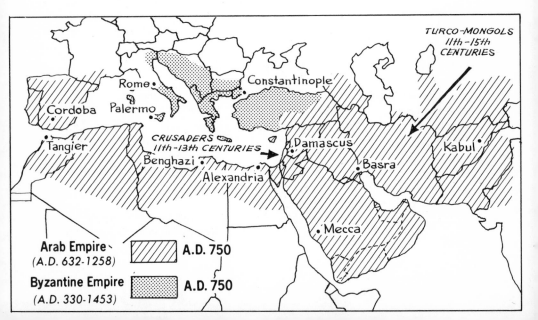

fluence of Islam is that Arab coins were being used as far away as Scandinavia less than one hundred years after Muhammad's death.

Under Islamic rule, Christians and Jews were allowed religious freedom. They were subject to more taxation than were the Muslims, but they were allowed to choose their own occupations and to pursue their own interests with a certain amount of freedom. This *laissez faire* attitude led to cultural enrichment for members of all three faiths and to what has been called the "Golden Age of Islam."

The Arabs who had moved into North Africa, Spain, and Egypt were greatly interested in the new cultures with which they came into contact. Eager to absorb the learning and traditions of the newly acquired territories, they turned their attention to academic pursuits. The period that followed was one to which the present Middle East owes much.

Muslim scholars translated the classics of Rome and Greece into Arabic. These works, in time, circulated through Muslim Spain and then on into Europe, where they formed part of the basis for the eventual European Renaissance. As scholars, the Arabs developed algebra, the medical sciences, art, and literature. One of the most beautiful forms of architecture in history also came from this "Golden Age." It can still be seen in the Islamic places of worship known as mosques which were built throughout the Empire.

The Muslims' interest in learning, as well as that of the Jews and Christians living under their rule, was so great that the libraries of two of the universities in the Empire outranked all other existing libraries. There were over a half million volumes in each of them, which were located in Cordoba, Spain, and in Baghdad.

But even as the Muslims prospered and grew intellectually, problems were developing within the Empire which would eventually lead to its collapse. Early in the eighth century A.D., a dispute arose over the religious leadership of the Muslims. Following Muhammad's death, his trusted friend and confidante, Abu Bakr, had been appointed Caliph, or successor, to Muhammad. Abu Bakr was in turn succeeded first by 'Umar, and then by 'Uthman. When 'Uthman died, Muhammad's son-in-law, Ali, became the fourth Caliph, and it was at this point that the dispute over succession to the Caliphate began.

The Muslim governor of Syria, Mu'awiyah, challenged Ali's right to be Caliph and charged him with murdering 'Uthman. A battle ensued in which Ali and his followers were defeated. The Syrian governor then forced Ali to agree to an arrangement, whereby Ali would become the nominal leader of the Muslims but real political power would remain in the hands of local sultans. When Ali died, Mu'awiyah became the Caliph and removed the seat of government, or the Caliphate, from Medina in the Arabian Peninsula to Damascus.

This dispute over the succession to Muhammad caused a rupture in Islam which in turn divided it into two major sects: the Shi'ites who

believed that Caliphate should be filled only by direct descendants of the
Prophet, and the Sunnites who felt that the succession should continue to
be, as it had been with the selection of Abu Bakr, a matter of election.

While the religious center of Islam continued to be the two holy
cities of Medina and Mecca, the political center, or Caliphate, remained
in Damascus until 750, when al-Abbas, an uncle of Muhammad, overthrew the Syrian Caliphate. He moved the Caliphate's seat to Baghdad,
where it remained until the area came under attack by the Mongols.

These religious disputes and the resulting jealousies led to a gradual
waning of the "Golden Age" of Islamic scholarship and hastened the de-
terioration of the Islamic Empire.

The Crusades

A new struggle over Palestine developed. This was not a conflict between powers of the area, but rather between the Muslims of the East and
the Christians of Western Europe. As with many wars that have been
fought throughout history, the Crusades began with what the Christians
of Europe felt was a highly laudable motive. For centuries following the
conquest of the Middle East by the Muslims, Christians had been allowed to make pilgrimages to the Christian Holy Places in and around
Jerusalem without fear of being molested. The Muslim Empire also controlled Asia Minor, and pilgrims could pass freely between Constantinople and Palestine.

In 1071, however, tribes known as Seljuks from Turkestan conquered Asia Minor from the Arab Muslims, and though the Seljuks
adopted the Muslim religion, they did not adopt its practice of allowing
all persons religious freedom. Pilgrims traveling between Western Europe
and the Holy Land came under constant attack by the Seljuks, and many
tales were circulated throughout Europe concerning the atrocities committed against foreign Christians in Palestine.

In 1095, Pope Urban II while speaking at Clermont, France, urged
the Christians of the West to march to Jerusalem and wrest the city and
its Holy Places from the hands of the Muslims. Fired by the stories that
they had heard and by the promise of salvation should they die repentant
in their quest to save Jerusalem, thousands of peasants from France and
Germany poured across Europe towards Constantinople.

The Peasants' Crusade was unorganized and ill-equipped to fight the
Seljuks, but this did not stop them from venting their feelings on others
who rejected Christianity. As they rode eastward, their first victims became the Jews of Eastern Europe. To the peasants, the Jews too were infidels in that they did not accept the teachings of Christ. In Eastern
Europe, hundreds of synagogues were burned, mass murders were committed, and those Jews who escaped death were subjected to degrading
and inhuman treatment.

Few of the thousands of peasants who began the march to Constantinople actually reached the city. The penniless and hungry peasants who did arrive there were viewed with alarm by the Byzantine Emperor Alexius, who had asked Pope Urban II for assistance in fighting the Seljuks. Alexius, therefore, made arrangements for the peasants to be quickly transported into Asia Minor where they were subsequently slaughtered by the Seljuks.

Meanwhile, in Europe the nobles who had also been stirred by Urban II's plea to aid the Byzantine Empire had organized four armies and set out for Constantinople in what is properly considered the First Crusade. They were readily welcomed by Emperor Alexius who aided them in entering Asia Minor in the spring of 1097. By the following winter the Christian nobles had captured all of Asia Minor from the Seljuk Turks and were moving southward. The following year the Crusaders captured Edessa in Armenia, and Antioch and Tripoli in Syria. Each became a tiny Christian state in the predominately Muslim territory. Elated by these successes, the noblemen marched southward to Jerusalem where they placed the city under a five-week siege. In mid-July of 1099, the nobles stormed the city's walls, entered Jerusalem, and carried out one of the most brutal bloodbaths ever to take place in the city. Thousands of Jews and Muslims were slain.

On Christmas Day of the following year, the Crusaders proclaimed Jerusalem and its environs a Latin kingdom thereby solidifying their hold over the narrow strip of coast running north from Jerusalem to Antioch. Frequent clashes between Muslims and Christians followed, and when Edessa was recaptured by the Muslims in 1147, a call went out to Europe for a Second Crusade. The call was again answered by the noblemen, but the Second Crusade proved unsuccessful, and Edessa remained in Muslim hands.

In 1187, Salah al-Din, a Kurdish warrior from northern Syria, moved southward through Syria bringing much of the area under his control. He hoped to conquer Egypt also, and as he moved towards this goal, he captured Jerusalem. Though the Latin kingdom set up by the First Crusade continued to exist, it was now limited to the coastal area between Jaffa and Tyre. A Third Crusade was called to reclaim Jerusalem. It eventually led King Richard the Lion-Hearted of England to the gates of Jerusalem. Though Richard was unable to recapture the city, he did reach an agreement with Salah al-Din that allowed unarmed pilgrims freedom to visit the Christian Holy Places in the city.

For a brief period between 1229 and 1244, Jerusalem, Nazareth, and Bethlehem were held by the Christians, but when Muslims in these cities were denied religious freedom, they rose up and ousted the Christians. Meanwhile, Salah al-Din had died in Egypt leaving as his successors the Egyptian dynasty known as the Ayyubids. Continuous fighting with the Crusaders plus power struggles within the government in Egypt had begun to weaken the Ayyubids. The Ayyubid dynasty came to an end in

1250 when the Sultan died, and in the ensuing confusion over who was to succeed him, the Mamluks seized the government. The Mamluks had formerly been the bodyguard slaves of the Sultan Salah al-Din and his descendants. The reign of the Mamluks over Syria and Egypt lasted until the establishment of the Ottoman Empire in 1517.

Besides having to contend with the Crusaders, the Mamluks were faced with a new threat which was mounting to the east of Syria. The Mongols of Central Asia led by Genghis Khan were already advancing southward when the Mamluks came to power in 1250, and by 1258, the Mongols had laid waste the land in northern Syria. They besieged the city of Baghdad, captured it, and utterly demolished the central portion of the city. They then marched through southern Syria and Palestine to the Mediterranean seaport of Jaffa, where they were finally defeated by the Mamluk Sultan, Baibars.

Other minor Crusades, including the ill-famed Children's Crusade, had been carried on during the period of the invasion of the Mongols. It was left to King Louis IX of France to lead the final two Crusades, both of which failed, and in 1291 the Christians of Europe abandoned their attempts to reclaim the Holy Places of Jerusalem.

The Crusades had not endeared Christians to the Muslims and the Jews. Both religions had suffered persecution under the Christians, and since members of both religions were considered infidels, the blood of Jews and Muslims had intermingled in the senseless slaughters which had taken place. It was probably among the Arab Muslims, however, that the greatest animosity was generated. They had always allowed the Christians traveling to the Holy Land the right to practice their faith freely and to worship unmolested at their shrines. For it had been the Seljuk Turks, not the Arab Muslims, who had denied the Christians the right of pilgrimage.

The Ottoman Empire

For the next two hundred years the Mamluks of Egypt retained control of Syria, Palestine, and Egypt. To the north, however, the Turks were slowly regrouping their forces, and though they had no strong foothold in the eastern Mediterranean, they looked with covetous eyes on the area which would provide them an access route to Arabia. This country held the key to much of the wealth of the East, and over its caravan routes from the Persian Gulf to Damascus were carried much of India's spices, silks, and ivory. Control of these routes would bring untold wealth and power to the Turks.

Under the Ottoman Sultan, Selim I, the Turkish dreams of expansion into the Middle East were realized, and in 1517, the entire eastern Mediterranean and Egypt came under their domination. In 1498, Constantinople itself had fallen to the Turks. Their rule was soon extended over most of North Africa and all but the central portion of the Arabian

Peninsula. Selim's rule was followed by that of Suleiman, who extended the Ottoman Empire into parts of Austria, Hungary, and Russia.

By the beginning of the seventeenth century, the Ottoman Empire had reached its zenith in terms of size, power, and prestige. Since much of the territory conquered by the Turks had been part of the former Islamic Empire, the Sultan proclaimed Islam as the official religion of the Ottoman Empire. The Sultan then held the dual role of the temporal ruler of the vast territories controlled by the Turks and of Caliph, or religious leader, of all Islam.

The governing of the Empire fell into two distinct categories. On the local level, the Sultan retained the system developed during the "Golden Age" of Islam. During that period certain distinctions were made between Muslims and non-Muslims which related directly to governing on the local level. If, for instance, a city contained recognizable numbers of Jews, Christians, and Muslims, religious leaders from each group were selected by the Sultan or one of his representatives. The religious leader was responsible for keeping order among the members of his faith in the city or area over which he had jurisdiction. He was also responsible for the collection of taxes levied by the Sultan. Each religious group was known as a *millet,* and each maintained its own courts and system of punishment for minor infractions. Muslims, Christians, and Jews were all tried in their own respective courts. The only exception to this rule was when a dispute arose between a Muslim and a Jew or Christian. Then the case was automatically referred to the Muslim court.

Responsibility for governing the overall Empire rested in the bureaucratic structure known as the Ruling Institution. The Sultan technically headed this body but, in fact, most of the power over it was re-

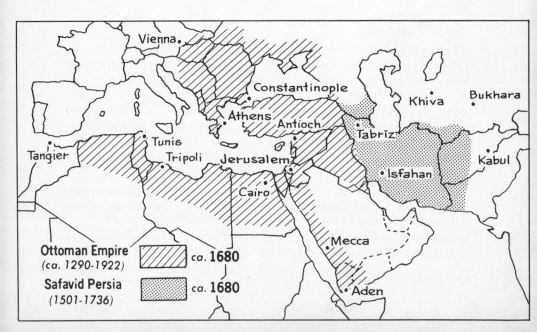

Ottoman Empire
(ca. 1290-1922)   ca. 1680

Safavid Persia   ca. 1680
(1501-1736)

tained by a kind of prime minister, known as the grand *vezir,* who was selected by the Sultan. The Ruling Institution was housed in the palace of the Sultan, and hundreds of civil servants and members of the military élite carried out the functions of administering the many provinces of the Empire and of working out plans to defend the Empire's borders from aggression.

This dual system of governing worked well during the sixteenth and early seventeenth centuries when the Sultanate was still responsive to the duties imposed on the ruler of such a large empire. By the end of the seventeenth century, however, the Sultanate had become self-indulgent, and the power of the Ottoman Empire began to decline steadily.

Though the Turks continued to rule over the Middle East and North Africa until the end of World War I, they never regained the strength and position which the Empire had had in its early days. Religious, military, and legal reforms were instituted in the early 1800's, but none of these measures were able to revive the Empire's waning influence. As World War I approached, the world watched as the Turkish Sultan aligned his empire with the Germans, and it waited to see what would become of "the sick man of Europe."

Western Influence in the Middle East

Initially, Western interests in the Middle East centered on the desire to establish and maintain trade routes through Syria, Iraq, and Iran to the Persian Gulf and overland through the area known as Suez to the Red Sea. By the late 1700's, the British were actively using the latter trade route much to the distress of the French who were wary of Britain's growing influence in Egypt. Following the demise of the French monarchy and the rise to power of Napoleon Bonaparte, France mounted an offensive campaign against the British in Egypt.

In 1798, Napoleon invaded Egypt in the hope of destroying British influence there. French troops penetrated the Nile Valley as far south as the city of Luxor. For three years they actively engaged in battle with the British in Egypt, but at last in 1801, Napoleon was forced to abandon the assault because of the growing problems he faced in Europe.

Egypt was the first of the Turkish provinces to break away from the repressive reign of the Ottomans. Muhammad Ali, an officer of Albanian descent in the Ottoman army, had been instrumental in expelling the French from Egypt in 1801. While the British continued to maintain military forces in Egypt, these troops at first seemed to pose no real threat to continued Ottoman rule. In 1805, the Turkish Sultan appointed Muhammad Ali "Governor of Egypt."

Two years after his appointment, the British attempted to capture Alexandria but were defeated. This victory, in addition to Muhammad Ali's successful suppression of what remained of the Mamluk dynasty in 1811, impressed the Turkish Sultan enough to allow Muhammad Ali a free hand in governing Egypt. Under his leadership, strong reforms were enacted. The educational system was revised, and Muhammad Ali urged Westerners to come to the province to aid in establishing new schools. The French were particularly receptive to this invitation, and many foreign schools were established in Cairo. As Governor, Muhammad Ali also initiated a program of agricultural development that included the building of irrigation canals, dams, and barrages which helped to control the annual flooding of the Nile.

During Muhammad Ali's rule, a young Frenchman, Ferdinand de Lesseps, was posted as vice consul in the city of Alexandria. He had observed that the overland trade route from Alexandria through Suez to the Red Sea was improved by the construction of a railroad built under British auspices. Travel time between England and India had been reduced to forty days, but the railroad could not transport bulky equipment or machinery, and de Lesseps began to dream of a canal which would cut through the Suez connecting the Mediterranean with the Red Sea.

He proposed the building of such a canal to Muhammad Ali, but his plan was rejected because of the fear that such a canal would be further incentive for the Western powers to try to gain control of Egypt. The British also objected to the canal for they felt it would threaten Britain's interests in India.

In 1854, however, Muhammad Ali's successor, Said, granted a concession to de Lesseps to build the Suez Canal. The British blocked all attempts to begin work on the Canal and even refused to buy the 80,000 shares of stock which had been reserved for them. These 80,000 shares amounted to one-fifth of the total stock to be sold and would have given the British a controlling voice in the management of the Canal.

Work on the Canal began only after de Lesseps himself had managed to sell $20 million worth of stock during a trip to France. Said purchased the 64,000 shares which had been allotted to Egypt, and his successor, Ismail, bought all the unsubscribed stock, besides the shares which the British had rejected. In all, Egypt's stock in the Canal amounted to over 182,000 shares, or almost one-half of the total shares sold.

There were many problems connected with the building of the Canal including the need for 25,000 men to excavate the path that the Canal was to take. It was Ismail's task to supply these men, which he did, but in 1864 he demanded that work on the Canal cease when he learned that a rumor was being spread that slave labor was being used to complete the job. He was severely criticized by Napoleon III for his failure to supply the Canal's labor force, and he was ordered to pay $17 million in costs for breaking his contract. The money was put to good use, however, and was allotted for the purchase of machinery which accelerated construction. In 1869, the Suez Canal was completed and was opened to shipping.

By this time, Ismail had overextended his credit in other directions, including development projects he had begun in the Sudan, and by the early 1870's, Egypt faced bankruptcy. In 1875, the British offered to buy Egypt's stock in the Canal. They hoped that by gaining these shares, they would be able to prevent the French from acquiring a controlling interest in the Canal. In 1876, Egypt declared bankruptcy, and the Canal was placed under international control.

It had become readily apparent following the opening of the Canal in 1869 that the countries of the West would benefit most from its construction. By the end of the nineteenth century, the eastern end of the Mediterranean had become economically important for France and England, as well as for other Western nations who traded with India and Southeast Asia.

But even as the British and French engaged in their battle for economic control in the Middle East, America was taking its own first tenuous steps towards establishing influence in the area. This was done, not under official government auspices, but rather by American Protestant missionaries who hoped to establish churches through which to reach the Muslim population. The first two ministers sent out by the American Board of Commissioners for Foreign Missions were the Reverends Pliny Fisk and Levi Parsons. They arrived in Jerusalem in 1820 but were unsuccessful in their attempts to establish either a permanent church or school in the Holy City. Ottoman law forbade Christians the right to reside in Jerusalem. The memories of the Crusades had not dimmed. The two young missionaries decided, therefore, to establish their headquarters in Beirut.

Almost two centuries earlier, French Jesuits had been active in Syria and Lebanon in the field of education. The Jesuit Order had been suppressed by the Pope, however, in 1773, and they were forced to close their schools and to leave the country. News of the arrival in Beirut of the Protestant ministers revived the interest of the Jesuits, by now reestablished by Rome. They and the French Lazarists returned to the Middle East.

In 1833, Muhammad Ali's son, Ibrahim, gained control of Syria. As his father had done in Egypt, Ibrahim urged Westerners to come to Syria and Lebanon to build schools. He allowed the French Jesuits to build the University of St. Joseph in the city of Beirut. Ibrahim also allowed a number of American Presbyterian missionaries to settle there, and by 1866 they had opened the Syrian Protestant College. Later, control of the College passed from the hands of the Presbyterians, and it became a private institution known as the American University of Beirut.

It cannot be said that the work of conversion by the missionaries who arrived in the Middle East in the mid-1800's was spectacularly successful. All proselytizing among Muslims was proscribed by law. As for the Christians living there, many were Eastern Orthodox, who were generally antagonistic to both Rome and the Protestants, or Eastern Rite Catholics who were in communion with the Roman Catholic Church.

At first the Arab Christians welcomed their Western counterparts, but it soon became apparent that there were great cultural differences between the Christians of the West and the Christians of the East. In matters of religion a wary attitude prevailed, and it was only in the field of education that a common bond was formed. By the turn of the century, mission schools dotted the Middle Eastern landscape from Iran to Egypt.

As the nineteenth century drew to a close, three of the most prominent Western nations — Britain, France, and the United States — had all developed ties with the Middle East. No longer was the area viewed solely as the romantic and mysterious East. It had become instead an increasingly important area strategically and economically. It was also destined to become the chess board upon which the power politics of the early twentieth century would be played. The countries of the Middle East would be used by the West as pawns.

The Emergence of Nationalism

By the beginning of the twentieth century, the Turkish Empire had become known as "the sick man of Europe," and internal disputes between the Sultan and his army were seriously jeopardizing its future. The Arabs, whose countries had never been clearly defined by settled boundaries or independent governments, now began to stir with the desire for autonomy. Nationalism, the same force which had swept across Western Europe almost a century earlier, now began to emerge in the Middle East.

There were problems of identity which accompanied this nationalistic movement. For instance, throughout the centuries the term "Syria" had been applied not only to what we know today as the modern nation of Syria, but also to the area of Lebanon. The territory known as Palestine had been controlled at various times by Syria and at other times by Egypt. The modern state of Jordan had not existed prior to this time. The northern portion was linked with the Arabian Peninsula. Common bonds did tie the entire region together, however, and these included the use of Arabic throughout the region, the common religion of Islam, and the heritage left by the Islamic Empire.

While nationalism was becoming a potent force in the Arab world, another nationalistic movement, known as Zionism, was emerging among the Jews of Eastern Europe. The Zionist movement had begun in part as a reaction to the ghetto existence forced on the Jews of Eastern Europe and Russia, but its major impetus came from the efforts of a Jewish journalist, Theodore Herzl, who covered the famous Dreyfus trial in France in 1893. A Viennese Jew, Herzl was stunned by the realization that anti-Semitism, as it was displayed at the Dreyfus trial, was a widespread force in Western Europe. During the trial, Herzl became convinced that it was necessary for the Jews throughout Europe to act in concert to protect their civil rights. Following the trial, he returned to

Vienna where he wrote a short book entitled *Der Judenstaat (The Jewish State)*, in which he developed the thesis that it was necessary for all Jews to work towards the creation of a homeland where they would be secure from persecution.

For many Jews who read his book, Herzl's homeland could be only one place: Palestine. The return of the Jewish people to the land of their spiritual forefathers had always been a part of the religious tradition of Orthodox Jews, but the return to Palestine had generally been associated with a return led by the Messiah. This Messianic concept foretold the rise of a leader from among the Jews who would lead them back to the environs of Jerusalem, where they would live in peace and prosperity till the end of their days.

It is important here to make clear two terms which will be used often in this text. The term *Jew* refers to any person who voluntarily adheres to the universal moral values found in the monotheistic religion known as Judaism. The term *Zionist* refers to any person who supports the nationalistic movement aimed at the creation and continuity of a state which is exclusively Jewish. Zionists do not necessarily have to be professed Jews, nor are all Jews necessarily Zionists.

In 1897, the first meeting of the Zionist Congress met in Basel, Switzerland. Many Jewish leaders from throughout Europe rallied to Herzl's call for a Jewish state. Others, however, rejected it on the grounds that only through the leadership of the Messiah could the Jews return to Palestine. Even Herzl himself at one point put forth a recommendation that the Zionists accept a tentative offer from the British to settle in Uganda, but this suggestion was ill-received, and he soon dropped it.

The participants at the Basel meeting founded what was known as the World Zionist Organization, whose primary purpose was to promote the idea of a national homeland among all Jews. Herzl became the first president of the organization, and in that capacity he pressed hard to persuade the Turkish Sultan to designate Palestine as a homeland for the Jews. The Sultan refused, and in 1904 Herzl died without having gained territorial rights in Palestine. He had, however, succeeded in implanting among many Jews the idea that they must seek a homeland which would eventually become a Jewish state.

Arab nationalism, on the other hand, was not so well organized as Zionism at the turn of the century. The Muslim Arabs who had lived under Turkish domination for four hundred years owed both political and religious allegiance to the Sultan. Though distressed by his policies, the Muslims were unwilling to rebel against him on the grounds that he was the Caliph, the religious successor to Muhammad. Arab nationalism, therefore, took root primarily among the educated middle class which was slowly emerging in Syria, Egypt, and Lebanon. Many of these Arabs were Christians who had been exposed to Western ideas, including nationalism, by missionary teachers from France and the United States.

Many others, however, including men like Mustafa Kamil, an Egyptian lawyer, were Muslims. Kamil was instrumental in founding a nationalistic political party known as al-Watani, which worked in Egypt in the latter part of the nineteenth century to establish a sense of national identity among the Egyptians.

Until the break-up of the Turkish Empire and the movement of foreign powers such as Britain and France into Syria, Palestine, and Transjordan, the spirit of nationalism touched few Arabs. Following World War I, however, with the Caliphate removed from Constantinople and with the movement of foreign powers into the area, Arabs of all religious persuasions and from all classes in the social spectrum slowly began to desire statehood. Many joined together to work towards the goals of independence and self-government.

CHAPTER I
Part 2

A Short History
of the Near East

1914 to May 14, 1948

World War I — A Time of Broken Promises

The period during and after World War I was a time filled with broken promises. From 1915 through 1919, the major Western powers made promises of independence to the Arabs, agreements on the division of the Ottoman Empire between themselves, and promises to the Zionists that they would be allowed a homeland in Palestine. Not all of these assurances could be kept, obviously, for they often conflicted. Those promises which were actually realized proved to be the ones most advantageous to the Western powers.

At the outbreak of World War I, Turkey called upon the Arab Muslims of the Middle East to join with the Sultan in fighting a holy war, or *jihad*, against Britain and France. The Sultan believed that the Arabs would come to his aid on religious grounds since they owed him allegiance as the Caliph. Such was not the case, however. The Sharif Hussein of Mecca, guardian of the Holy Places of Islam, was a powerful figure among the Muslims, and it was to him that many turned when the war broke out.

In August 1915, the Sharif Hussein entered into a lengthy exchange of correspondence with the British High Commissioner of Egypt, Sir Henry McMahon. Hussein initiated the exchange in order to extract from the British a promise that they would recognize Arab independence following the war. In return for this promise of recognition, Hussein agreed to use his influence among the Arabs to convince them to assist the Allies in their war against the Turks and not to join with the Turks.

Hussein and McMahon at last agreed that all of the Arabian Peninsula and most of the territory north of the peninsula to Asia Minor would

be granted independence. The exceptions were the Cilician districts of
Mersin and Alexandretta in Lebanon, the part of Syria west of a line between Aleppo and Damascus, and southern Iraq from Baghdad to Basra.
In the fourth letter of the exchange, after noting the above modifications,
McMahon wrote: "Subject to the above modification, Great Britain is
prepared to recognize and support the independence of the Arabs in all of
the regions within the limits demanded by the Sharif of Mecca."

Several more letters were exchanged in which the Sharif explained to
McMahon why the territories which would be under Western control
should also be freed, but McMahon replied that it was necessary to retain
these areas because of promises the British had made to the French and
for security reasons. The two men finally reached agreement, and though
no specific mention was made about the future of Palestine, the correspondence certainly implied that it too would be given independence
after the war.

Hussein's forces, though encountering extreme difficulties, were successful in overpowering the Turkish forces first in Arabia and later in
Syria. In the meanwhile, however, new agreements were being made
which negated the Hussein-McMahon correspondence completely. It is
evident that even while Sir Henry and the Sharif Hussein were corre-
sponding over settlement of the future of Arabia and the central portion
of the Middle East, Britain was considering alternate plans for the area,
should the Allies prove victorious over the Turks. Unknown to the
Arabs, the major powers engaged in a series of secret meetings, and in the
spring of 1916, they agreed to divide the Ottoman Empire among themselves.

In the Sykes-Picot Agreement which was signed in May 1916,
France was to receive Syria and the province of Lebanon, plus parts of
Iraq in which it had a special interest. Russia, long desirous of a warm-
water port, wanted Constantinople and the Straits of Bosphorus. Britain
would control the remainder of Iraq, Transjordan, and Gaza. Palestine
was to be subject to an international administration, both British and
French. The Agreement was kept secret, for the Allies could ill afford to
lose the aid which they were receiving from the Arabs. Though not well
trained in military tactics, the Arabs were performing quite effectively the
task of winning back their lands from the Turks, with the help of such
men as T. E. Lawrence, known to the world as "Lawrence of Arabia."

The secrecy of the Agreement did not last long, however, and following the Bolshevik uprising in Russia in 1917, the news of the infamous
agreement was broadcast to the world by the Communists who wished to
demean the former Czarist regime. The Arabs were at first puzzled, then
angered by these revelations, and the Sharif Hussein immediately wrote
to McMahon asking for an explanation. The High Commissioner sent
him a reassuring reply over the signature of A. J. Balfour, Britain's
Foreign Secretary. Hussein, who had never seen the text of the Sykes-

Picot Agreement, trusted British integrity and accepted the Foreign Secretary's word.

Britain's Prime Minister, Lloyd George, and France's Premier, Georges Clemenceau, also made statements assuring the Arabs that the independence and territorial integrity promised them in the Hussein-McMahon correspondence would be honored. Arab optimism grew even stronger when on January 8, 1918, President Wilson presented his Fourteen Points to the U.S. Congress. Many of the Points related to the future of the Middle East, but it was Point XII from which the Arabs drew their greatest assurance. It stated: "The Turkish portions of the present Ottoman Empire should be assured a secure sovereignty, but other nationalities which are now under Turkish rule should be assured an undoubted security of life and an absolutely unmolested opportunity of autonomous development. . . ."

The Balfour Declaration

Early in the war, the Zionists, anticipating that Britain would control Palestine when the conflict ended, began a long and intense campaign to gain British support for the establishment of a national home for the Jews in Palestine. One of those who worked hardest was Chaim Weizmann, a Russian Jew by birth who had attained prominence in England as a chemist and who had done much to aid Britain's war effort by discovering a synthetic explosive. Another was a scion of a famous banking family, Baron Edmond de Rothschild, a French Jew who had provided large sums of money to Eastern European Jews to be used for the purchase of land in Palestine.

On the basis of the Zionist efforts which had proved quite successful in molding opinion and in order to gain the support of world Jewry for the British war effort, Lord Balfour, Britain's Foreign Secretary, on November 2, 1917, issued the following statement, addressed to Lord Lionel Walter Rothschild, a private British subject, related to the French Rothschilds.

*   *   *

Foreign Office
November 2nd, 1917

Dear Lord Rothschild,

I have much pleasure conveying to you, on behalf of His Majesty's Government, the following declaration of sympathy with Jewish Zionist aspirations which has been submitted to, and approved by, the Cabinet.

"His Majesty's Government view with favour the establishment in Palestine of a national home for the Jewish people, and will use their best endeavours to facilitate the achievement of this object, it being clearly understood that nothing shall be done which may prejudice the civil and religious rights of the existing

non-Jewish communities in Palestine, or the rights and political
status enjoyed by Jews in any other country."
I should be grateful if you would bring this declaration to the knowledge of the Zionist Federation.

Yours sincerely
Arthur James Balfour

*   *   *

The Declaration itself was a unilateral British public law instrument.
It is doubtful that the Declaration would have been upheld as a valid document had it been questioned in an international court at the time it was
issued. In 1917, Britain had no legal justification for offering any part of
Palestine for use by any nation or people, since the war had not ended, no
peace agreement had been signed, and no division of what was still technically part of the Ottoman Empire had been made.

Not only were these facts to be considered, but it was also apparent
that the statement had purposely been made ambiguous and open to
many interpretations. Consider, for example, the phrase ". . . nothing
shall be done which may prejudice the civil and religious rights of the existing *non-Jewish* communities in Palestine. . . ." At the time of the Declaration's issuance, no census had been taken of the area, but it was later
estimated that about 91 percent of the population in Palestine was either
Arab Muslim or Arab Christian, while only nine percent of the population was Jewish. The non-Jewish communities, therefore, comprised the
overwhelming majority of the people living in Palestine.

Another ambiguity was the use of the word *home.* Chaim Weizmann
mentions in his autobiography, *Trial and Error,* that Zionists who
worked with the Foreign Office in drafting the Declaration had pressed
for the use of the word *state.* Certain British Jews, among them Edwin
Montagu, Britain's Secretary of State for India, did not agree with Zionist aims, however, and it was probable that pressure from these Jews
resulted in the insertion of the word *home* rather than *state.*

Another interesting point is that these developments occurred after
completion of the Sykes-Picot Agreement. With the issuance of the Balfour Declaration, it appeared that England had taken upon itself the future of Palestine, even though its government had agreed with the
French that together they would provide for an international administration of Palestine.

The Peace Talks at Versailles

When the war ended in November 1918, the British, as the Zionists
had foreseen, were in military control of Palestine. At the Peace Conference held in February 1919, at Versailles, it became readily apparent that
the division of the Ottoman Empire was to be the Conference's major
problem.

The Arabs, represented by Sharif Hussein's son, Faisal, anticipated that they would be granted independence. The French, relying on the Sykes-Picot Agreement of 1916, anticipated that they would be granted control of Syria, Lebanon, and part of Iraq. The Zionists, determined that the Balfour Declaration would be honored, anticipated that soon they would have a national home in Palestine. And the British, who had committed themselves to all of the above claims, found themselves in a difficult diplomatic position.

The debate regarding the disposition of the Ottoman Empire was lengthy and heated. Britain's Lloyd George pointed out that the French were committed to the Hussein-McMahon correspondence because they had acknowledged that prior arrangement when they entered into the Sykes-Picot Agreement. Each faction involved was determined to look after its own vested interests in the Middle East, with the exception of President Wilson who represented the United States. As yet, the United States had no real economic or military interests in the area.

When Faisal realized that the Arabs were going to have little to say about their own future, he urged the members of the Conference at least to find out how the Arabs in Syria and Palestine felt about the plans for their political future. President Wilson backed this suggestion, and agreement was finally reached that an inquiry would be conducted among the Arabs.

The King-Crane Commission and the Mandate System

The Commission assigned to conduct the inquiry was to include representatives from France, Britain, and the United States. Members were to have had no prior experience in the Middle East so that their work would be unbiased. France refused to join the Commission, however, and England withdrew its representatives before the Commission left for the Middle East. It was then left to the American delegation, headed by Henry C. King and Charles R. Crane, to make the investigation, and their findings were published as the King-Crane Commission's Report. The Report was presented to the members of the Versailles Conference, and its findings showed that the Arabs overwhelmingly favored independence. If complete independence was not possible, those living in the area stated that they would prefer to be placed under a Mandate directed by the United States.

The Mandate system was a new concept in international law. Under such a system, a major power took responsibility for a dependent country and worked with its leaders until the country had developed its governmental structures sufficiently to carry on its own internal and external affairs. When this point was reached, the Mandatory power would withdraw its personnel, and the country would become totally independent.

The King-Crane Report also stated that the only way the Balfour Declaration could be implemented in Palestine was by military force, and if it were, it would be at the expense of the Arabs already in Palestine.

Despite the recommendations of the King-Crane Report, the League of Nations adopted the Mandate system and made France the Mandatory power in Syria, rather than the United States, as the Syrian Arabs had requested. Britain was awarded a Mandate for Palestine and Iraq. The Balfour Declaration was incorporated into the text of the Palestine Mandate by the League of Nations. This inclusion changed the status of the Declaration from that of unilateral British public law to multilateral public law. The awarding of the Mandates took place in April 1920.

The Mandates

Following the announcement of the awarding of the Mandates in 1920, riots broke out among the Arabs living in Jerusalem and Damascus. In Syria, nationalism had grown considerably since the end of World War I, and the French found it necessary to occupy the country militarily. The policy of the French towards Syria soon became characterized by a "divide and rule" approach. By 1925, the French Mandate personnel had divided Syria into four separate units. They enlarged the former Turkish province of Lebanon by adding to it the cities of Tripoli, Sidon, and Tyre. The other units included Latakia, which was the area lying along the Mediterranean coast in the northwestern section of Syria, Jabal Druze in the west, and the area surrounding Damascus which became known as the Syrian Republic.

The French had purposely separated the area near Damascus from the rest of the Mandated territory, because they wished to isolate the Syrian nationalists who had become a strong and vocal force in the city.

Britain maintained a somewhat more liberal administrative policy in Iraq, but here, too, nationalists were determined to win independence for the country. In 1922, following demonstrations led by Iraqi nationalists,

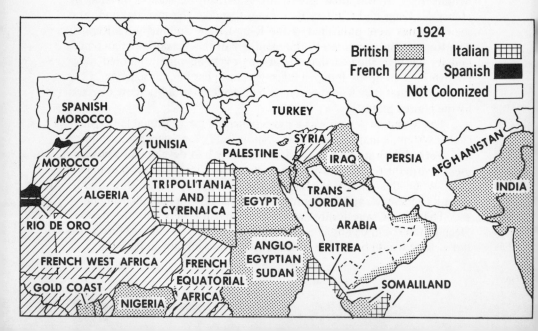

the British signed an agreement stating that Iraq would gain its independence within ten years. This promise was kept, although the British continued to maintain a strong influence in the area even after the Mandate ended. The British also asked Faisal, the son of Sharif Hussein who had represented the Arabs at the Versailles Conference, to act as King of Iraq. He accepted the position, but in fact he had little power.

The area then known as Transjordan was not placed under Mandate. No such state had existed previously, but during the Versailles Conference, borders for the state were arbitrarily drawn by the British, and Abdullah, another son of Sharif Hussein, was prevailed upon to become king. Though the British did not have a Mandate over the area, they maintained a strong presence in Transjordan, for they wished to protect their interests in the Suez.

Prior to the time that the Mandate went into effect in Palestine there were riots in Jerusalem. In 1921, more serious rioting took place near the seaport of Jaffa, in Palestine. Here, too, nationalistic feelings were strong among the Arabs, and resentment was growing. The Palestinian Arabs disliked the British administration and were already experiencing grave misgivings about Jewish immigration into the area.

The British, in an effort to assess just how grave the situation in Palestine might be, sent Sir Winston Churchill, then head of the British Colonial Office, to the area in 1921. Churchill's report on the situation was published as a "White Paper," or policy statement, in June 1922. In the paper he reiterated Britain's intention of helping the Jews to found a national home in Palestine. He also stated, however, that the British foresaw that at some future date Palestine would become a binational state.

The Zionists were unhappy over the views expressed in the White Paper, for they already visualized a Jewish state, and they had no intentions of settling for a binational state to be shared with the Palestinian Arabs. The Arabs, now aware that the Zionists viewed the Balfour Declaration and its inclusion into the Mandate as the first step towards an exclusively Jewish state, were equally unhappy with the views expressed by Churchill. They had hoped that upon reviewing the situation in Palestine, he would recognize their right to a Palestinian state and would disavow the Balfour Declaration.

There had never been a formal census of the population of Palestine. The British decided, therefore, that before the Mandate went into effect an official census should be made. The results of the 1922 census showed that at the time there were slightly more than 655,000 Arabs and almost 84,000 Jews living in Palestine. According to Churchill's White Paper, about 25,000 of these Jews had migrated to Palestine since the beginning of the British occupation following World War I. Also, when the British Mandate went into effect in September 1923, it was estimated that approximately 94 percent of the land in Palestine belonged to Arabs.

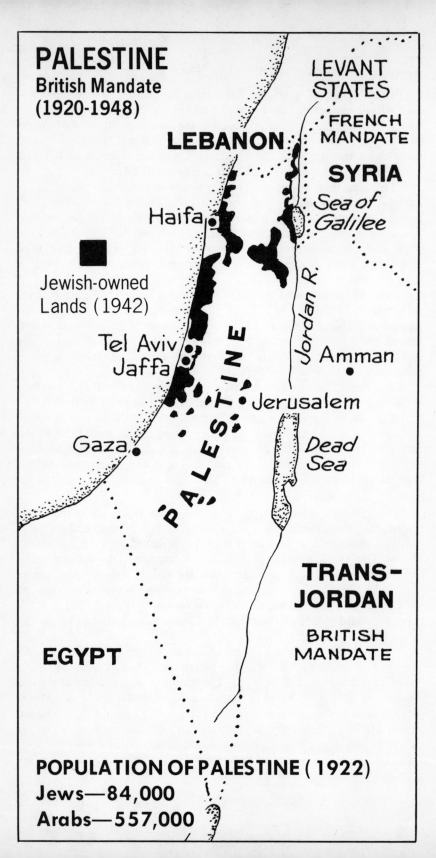

PALESTINE
British Mandate
(1920-1948)

LEVANT STATES

LEBANON

FRENCH MANDATE

SYRIA

Sea of Galilee

Haifa

■
Jewish-owned
Lands (1942)

Tel Aviv
Jaffa

Jordan R.

Amman

PALESTINE

Jerusalem

Gaza

Dead Sea

TRANS-JORDAN

BRITISH MANDATE

EGYPT

POPULATION OF PALESTINE (1922)
Jews—84,000
Arabs—557,000

Palestine Becomes a Special Problem

While the other nations of the Middle East were making some progress towards creating governmental structures which would lead to future independence, Palestine became a special problem. Both Arabs and Jews assumed that when the British Mandate ended in Palestine, they would be in control of the government. Little was done during the 1920's to train Arabs for governmental jobs, nor were there many Jews working in the offices of the Mandate personnel.

Throughout the 1920's, immigration of Eastern European Jews into Palestine rose steadily. Though many of the more educated and nationalistic Palestinian Arabs were alarmed at this, Arabs living in the rural areas did not at first become upset by the collective farms, or *kibbutzim,* which were being developed throughout the country by Jews. The rural Arabs reasoned that their forefathers had lived side-by-side in peace with Palestinian Jews for twelve centuries and that they could also.

Coupled with this upsurge in Jewish immigration, there was an influx of capital raised by the World Zionist Organization. This capital was carefully invested in land which had been thoroughly examined either for present productivity or for possible reclamation. Often the land was purchased from absentee Arab landlords who resided in Lebanon or Syria.

In 1929, in accordance with Article IV of the British Mandate, an organ known as the Jewish Agency was established in Palestine. The Jewish Agency was to provide for ". . . economic, social, and other matters as may affect the establishment of the Jewish national home and the interests of the Jewish population in Palestine." The Agency became, in part, the training ground for Jews in Palestine who were thinking of a future date when a Jewish state would be created and when there would be need of governmental administrators.

The tension among the Arabs, which had mounted as immigration of Jews increased, erupted in August 1929 in the form of anti-Jewish riots. Attacks were made against Jews in the urban areas, particularly in Jerusalem and Hebron. When the British finally restored order, 113 Jews and 116 Arabs had been killed. Once again a commission was sent to the area by the British to study the situation, and in 1930 a policy paper known as the Passfield White Paper was issued. The Paper recognized certain serious problems which hitherto had been ignored. One was the alienation of Arabs from Jews, because Arabs were consistently refused employment in Zionist colonies. Another was the fact that large portions of land, though sometimes unpopulated, were being purchased by the Jewish National Fund, an agency established in 1902 specifically for the purpose of buying land in Palestine through funds donated by world Jewry. The Paper also pointed out that future immigration would depend on the amount of unemployment found within the Arab and Jewish populaces in Palestine. By 1930, the Arab population had risen to 818,000, due primarily to natural growth. The Jewish population, on the other hand, had practically doubled from the nearly 84,000 Jews listed in the 1922 census to over 164,000 Jews in the 1930 census.

Finally, the Passfield White Paper reaffirmed Britain's determination to fulfill her obligations as the Mandatory power, and it rejected the extreme demands of the Arabs who were asking for nullification of the Mandate. It also noted that Zionist leaders must take responsibility in helping to solve the immediate problems in Palestine, including those caused by increased Jewish immigration.

Zionist reaction to the Paper was intense, for they felt the British were reneging on the promises made in the Balfour Declaration. Dr. Chaim Weizmann, then President of both the World Zionist Organization and the Jewish Agency in Palestine, met with Britain's Prime Minister, James Ramsay MacDonald, and conveyed the bitter disappointment of world Zionism to him. At first, the Prime Minister appeared unmoved, but pressure began to build both in England and throughout the world, and on February 13, 1931, MacDonald addressed a letter to Dr. Weizmann which seemed to negate the Passfield White Paper. Generally, it provided the Zionists with assurance that the terms of the Mandate would be fulfilled.

The Pre-War Years

As the 1930's passed, the world watched uneasily as Hitler rose to power in Germany. The uneasiness of the world was reflected in the rise of Jewish emigration from Germany and other countries of Eastern Europe. Many of these Jews emigrated to Palestine, and by 1935, Jews accounted for 28 percent of Palestine's population. The rumors of persecution and repression went unheeded by the Western powers, and for many Jews the only escape from the tragic situation was emigration to Palestine. Thus, what had started out as a political movement based on Biblical prophecy soon became a political necessity based on survival of European Jewry.

During these same years, many of the Arab nations were experiencing a growth in their popular nationalistic movements. Palestine was no exception, and two quasi-political parties developed in the early 1930's led by members of two prestigious Palestinian Arab families.

The Palestine Arab Party was headed by Hajj Amin al-Husaini, the *Mufti,* or religious leader of Muslims, in Jerusalem. The Mufti's party drew members of the upper class Arab Palestinians, many of whom represented old established families in Palestine. The Palestine Arab Party was pan-Arab in orientation, with the Mufti involved in nationalistic movements in Iraq, Egypt, and Syria.

The National Defense Party, on the other hand, was headed by members of the Nashashibi family. Members of the party were mainly from middle class families involved in commerce. Their first concern was not pan-Arabism, but rather development within Palestine itself.

Towards the end of 1935, Palestinian Arabs from both parties became alarmed by the ever increasing number of Jews migrating to Palestine. They were also aware that now the Jews were smuggling arms into the country to be used for defense purposes. In November of that year, the first real armed guerrilla resistance on the part of Arabs took place in Palestine, but it was quickly quelled by the British.

The following year, both major parties and several smaller ones which had begun to emerge banded together. Leaders of various Arab National Committees united to form an Arab Higher Committee. Its purpose was to force the British to implement stricter quota limitations on Jews entering Palestine. From August until October, approximately 8,000 guerrillas engaged in acts of terrorism aimed at both the British police and the Jewish settlements.

Then in October, a general strike was called in the hopes that it would so paralyze the economy in Palestine that the British would be forced to limit immigration. The strike proved effective in that the British promised they would send a Royal Commission to Palestine to discuss and investigate the grievances of the Arabs.

Having succeeded in focusing British attention on the Arab side of the dispute in Palestine, the Arab Higher Committee all but disbanded, insofar as the more moderate leaders, including the representative of the Nashashibi's National Defense Party, resigned from the Committee. This left the Committee dominated by the Mufti and his followers, who advocated violence as a solution to the Palestine question. The Mufti even went so far as to warn the British that if they did not change their policies in Palestine, which he considered pro-Zionist, the Arabs would in the future ally themselves with Britain's enemies, including Hitler. In years to come, the Mufti would indeed approach Hitler and would request aid in solving the "problem in Palestine," but despite his claim that he had the backing of the entire Arab world, his following was neither too large nor too powerful.

The British sent the Peel Commission to Palestine, as it had promised, and its report was published in July 1937. The report reflected generally the feelings of both the Palestinian Arabs and Jews. It stated that basically the cause of the disturbances was fear on the part of the Arabs that the Zionists were successfully establishing a Jewish state within Palestine in direct conflict with the Arabs' own hopes for self-determination and national independence. Both aims obviously could not be met within Palestine, and so the Peel Commission recommended for the first time that Palestine be partitioned.

It suggested that a Jewish state and an Arab state be established and that an area to include the cities of Jaffa, Jerusalem, and Bethlehem be kept separately under British supervision. The Arabs completely rejected the Commission's report. The Zionist leadership, however, after much discussion accepted the report, for it was the first clear statement proposing a Jewish *state* in Palestine, and not merely a Jewish *home*. Initially, the British government accepted the Commission's report, but after much debate it was finally rejected in November 1938.

During the early 1930's events were also taking place in the Jewish community in Palestine which would directly affect British policy for the remainder of the Mandate. As early as the end of World War I, Jewish settlers in Palestine had established defensive military units in order to protect themselves from attacks by Palestinian Arabs. By 1929, the *Haganah,* or Jewish Defense Organization, was clandestinely collecting funds and ammunition needed for self-defense. After World War I, the British had limited the distribution of arms in Palestine, but they had promised the Jews protection from attacks by the Arabs. The riots of 1929, however, proved to the *Haganah* that the British could not keep that pledge, and they felt it was up to the Jewish settlers to defend themselves. The *Haganah* was organized to include most of the Jews in Palestine and each community, each *kibbutz,* and each settlement had its own unit responsible for the defense of its Jewish settlers.

By 1934, the *Haganah* had widened its activities considerably. Specially chosen members were being sent to Eastern Europe to assess the situation of the Jews living in Poland, Rumania, and Bulgaria. Shocked by the repression they found there, the *Haganah* began making plans to help Jews leave Eastern Europe and to help in whatever ways they could to aid these refugees in entering Palestine, either legally or illegally.

The young members of the *Haganah* were often able to get many Eastern European Jews to Mediterranean ports, but they were less successful in obtaining the necessary immigration certificates issued by the British to control the entry of Jews into Palestine. They, therefore, chartered or bought ships, took aboard as many Eastern European Jews as possible, and began to smuggle them into Palestine.

In 1938, a special committee, the *Mossad le Aliyah Bet,* or the Committee for Illegal Immigration, was formally set up by the *Haganah.* Illegal immigration in Palestine, which until that time had only been on a limited scale, now began to increase in size and scope. By the end of 1938, nearly one thousand illegal immigrants were entering Palestine each month. The British made every attempt to stop this immigration, and all ships caught transporting Jews without the proper entry papers were taken to the island of Cyprus, where the immigrants were placed in detention camps.

In April 1937, a division took place in the *Haganah* which eventually led to some of the most bitter and frustrating events yet to plague Palestine. The philosophy of the *Haganah* was based on *havlagah,* the Hebrew word for self-restraint. The *Haganah* had been constructed initially for purposes of self-defense, not for retaliation against Arab raids. The responsibility of its members was to protect Jewish settlers in Palestine who were working to build *kibbutzim* and to reclaim the land. However, there were those in the *Haganah* who disagreed with this philosophy.

A Russian-born Jew, Vladimir Jabotinsky, chafed under the *Haganah's* policy of self-restraint. In the early 1920's, Jabotinsky had founded the Revisionist Zionist party in Palestine. One of the goals of the party was to bring into existence an independent Jewish state, which would incorporate the historical boundaries of ancient Israel and which would stretch from the Nile to the Euphrates. Jabotinsky felt that the only way such a state could become a reality was through force of arms. Within the party he created a military movement made up of young Jews, known as the *Betar*. The movement emphasized military tactics, including guerrilla warfare, and Jabotinsky envisioned its young members as the hope for realizing the goal of an independent and new state of Israel.

By 1937, the differences in philosophy between the *Haganah* and followers of the Revisionist Zionist party had become pronounced, and in April, about 800 members of the *Haganah* broke away to form a new group. The new group, led by David Raziel, was known as the *Irgun Zvai Leumi,* or National Military Organization. Members of the *Irgun* swore that they would not accept the authority of the Jewish Agency, nor would they be content merely to defend themselves from attacks by Arabs.

The *Irgun's* policy was twofold: reprisal against Arabs who attacked Palestinian Jews, and direct attacks on any installations of the British civil government in Palestine. The attacks of the *Irgun* were later to embarrass the Jewish Agency, terrorize the Palestinian Arab populace, and force the British to withdraw hastily from Palestine.

The White Paper of 1939

Reaction of the Peel Commission's Report of 1937, which had called for the partition of Palestine, had been intense. By 1938, the British Government had rejected the position taken in the Report. The reasons given were that the financial and administrative problems, which such a partition would involve, were too great. Under pressure by Zionists and Arabs to present an alternate policy, the British issued a new policy statement in May 1939.

The White Paper of 1939 declared that the British now intended to create an independent state in Palestine in which both Arabs and Jews would share governmental responsibility to insure that the interests of both communities would be met. The Paper also called for immigration quotas which would limit the entry of Jews into Palestine to 15,000 persons a year for the following five years. Thereafter, immigration of Jews would be left up to the discretion of the Palestinian Arabs. Cognizant of the pogroms taking place in Europe, however, the British also insisted that 25,000 Jewish refugees be allowed to enter Palestine as soon as it was feasible. The one right which the British retained was the regulation of land transfers in Palestine which had been entrusted to them under the original Mandate.

The Arab leaders rejected the 1939 White Paper and declared that they wanted Palestine to become an Arab state at once and that the immigration of Jewish settlers had to be stopped immediately.

The Zionists reacted violently against the 1939 White Paper and ardently opposed it both in Palestine and in Britain. On May 17, 1939, the day that the White Paper was to be announced, the Palestine Broadcasting Studios were bombed, and the White Paper was not read over the air as had been anticipated. The next day immigration offices in Haifa, Jerusalem, and Tel Aviv were broken into, and documents concerning Jewish immigration were burned.

The publication of the 1939 White Paper left the Jews in Palestine incredulous, for they considered it a break of the promises made to them through the Balfour Declaration. The various elements within the Jewish community in Palestine now worked, each in its own way, to assure that a Jewish state would be proclaimed in Palestine. The *Irgun* directed its sabotage and terrorist activities almost solely towards the British. The *Haganah* increased its efforts to facilitate the illegal entry of European Jews into Palestine. The Jewish Agency pressed for more legal immigration certificates, and when the war broke out a few months later, the Agency urged Palestinian Jews to register for service in the British Armed Forces. If civil war later erupted in Palestine, then training in the British Army would be invaluable, and volunteering for such service would prove the loyalty of the Jews to the Allied cause.

World War II

If World War II had not broken out, it is difficult to predict what might have happened in Palestine. Perhaps the strong feelings of the Arabs and the Zionists might have precipitated a civil war, with the British caught in the middle. Perhaps the Zionist and Arab terrorist activities would have created a situation of anarchy and destroyed all British influence in the area.

In fact, however, neither situation occurred for as the war approached, the Allied Powers, realizing their need for support from the eastern end of the Mediterranean, turned once again to the Levantine states. Promises were made that the several states under Mandate would receive independence in return for their support in the war effort. Iraq had already been released from its Mandate under the British in 1932. Lebanon achieved independence at the height of the war in 1943. Syria and Transjordan both gained independence in 1946. In Palestine, no agreement could be reached, however, because of the unstable situation there. Only Egypt, which had been granted nominal independence in 1922, but which still maintained a strong British presence, would have to wait until 1956 before gaining full independent status.

By the end of the war, some 35,000 Jews from Palestine had served in the regular British Army, while another 15,000 had served in the capacity of special police in Palestine. The Arab Palestinians also served with the British, but insofar as they had no personal feelings towards the Germans, they did not volunteer in the same proportions. Only 9,000 Arab Palestinians saw duty with the British.

But even as the war progressed, the British found themselves faced with the continuing problem of illegal immigration into Palestine. Though the world was becoming aware of what was happening in German concentration camps and knew that the British were taking every step to stop illegal entry into Palestine, no country came forth with an offer to resettle the European refugees. Even after the war when the full story of Hitler's horrors was broadcast to the world, only the Dominican Republic would step forward with a concrete offer of asylum to Jewish refugees.

The *Haganah,* well aware of the hideous situation faced by Jews in Europe, increased their efforts to force illegal immigration. Finally, in November 1940, the British announced that any refugees caught attempting to enter Palestine illegally would be deported to the British colony of Mauritius in the Indian Ocean, where they would remain until the war ended. Three days after the announcement of this new policy, world attention was riveted on Palestine and the problem of illegal entry. The British had captured two refugee boats, the *Milos* and the *Pacific,* trying to land in Palestine. Over 1700 passengers were aboard the two ships.

The "Exodus," immortalized in Leon Uris's novel, carried Jewish immigrants to Palestine.

Because of the poor state of repair of both ships, the refugees were transferred to a French ship, the *Patria,* which was to take them on to Mauritius.

The *Haganah,* perhaps in an attempt to disable the ship so that the refugees would be allowed into Palestine, planted explosives on the *Patria* while it was still anchored near Haifa. The charge, instead of merely disabling the vessel, blew a large hole in it, and within minutes the ship had sunk. Two hundred and fifty of the passengers on board were killed. The world saw what was happening, yet turned a deaf ear to the appeals of the Jews. Had the countries of the West offered to aid these victims, perhaps the Arabs and Jews in Palestine might have been able to settle their differences. In fact, however, the illegal immigration of Jews became an ever growing problem.

Nor was the Zionist struggle for Palestine limited to Palestine itself. A special meeting was held in the Biltmore Hotel in New York City in 1942, and Zionist leaders from throughout the United States were brought together. The meeting ended with a complete rejection of the White Paper of 1939 and a call for an independent and sovereign Jewish state in Palestine. The immediate results of the meeting were a solidification of opinion within the American Jewish community about the future of Jews in Palestine and a campaign to influence both the American public and its lawmakers to approve the establishment of a Jewish state in Palestine.

Until this time America had stayed out of the controversy. Now, however, the Presidency, the Congress, and the communications media began to respond to Zionist pressures which focused on the American tradition of supporting minority groups and on the strong feelings of guilt which prevailed in the country over America's failure to alleviate the plight of the Jews in Europe during the ruthless Nazi purges. So successful was this campaign that by 1944, the election platforms of both the Republican and Democratic parties called for unlimited Jewish immigration into Palestine and the reconstitution of Palestine as a Jewish state.

Eventually, the British did have to accept the offers of Palestinian Jews to aid in the war effort. When Tobruk, on the northeast coast of Libya, was besieged by the German General Rommel between March and November 1941, special commando units of the *Haganah* were pressed into service.

Meanwhile, in Palestine another rift had taken place, this time within the *Irgun Zvai Leumi.* The *Irgun* was now directing its attention towards disrupting British administration in Palestine by attacking the installations of the civilian government. They raided supply depots to obtain British arms and ammunition. They also aided the *Haganah* in the illegal entry of immigrants into Palestine. Dissidents within the *Irgun* led by Abraham Stern left the *Irgun* early in 1941.

Stern and his followers became known as the *Stern Group,* and they were feared and hated not only by the British, but also by the Palestinian Jews. The *Stern Group's* philosophy was that all obstacles to freedom for Jews must be removed whether they were Nazis, the British, or Palestinian Jews employed by the British police. In Stern's opinion the latter were collaborators. The single most spectacular terrorist activity carried out by the *Stern Group* during the war was the assassination of Lord Moyne, the British Minister of State in the Middle East. In November 1944, he was shot to death in Cairo by two young members of the *Stern Group*.

The activities of these terrorist groups, the *Irgun* and *Stern*, increased considerably when the war ended. Acts of sabotage which caused the disruption of communications and transportation were commonplace. At first, exhausted by the war effort and still concerned primarily with illegal immigration, the British did little to retaliate.

Finally, however, with their patience stretched to its limits, the British occupied the headquarters of the Jewish Agency in late June 1946. The Jewish Agency was the focal point of all Jewish activities in Palestine, and occupation by the British meant that future planning and the allocation of funds from the World Zionist Organization would be suspended. A month later, in retaliation terrorists blew up a wing of the King David Hotel which quartered the offices of the British Mandate personnel in Jerusalem. Ninety persons died, and over one hundred were injured in the explosion. Among the casualties were many Jews and Arabs. The British evacuated all of its nonessential personnel from Palestine, with the remaining staff housed in compounds surrounded by walls of barbed wire.

One Final Try

The British, exhausted by the war effort and the continual harassment encountered in Palestine, called on the United States to help examine the situation in the mandated territory and to make recommendations concerning its future. To reconcile American and British viewpoints, an Anglo-American Commission of Inquiry was established to study the situation at firsthand. On November 13, 1945, before the mission began its work, British Foreign Secretary Bevin drew a distinction between the establishment of a Jewish *state*, ". . . which we did not undertake to establish," and a Jewish *home*, ". . . that we must fulfill." The Zionist organizations throughout the world protested Bevin's statement strongly and pressed even harder for a Jewish state. On the heels of this statement, the U.S. Congress passed a resolution calling for unrestricted immigration of Jews into Palestine.

The joint report of the Commission was issued in May 1946, and its findings concluded that Palestine alone could not meet the emigration needs of the victims of the war. It suggested, therefore, that the United States, Britain, and other Western countries do all in their power to facilitate the entry of Jewish war victims and their resettlement in nations

other than Palestine. The report noted, however, that Palestine could ac-
commodate up to 100,000 displaced persons and that such persons
should be granted certificates authorizing their entry into Palestine. It
also discouraged the concept of establishing separate or exclusive states
in Palestine and stated that ultimately a form of government should be
established in Palestine which would guarantee protection of the rights of
both Arabs and Jews. Finally, the report concluded that because of the
continuing hostility in the country, Palestine was not yet ready for self-
government, and that the Mandate should continue until a trusteeship
agreement could be worked out in the United Nations.

The British and American governments agreed, at least in principle,
with the recommendations of the Commission, and in an effort once
again to find out how the Jews and Arabs in Palestine felt, the British
called for a conference to be held the following fall. The London Conference was to have brought together members of the Jewish Agency for
Palestine, the Palestine Arab High Executive, and members of the Arab
League.

When the Conference convened in September 1946, only representatives from the Arab League were in attendance. They rejected the
proposals of the Commission and again reiterated their stand that Palestine should be a state with an Arab majority. They did insist that Jews in
the country would have full citizenship rights.

Unable to reach an agreement, the Conference was adjourned in October. When it reconvened in late January 1947, it was obvious that
agreement over Palestine would not be reached. At last convinced that
they could not reconcile the Arab and Jewish demands, the British announced on February 18, 1947, that they would submit the entire problem to the judgment of the United Nations.

The United Nations and Palestine

At this point, it would be well to review the situation throughout the
Middle East. Many of the nations which had been placed under Mandates at the end of World War I were now independent. Even so, the British continued to maintain a strong presence in Egypt and Transjordan,
and they were also still quite influential in Iraq. The French had been
forced out of Lebanon and Syria, with both those countries working to
strengthen their own governmental structures.

Oil had been discovered in Iraq, Saudi Arabia, and Kuwait. Though
production had been interrupted by the war, it was evident that future
revenue from oil would, within a decade, begin to place these countries
on a sound economic footing.

In March 1945, Egypt, Iraq, Jordan, Lebanon, Syria, Saudi Arabia,
and Yemen had joined together to form the Arab League. Its purpose
was to strengthen ties between the Arab states and to allow for coordination of the various countries' economic and political activities. In the

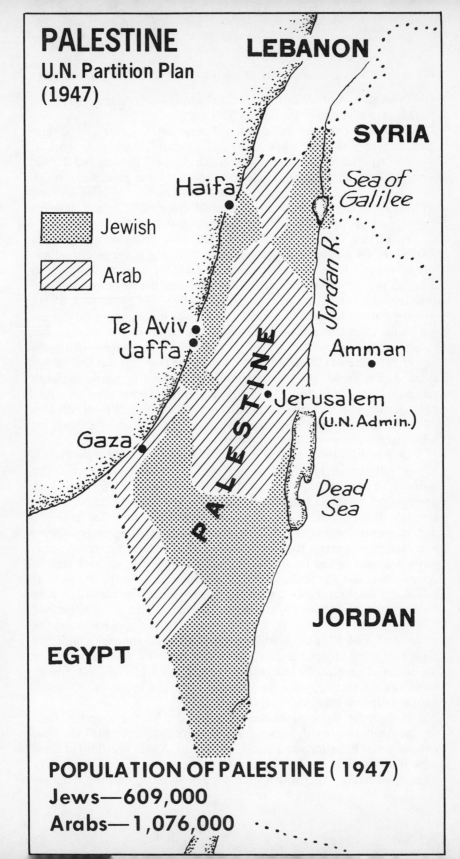

PALESTINE
U.N. Partition Plan
(1947)

LEBANON

SYRIA

Jewish

Arab

Haifa

Sea of
Galilee

Jordan R.

Tel Aviv
Jaffa

Amman

Jerusalem
(U.N. Admin.)

PALESTINE

Gaza

Dead
Sea

JORDAN

EGYPT

POPULATION OF PALESTINE (1947)
Jews—609,000
Arabs—1,076,000

same year, five Arab countries, Iraq, Lebanon, Saudi Arabia, Syria, and Egypt, were admitted to the United Nations.

Syria and Lebanon had developed representative forms of government. Egypt and Iraq, while still ruled by monarchies, were working towards representative government. Saudi Arabia, Yemen, and Jordan were ruled by absolute monarchies. Even with these governmental differences, the states of the Arab League looked on the Palestine problem with concern, and all condemned the establishment of a Zionist state in a territory which for twelve centuries had been dominated by Arabs.

As for the situation in Palestine itself, both Palestinian Arabs and Zionist Jews had rejected any plans for the partition of the country. Each wished either a Jewish state with an Arab minority or an Arab state with a Jewish minority. Both rejected any extension of the Palestine Mandate, together with the British offer to provide a five-year trusteeship, a plan proposed at the London Conference. No future lay ahead for further negotiations except to put the problem in the hands of the international community as represented by the United Nations. The complicated problem of Palestine was therefore placed before the two-year-old United Nations. At the outset, the United Nations was primarily western in both representation and outlook. In 1947, many of the countries, which would subsequently join it, were still colonial in status. This was especially true of the African and Asian countries, where nationalism and the desire for self-determination were beginning to stir.

On April 28, 1947, the first meeting of a special session of the General Assembly met at Lake Success in New York to discuss Palestine. The outcome of the special session was the appointment of a United Nations Special Committee on Palestine (UNSCOP). The Special Committee met throughout the summer, and on August 31, 1947, it published its report and recommendations. The Committee did not reach agreement, however, except on general recommendations, and the report included a majority proposal calling for the partition of Palestine into an Arab state, a Jewish state, and a specially administered trusteeship for the city of Jerusalem and environs under United Nations auspices. The majority's plan for partition of Palestine was also to include a Treaty for Economic Union between the two newly created states. The minority report, on the other hand, called for the establishment of a federal state with both factions remaining independent in a federated structure with Jerusalem as the capital. The minority report then went on to outline how the government would be set up, plans for a Constitution, and provisions for international supervision of the Holy Places.

Both of the reports included recommendations for boundary lines for the Arab and Jewish sections of the divided state. In 1947 the total population of Palestine was 1.8 million persons. About one-third of these were Jewish natives and immigrants, while the remaining two-thirds were Palestinian Arabs. Also at that time, the Jewish settlers owned about six percent of the land in Palestine, while the remainder was owned by Arabs. The majority report divided Palestine so that about 43 percent of the area would constitute the Arab state. Within the territory about 100,000 Jews and 650,000 Arabs resided. The Jewish state would comprise 56 percent of the land within Palestine, and in that area lived a Jewish population of 498,000 and an Arab population of 497,000.

The proposal put forth by the majority of the UNSCOP personnel was accepted by Jewish leaders and rejected by the Arabs. The Arab rejection was based in part on the fact that the United Nations was not a legislative body and could only "recommend" a solution to the problem of Palestine. Even if the General Assembly were to vote for partition, the body had no power to implement the decision, and it could not make the decision binding on either party.

Despite this very real objection, the vote for partition came to the floor of the General Assembly in November 1947. When the plan was presented, there was a great deal of uncertainty that it would pass. A delay in voting on the plan, however, allowed influential governments and special interest groups who favored the creation of a Jewish state additional time to lobby. This lobbying changed the decisive vote of three member nations (Liberia, Haiti, and the Philippines), who had previously opposed the partition. When the voting was complete, the partition of Palestine was approved by a vote of 33 for, 13 against, and 10 abstentions. Included in the resolution was the stipulation that the British Mandate for Palestine would be terminated no later than August 1, 1948.

The partition plan had been voted on by the international community, a deadline for withdrawal of the Mandatory power had been set, and the future of Palestine had been decided. The next five months in Palestine, however, would be painful ones with the situation there deteriorating to the point of anarchy.

Grim Winter in the Holy Land

The British, now assured that the responsibility for Palestine would soon be lifted from their shoulders, announced shortly after the vote for partition that they would withdraw from Palestine on May 14, 1948. In actuality, the British withdrawal began almost immediately. Strategic administrative posts throughout Palestine were systematically abandoned by the British forces who were now unwilling to risk the loss of more arms or men. As the British withdrew from these command posts, either the Arabs or the Jews and often both parties moved into the areas to claim them.

As is evident from the map of the United Nations Partition Plan for Palestine, the area which was to be the Jewish state, though it included over 56 percent of the territory of Palestine, was an area which obviously would be difficult to defend, if the almost 500,000 Arabs remaining in the Jewish state formed a fifth column in support of the 700,000 Arabs residing in the adjoining state of Palestine. The Jews would be forced into the difficult position of defending themselves both from outside aggression and from the Arabs within their country. And, if they did not prove successful in defending their state, it would almost certainly mean either a loss of territory or capitulation to Arab demands for a larger Palestinian state.

Realizing the seriousness of the situation which would face them at the end of the Mandate, the Jews began carrying out a two-pronged plan which would place them in a definite position of strength by the following spring. Jewish forces moved into as many strategic command areas as possible after they were evacuated by the British. They also carried on a protracted struggle with the Arabs over the control of the road which ran between Tel Aviv and Jerusalem. The road was a particularly vital link between the Jews living in the coastal areas and the nearly 100,000 Jews living in and around Jerusalem. The second part of the Jewish plan to solidify and strengthen their position was a systematic effort on the part of the *Haganah* to convince Arabs living in the territory which was destined to be part of the Jewish state that they should leave their homes and lands.

During the early part of the winter of 1948 the *Haganah's* attention was directed primarily towards organizing and training troops. At the same time the terrorist organizations, the *Irgun* and the *Stern Group,* took part in guerrilla raids directed against individual Arabs. Throughout January and February, a series of attacks and retaliatory raids between the Jewish guerrillas and the Arabs took place in the cities of Jaffa, Jerusalem, Ramleh, and Tel Aviv. It was a long and bloody winter, and according to a United Nations document issued on February 16, 1948, there were 2,779 casualties in Palestine between December 1, 1947, and February 1, 1948. The casualties included 1,462 Arabs, 1,106 Jews, and 181 British subjects.

Partition Reconsidered

With the mounting belligerency in Palestine, prospects for a peaceful partition dimmed. The United States, which had been one of the leaders in calling for the Partition Plan of the previous November, began to reevaluate its position. On March 19, 1948, the United States formally admitted to the U.N. Security Council an alternate plan calling for a temporary trusteeship over Palestine in place of the partition of the Mandate. The Council decided to call a special session of the General Assembly to reconsider the partition plan, and the session opened on April 16, 1948. The Palestinians accepted the proposed trusteeship, for they felt that they might be given another chance to express their viewpoint to the General Assembly. The Zionists rejected it, for they feared it would jeopardize their plans for a Jewish state.

Despite the fact that the General Assembly had convened to reconsider the future of Palestine, the British continued to prepare for with-drawal, and the attacks and reprisals between the Jews and the Arabs escalated. The Jews, aware that they must control more land than had been allotted them by the Partition Plan, stepped up their operations against the Arabs. There followed a series of incidents which resulted in the exodus of over 300,000 Arabs from their homes in Palestine before the May 14 deadline date, which would mark the end of the Mandate.

The first, and certainly the most shocking of these incidents, was the massacre of 254 Arab men, women, and children on April 10 in the village of Deir Yassin. The massacre was not perpetrated by the *Haganah,* though they had helped to occupy the village, but rather by the *Irgun* and *Stern Group.* When a United Nations fact-finding team was fi-nally allowed to enter the village, they found mutilated bodies of the Arabs, many of which had been thrown into a well. News of the massacre spread quickly and with it a growing terror that other Arab villages might meet the same fate. Thus, what had been until this time a small and spo-radic movement of Arabs out of the areas of conflagration now turned into a large-scale flight of Palestinians to what they considered safer ground.

Nor were terrorist raids carried out only by the Jews. On April 19, in reprisal for the Deir Yassin raid, Arab guerrillas attacked a convoy which was carrying supplies to the *Haganah* garrison in the Haddassah Hospi-tal, located on Mount Scopus in Jerusalem. A total of 77 doctors, nurses, teachers, students, and members of the *Haganah* were killed. But such re-prisals upset the Palestinian Arabs as much as they did the Jews, for the Arabs knew that such raids would lead inevitably to further retaliatory attacks by the *Haganah.*

The Arab Higher Committee, which in 1936 had represented various Arab nationalist groups throughout Palestine, was no longer represen-tative of the Palestinian Arabs. The vitriolic statements of the Mufti, Hajj Amin al-Husaini, added to the uncertainty of the already chaotic situa-tion. Throughout the Arab world, promises were being made that other Arab countries would come to Palestine's aid should war break out. But, there was also divisiveness among the Arab nations, and no one could foresee how such a war would end. And so, confused and frightened, the Arabs of Palestine continued to leave their homes and lands to seek ref-uge in areas which they considered safe.

Meanwhile, the Jews continued to solidify their positions in antici-pation of May 14, 1948. In late March, the *Haganah* was able to smuggle into the country arms and ammunition, acquired through an agreement with Czechoslovakia. These arms, in addition to those obtained from raids on British supply depots, would prove decisive factors in the strug-gle to come. But most decisive would be the organization and the training of the *Haganah* forces which had been preparing for the end of the Pales-tine Mandate since April 1923.

At Lake Success, the United Nations General Assembly was still in session trying to determine a course of action other than the partition of Palestine which could be implemented in the troubled territory. On May 14, 1948, the Assembly concluded its discussion of Palestine and adopted a new resolution, which would have delayed the actual partition. The resolution called for the selection of a mediator by the major powers. This mediator was to be assigned the tasks of promoting a peaceful adjustment to the Palestine problem, of insuring the maintenance of essential public services, and of assuring the protection of the Holy Places.

But less than an hour after this resolution was adopted, Israel unilaterally proclaimed its statehood. Recognition of Israel's statehood by the President of the United States, Harry S. Truman, followed almost immediately. This recognition came as a complete surprise to the U.S. Department of State officials at Lake Success, for they had just given the United States' support to the new United Nations' resolution calling for delay of the partition.

CHAPTER I
Part 3

A Short History of the Near East

May 15, 1948 to November 22, 1967

The 1948 Arab-Israeli War

The Arab states surrounding Palestine had already promised that they would fight Jewish claims to statehood. Twenty-four hours after the proclamation, the forces of various Arab states invaded Palestine. The Arabs claimed that Israeli forces had taken territory which was to have been allotted to the Arabs under the partition plan. The Israelis, however, claimed that the attack by the Arab states was unprovoked.

The war lasted less than a month, and on June 11, 1948, a truce was signed. At the time of the truce, the Arabs held roughly the land that was to have been Arab Palestine. The truce was breached intermittently until on July 9th, fighting resumed. During the ten days that followed, Israeli troops occupied Ramleh and Lydda and a large portion of western Galilee. Fighting was brought to an end by the United Nations on July 18th, and the positions held by Israeli and Arab military forces solidified and ultimately became the demarcation lines under separate armistice agreements signed the following year.

At the end of July, Israel held 77 percent of what had been Palestine; the Arabs held 21 percent. The Gaza Strip, which comprised about one percent of the territory, was occupied by Egyptian forces. The city of Jerusalem was to have been an internationally controlled area, or *corpus separatum,* but by the time of the armistice, it was instead a divided city. The Arabs held the Old City, containing most of the Holy Places, and the Israelis controlled the New City.

The United Nations, deeply concerned that the positions held by the respective armies would in the future create even greater problems, selected Count Folke Bernadotte of Sweden as its truce mediator. Before he

ISRAEL
(1948-1967)

LEBANON

SYRIA

Haifa

Sea of Galilee

○ Arab Refugee Camps

WEST BANK

Jordan R.

Tel Aviv-Yafo

Amman

Jerusalem

Gaza

Dead Sea

ISRAEL

JORDAN

EGYPT

POPULATION OF ISRAEL (1948)
Jews—879,000
Arabs—140,000

was able to change the precarious truce arrangements into a real armistice, Count Bernadotte was assassinated in Israeli-held Jerusalem on September 17, 1948, by members of the *Stern Group*. In November, the United Nations called upon all of the Arab states which had participated in the fighting and on Israel to agree to an armistice. With the help of the U.N.'s Ralph Bunche, third-party talks were held on the island of Rhodes during that winter, and eventually separate agreements were drawn up between Israel and the Arab states.

But even as fighting ceased, disputes began to develop over what remained of Arab Palestine, namely the West Bank of the Jordan River and the Gaza Strip. The Egyptians, who controlled Gaza, sponsored what was called the Arab Government of All Palestine. The Mufti, al-Husaini, was elected President of a national assembly in the Gaza Strip, which purported to have sovereignty over Palestine. In Transjordan, however, King Abdullah convened a meeting of influential Palestinian refugees in October 1948. At that conference, Abdullah rejected the Mufti's claim to the Presidency of the Arab Government of All Palestine. The king convinced the Palestinians to accept a plan whereby Palestine was placed under a protectorate agreement with Transjordan. At a later meeting in mid-December, leaders of the Palestinians on the West Bank formally called for annexation of the West Bank by Transjordan. The process was completed in April 1949 when King Abdullah appointed a Jordanian parliament with seven of the twenty seats held by Palestinians. This annexation was in direct opposition to resolutions passed by the Arab League and was bitterly opposed by most of the Arab states, for it appeared to give *de facto* recognition to Israel's boundaries and to solidify the existing partition of Palestine. Though armistice agreements had been signed in the spring and summer of 1949, no peace treaty had been drawn up, and the Arab League still hoped that should such a treaty be made, it would reflect the partition plan called for in the United Nations resolution of November 27, 1947.

The Arab Refugees

This failure to achieve a permanent settlement to the Arab-Israeli dispute has plagued the Middle East since 1948. At the core of the problem is the displacement of some 700,000 Palestinian Arabs who fled before, during, and after the war of 1948. Neighboring Arab states allowed the Palestinians to live in emergency refugee camps set up along their borders, but only Jordan offered to allow the Palestinians to become citizens. Gradually, the temporary camps became permanent.

Many arguments have arisen over the refugees of Palestine. Claims have been made that the Arab states refused to absorb the refugees in order to maintain the conflict with Israel. In part, this is probably true. However, one should also consider the problems faced by the Arab states which were asked to take in these refugees. All of the states were newly independent, and each shared the problems which independence often brings. All were faced with major economic problems. To absorb the tens of thousands of refugees would have meant providing adequate housing, food, health facilities, and education which could only be done at the expense of each state's own people. Ironically, it was Palestine from which the refugees had fled, that was one of the most developed countries of the region in 1948.

Many Palestinians were professional people, and over the years they managed to integrate themselves into the professional, commercial, and political life of their host countries. Many, too, migrated to Saudi Arabia, Kuwait, Europe, and even the United States. But it is estimated that about 70 percent of the refugees had formerly depended on farming for their livelihood, and these people could not readily find employment because of the lack of arable land available in the Arab states. Of equal importance, however, is the fact that most of the Palestinians did not wish to become citizens of another state. Many of those who had fled to Gaza and Jordan could view what had been their farms and homes from the armistice lines, and most wished to return to them.

On a political level, it was the United Nations which first took action to try to resolve the unanticipated problem of 700,000 refugees. Debate began immediately in the General Assembly to determine the status of

A typical Arab refugee camp.

the refugees and their rights to repatriation or compensation for the lands which they had lost. On the economic level, relief services throughout the world worked together to provide the necessities of life, including food, clothing, medical supplies, and shelter, which were all desperately needed by the refugees.

On December 11, 1948, the United Nations General Assembly adopted Resolution 194 (III), which called for the creation of a Conciliation Commission for Palestine. It was to work out a just settlement to the refugee problems caused by the 1948 conflict. The resolution stated that refugees who wished to return to their homes should be allowed to do so at the earliest possible date, and that those who did not wish to return should be compensated for the property they had lost.

It is estimated that up to 40,000 Arabs were allowed to return to their homes in Israel between 1948 and 1950. For the remainder of the refugees, however, there was neither repatriation nor compensation for the lands which they had lost. In 1951, the Conciliation Commission for Palestine did produce a general formula for reparations to the refugees by Israel, but it was a formula which was unacceptable to both Arabs and Israelis. During the years that followed, the Commission registered some 450,000 claims on Arab property in Israel, but it was unsuccessful in collecting on these claims. However, it did prove successful in unfreezing some ten million dollars in Arab money which had been blocked in bank accounts in the new state of Israel.

During this time, Israel continued to request recognition of its right to national existence, while at the same time she rejected any border changes and the requests made on behalf of the displaced Palestinians. The Arabs, on the other hand, demanded a return to the boundaries which had been called for in the United Nations partition resolution. They also asked that the refugees be allowed to choose freely whether they wished to seek repatriation in Israel or to receive compensation for the loss of their property.

United Nations Relief and Works Agency

As the situation deadlocked, it became apparent that the urgent needs of the refugees would have to be met in a more consistent and unified manner than was possible through the assorted agencies which were then providing emergency relief. The International Red Cross and the American Friends Service Committee had been two of the major organizations to step in and offer aid immediately following the war. Other organizations had soon followed suit including the Lutheran World Relief, the National Council of the Churches of Christ, and the Pontifical Mission for Palestine. On December 8, 1949, a resolution (302/IV) was adopted by the United Nations General Assembly calling for the creation of a United Nations agency to provide relief, medical care, and education for the refugees. The agency, the United Nations Relief and Works

Agency (UNRWA), was also charged with the task of assisting the refugees so that they could become self-supporting.

It is a sad commentary on the entire Middle Eastern problem that today, UNRWA continues to exist providing relief aid to the ever-increasing number of Palestinian refugees. In spite of the annual United Nations resolutions passed each year since 1949 requesting Israel either to repatriate or to compensate the refugees, Israel has consistently been unable to honor the directions of the international community.

U.S. Interests in the Middle East

Throughout history, the Middle East has been regarded as a strategic area by the major powers of the world. Empires waxed and waned in the region and seldom was it free of domination by foreign powers.

From the late 1700's to the end of World War II, the two major western influences in the area were Britain and France. Both countries vied for control of the trade routes through Syria and Iraq to the Persian Gulf and through the Suez to the Red Sea. This contest for preeminence ultimately led not only to political but also to military involvement in the region.

Following World War I and the break-up of the Ottoman Empire, it appeared likely that the countries of the Middle East would obtain independence. Knowing that statehood would threaten their interests and influence in the area, however, the Western nations imposed a Mandate system over many countries of the Middle East. This system delayed independence but the spirit of nationalism among the Arabs was growing, and it was soon apparent that statehood could not be put off much longer. Throughout the 1800's and early 1900's, the United States had relied on French and British influence in the area to protect American interests there. In the early 1930's, however, oil was discovered in Iraq. Within a few years oilmen were certain that there were vast petroleum reserves underlying much of the area. Oil became an increasingly important industry in the Middle East, and American oil companies invested large sums for exploration and production of oil.

After World War II, oil became an even more important factor to the international community. This was in part due to the implementation of the Marshall Plan, which was designed to rehabilitate war-torn Europe. As the Marshall Plan was put into effect, the need for petroleum and its by-products rose rapidly in Western Europe, and again American oil companies provided much of the private investment needed to expand production.

Politically, America's interests in the Middle East focused on the many newly independent nations of the region. Until the late 1940's, Russia's influence in the Arab world had been minimal. With the war over and Russia firmly in control of many of the countries of Eastern Europe, the United States began to fear that the Communists would attempt to move into the Middle East. The United States was aware that if the Russians successfully penetrated the area, they would ultimately gain control of the oil exports of the countries there. In an effort to stave off this possibility, in addition to the other problems which Communist control would bring to the new nations, the United States began supplying aid to the Arab countries under the Point Four Program.

In 1950, American involvement in the Middle East became even greater when the United States entered into an agreement with France and Britain known as the Tripartite Declaration. In part, the Declaration was aimed at preventing an arms race between Israel and the Arab states. The three powers promised that controls would be placed on the shipment of arms to any state in the area in order to avoid an arms race. The three governments also resolved that should they find that a state was preparing to violate the frontiers or the armistice lines that existed, action would be taken both within and without the United Nations to prevent such violations.

The Egyptian Revolution

The political picture in the Middle East was greatly altered by the Egyptian Revolution of 1952. Though it had gained nominal independence in 1922, Egypt still retained a strong British presence because of an Anglo-Egyptian treaty signed in 1936 and renewed periodically thereafter. The treaty allowed the British to maintain forces in the Suez Canal

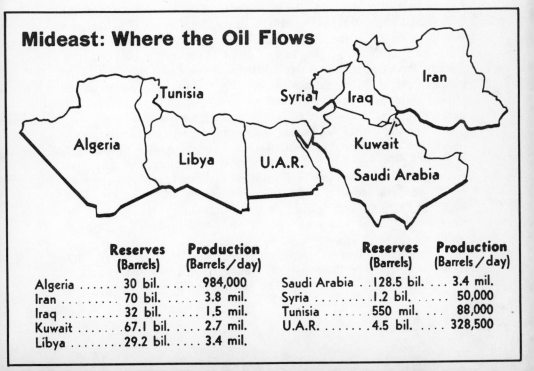

Mideast: Where the Oil Flows

	Reserves (Barrels)	Production (Barrels/day)		Reserves (Barrels)	Production (Barrels/day)
Algeria	30 bil.	984,000	Saudi Arabia	128.5 bil.	3.4 mil.
Iran	70 bil.	3.8 mil.	Syria	1.2 bil.	50,000
Iraq	32 bil.	1.5 mil.	Tunisia	550 mil.	88,000
Kuwait	67.1 bil.	2.7 mil.	U.A.R.	4.5 bil.	328,500
Libya	29.2 bil.	3.4 mil.			

Zone until 1956. In 1951, however, the treaty was unilaterally renounced by Egypt, and there followed an attempt to force the withdrawal of British troops.

By early spring of 1952, anti-British feeling was running high in Cairo. The Egyptians were not only against the British, but they were also strongly opposed to their ruler, King Farouk, who had brought the country to the brink of bankruptcy. On July 23, 1952, a group of young army officers overthrew Egypt's monarchy in a bloodless coup and seized control of the government.

Initially, General Muhammad Neguib, Commander-in-Chief of the Egyptian Army, headed the military junta which controlled the country. He was replaced in a power struggle, however, which ended on February 25, 1954, when Colonel Gamal Abdel Nasser, who had led the "Free Officers" in staging the peaceful revolution of 1952, became Prime Minister and Chairman of the Revolutionary Command Council. In this dual capacity he quickly moved to initiate reforms in the country's economy, an extensive program of land reform, and a building program to provide the country with more schools which it desperately needed. In October 1954, an agreement was reached between the Egyptians and the British that called for the removal of all British troops in the Suez Canal Zone by June 1956. Nasser was determined to rid the country of the remaining vestiges of British control and influence as rapidly as possible. He also sought to create greater unity among the Arab states, and by 1956 he had concluded defense agreements with both the more radical Syrian government and the more conservative Saudi Arabian government.

The United States was unsure of the new Egyptian ruler and the direction which Egypt would take in the future. Concern was also growing over Russia's intentions in the Middle East. Therefore, in 1955, America was instrumental in encouraging and finalizing the establishment of the Baghdad Pact. The Pact was one of mutual cooperation between Iraq, Turkey, Pakistan, Iran, and Great Britain. It was aimed primarily at the containment of Soviet expansion into the Middle East. Although the United States never formally joined the Pact, it virtually acted as a member by supplying both advice and aid to the member nations.

While the United States saw the Baghdad Pact as a means of containing the expansion of Communism, many of the Arab countries, particularly Egypt, saw it as a threat to greater Arab unity. The only Arab country to join the Pact had been Iraq, but pressure to join had also been placed on Syria, Jordan, and Lebanon. Nasser's denunciations of the Baghdad Pact gave him added prestige in the Arab world, but they distressed the United States and put it on guard toward the Egyptian leader.

The Baghdad Pact was signed on February 24, 1955. Four days later, members of the Israel Defence Forces launched an attack on an Egyptian army garrison in the Gaza Strip. The surprise raid proved extremely successful for the Israelis. For Nasser, however, the raid caused grave problems. Members of the Egyptian Army were convinced that one of the reasons the Israelis had carried out the raid so easily was because the arms used by the Egyptians were outdated. Those in command began pressuring Nasser to reequip the army with more modern weaponry and to do so as soon as possible.

The Suez Crisis

Nasser could ill-afford unrest within the Egyptian Army. He himself had come to power through the army, and he knew that he too could be deposed by a military *coup d'état*. The Soviets were aware of the crisis which Nasser faced, and in May 1955, they made their first tentative offer to supply arms to Egypt. Nasser neither accepted nor rejected the offer. Instead, in June he asked the United States and Britain for arms. Neither power actually rejected Nasser's request. Instead, they let the request reach the talking stage, and there it remained for three months.

Finally, unable to delay any longer because of additional Israeli raids in Gaza, Nasser agreed to the Soviet offer to supply arms to Egypt in September 1955. Instead of a direct Soviet-Egyptian arms deal, however, the agreement was made with Czechoslovakia for $200 million worth of military arms aid. A month later the Russians again offered to help Egypt: this time by supplying aid which would make possible the construction of a high dam at Aswan on the Nile River in Upper Egypt. The building of such a dam had long been a cherished dream of both the Egyptians and the British colonial government when it had held power in Egypt. Such a dam would not only add several hundred thousand acres of arable land to the four percent of Egypt's total land area then being cultivated, but it would also supply much-needed electrical power for industrial development in the country. Egypt did not accept the Russian offer, for Nasser was hoping that funds for the dam would be supplied by the World Bank and the United States and Britain. Eugene Black, President of the World Bank, visited Egypt in November and held discussions with leading Egyptians concerning a loan. He returned to the United States favorably impressed with the project and certain that Egypt would be able to repay the loan. Shortly thereafter, the United States and Britain both offered to assist in the building of the dam.

During the early months of 1956, Nasser's attention was focused on the Sinai and especially on the Gaza Strip. Several Israeli attacks took place in the area, and it was evident that the Egyptian Army still needed military equipment if they were to contain Israeli encroachment into the area. During the spring a second Egyptian arms deal was made with the Russians: this time directly with the Soviet Union. At the same time, Syria also completed an agreement to secure arms from the Russians.

Then on May 16, 1956, Egypt recognized Red China. It was probably this move which caused the United States to withdraw its offer to supply aid to Egypt for the Aswan High Dam. The United States appears to have felt that the recognition of Red China was done solely for the purpose of obtaining a new source of arms. At any rate, on July 19, 1956, the U.S. Secretary of State, John Foster Dulles, announced that the United States would no longer support the dam's construction. He stated that developments over the past seven months had not been favorable to the success of the High Dam project and that it was questionable whether Egypt had the ability to devote adequate resources to ensure the project's success. The British and the World Bank quickly followed suit and withdrew their offers of loans also.

A week later, Nasser announced the nationalization of the Suez Canal by Egyptian civilians. He ordered all British military personnel out of Egypt. The British who owned the controlling interest in the Suez Canal Company were astonished by the action. Nasser claimed, however, that the revenue which was then being received by the British would now be used instead to build the Aswan High Dam. Britain and France had both benefited greatly from the revenue earned by the Suez Canal Company, and they objected strongly to the Egyptian move. Israel, which had been denied passage through the canal since 1948, also objected strongly on the grounds that Egyptian control of the Suez Canal might jeopardize future Israeli shipping through the Straits of Tiran. In what has since been exposed as a coordinated effort on the part of the three nations, an attack took place on the Sinai Peninsula late in the fall. On October 31st, Israeli forces invaded the Sinai, and two days later Britain and France joined in the assault on Suez by landing paratroopers at Port Said. This aggression took place while the attention of the world was focused on the Hungarian revolt and the subsequent invasion of Hungary by the Soviet Union.

In spite of the tension caused by the situation in Hungary, the United States and the U.S.S.R. brought pressure to bear on the Suez aggressors through the United Nations, and cease-fire agreements were signed with Britain and France on November 7th, and with Israel on November 8, 1956. British and French troops withdrew from the Canal Zone in December, but Israel refused to withdraw its troops from the Sinai until satisfactory arrangements could be made to keep the Straits of Tiran open to Israeli shipping.

The position taken by the Eisenhower Administration during the Suez Crisis in 1956 compensated somewhat for its earlier refusal to provide financial assistance to Egypt for the Aswan Dam project. These tenuous good relations were nearly shattered, however, when on January 5, 1957, President Eisenhower appeared before Congress and presented a message which has since become known as the "Eisenhower Doctrine." Though intended to be a major step forward in healing relations with the Arab countries of the Middle East, the Doctrine instead alienated the moderate as well as the more radical Arab countries. In his speech, President Eisenhower stressed the threat which international Communism posed to the nations of the Middle East. After pointing out that America's basic national objective was ". . . a world peace based on justice," the President went on to state that Russia's intent was the opposite. International Communism, he contended, sought ". . . to mask its purposes of domination by expressions of good will and by superficially attractive offers of political, economic, and military aid." He then went on to ask the Congress to authorize the appropriation of $200 million to be used during 1958 and 1959 to assist any nation in the Middle East in developing economic strength which would help maintain national independence. The money would also be used to undertake programs of military assistance and cooperation. Finally, such assistance would include ". . . the employment of the armed forces of the United States to secure and protect the territorial integrity and political independence of such nations . . . against overt armed aggression and from any nation controlled by international Communism."

It was obvious that the Doctrine was aimed particularly at Egypt and Syria both of which had entered into arms agreements with the Soviets. There was, however, the further implication that any Middle Eastern country which might in the future accept aid from the Soviets would not be considered a friend of the United States. The Doctrine was a kind of international blackmail, and Arab reaction to it was mixed.

The Egyptians seemed to feel that the Doctrine was irrelevant. Having just been denied aid in building the High Dam, and having encountered aggression from England, France, and Israel, Nasser seems to have felt that the threat to his country was greater among Western nations than from international Communism. Other Arab countries appeared to follow Nasser's lead, and for the most part all thought the Doctrine was at best unimportant. This can be seen in the fact that even when President Eisenhower's request for aid was approved by Congress in a joint resolution on March 9, 1957, only two Arab countries, Libya and Lebanon, formally accepted the Eisenhower Doctrine.

The United Nations Emergency Force in Sinai

Prior to its troop withdrawal from the Sinai, Israel had demanded that its right to free passage in the Gulf of Aqaba be guaranteed. Three alternate solutions were offered to the United Nations. On March 5, 1957, U.N. Secretary Dag Hammarskjold announced that a United Nations Emergency Force would take over the provisional administration of the Egyptian side of the Suez Canal and the Straits of Tiran. The United States supported this arrangement which would guarantee the free passage of ships using the Canal. The *aide memoire* regarding this arrangement indicated that the U.N. Emergency Force, as it was to be known, was on Egyptian soil at the consent of the host country and could be removed at any time at the request of the Egyptian Government. Israel, on the other hand, would not permit a similar United Nations presence on her soil and announced that any future attempt to close the Straits of Tiran would be looked upon as a *casus belli,* or cause for war.

The troops sent to the Sinai by Israel were withdrawn from the area when the United Nations Emergency Force moved in to occupy the gun emplacements at Sharm el Sheikh, on the tip of the Sinai Peninsula. These forces now controlled the shipping which passed through the Straits of Tiran into the Gulf of Aqaba and allowed cargo bound for Israel free passage to its port at Eilat. The U.N. Emergency Forces were to remain there for the next decade supervising free passage through the Straits.

Unsettling Events of 1958

On February 21, 1958, Syria and Egypt announced that they were merging into a federation to be known as the United Arab Republic, with Nasser as President of the new state. The union was to allow for the coordination of economic policies between the two countries. Shortly after this merger took place, the new federation entered into negotiations with Yemen, and in March an agreement was signed which established a loose cooperative arrangement between the United Arab Republic and Yemen, known as the United Arab States.

In response to the merger of Syria and Egypt which indicated Nasser's growing prestige in the Middle East, Jordan and Iraq formed a federal union which was known as the Arab Federation. Jordan's King Hussein and Iraq's King Faisal were second cousins, and both were descendants of the Hashemite dynasty. Of the Arab states clustered at the eastern end of the Mediterranean, only Lebanon now remained uninvolved in mergers or agreements. These understandings were supposed to bring about greater unity, but in fact they proved divisive and led to polarization of attitudes in the area. Lebanon, however, stated it would join neither the United Arab Republic nor the Arab Federation, for it felt such moves would limit its independence and sovereignty. This angered many of the Arab Muslims in Lebanon who opposed the pro-Western stance of the Lebanese Government. A reorganization of the Lebanese Government in March 1958 only made the situation worse, for it removed the critics of pro-Western policies from office. By mid-May, disturbances had broken out throughout the country, and Lebanese officials blamed the riots on outside agitators from Syria. Fighting between the Lebanese Army and the rebels continued through June until finally the government, using the formal acceptance of the Eisenhower Doctrine as its criterion, asked the United States to send arms and police equipment into the strife-torn country. A special United Nations investigating team went to Lebanon to check reports that the riots were being caused by Communist-inspired Syrians. It reported on July 4th that there was no evidence of incursions into Lebanon and termed the conflict a civil war.

The turbulence in Lebanon triggered reactions throughout the rest of the Middle East. On July 14th, King Faisal of Iraq was killed in a military *coup,* and the Hashemite monarchy in Iraq was toppled. Immediately, the United States announced that it would halt all military aid which has been offered to Iraq under the terms of the Baghdad Pact. Iraq, in turn, denounced the Pact, withdrew from it, withdrew from the Arab Federation with Jordan, and shortly thereafter concluded a mutual defense pact with the United Arab Republic.

On the same date that the *coup* took place in Iraq, President Camille Chamoun of Lebanon requested that the United States send American troops into his country. By July 20th, over 10,000 U.S. Marines had been brought into Lebanon and were stationed in and around Beirut. At the same time, Jordan's King Hussein, fearing that his regime might also suffer the fate of his cousin Faisal's, requested that British troops be brought into Jordan, and on July 17th they were flown from Cyprus to Amman. Troops remained in both countries even though the Soviet Union and the Chinese People's Republic issued strong protests over American intervention into Lebanon's internal affairs. Finally, the United Nations General Assembly drafted a resolution calling for the removal of all troops, and both British and American forces left the area in early November.

Attempts to Promote Arab Unity Fail

Following the *coup d'état* in Iraq, King Hussein dissolved the agreement linking the two countries in the Arab Federation. Jordan now maintained the only monarchy in the eastern Mediterranean, and relations between King Hussein and the more revolutionary governments of the United Arab Republic and Iraq remained fragile. Unlike many of the other countries of the area, Jordan was still receiving a great deal of aid from the West, and this was an irritant to the more radical Arab governments. Slowly, however, relations between Jordan and the U.A.R. began to improve and diplomatic relations between the countries which had been broken off in July 1958 were resumed in August 1959. In December 1960, diplomatic relations between Iraq and Jordan were also restored.

Meanwhile, within the United Arab Republic there was growing disenchantment on the part of the Syrians. Economic progress which had been the basis for the union was not being achieved as quickly as the Syrian Baath party had hoped. This, however, was not the major reason for the growing discontentment. Large numbers of military advisers were being exchanged between the two countries and many Egyptians now held positions of prominence in Syria. Syria was being ruled now as a province of Egypt, and this worried many of the Baath leaders. Dissident elements within Syria precipitated a military *coup* on September 28, 1961, and by October 5th, Nasser had bowed to the new government's demand that the United Arab Republic be dissolved. Syria became known as the Syrian Arab Republic, while Egypt retained the title of the United Arab

Republic. Yemen dissolved its agreements with Egypt in December 1961, but the special relationship established between the two countries remained, and it came to bear on events which took place in Yemen the following year.

One of the first tasks President John F. Kennedy undertook after his election in 1960 was to improve relations between the United States and the Arab countries. He initiated a massive program of economic assistance to the U.A.R., and also encouraged fruitful relations with President Nasser by engaging in a personal exchange of letters with him. In their correspondence they discussed the many unresolved issues of the area. One of the outstanding issues, according to Nasser, was the continuing injustice to the Palestinian refugees, and he predicated a *rapprochement* with the United States on the solution to this problem.

In September 1962, a revolution took place in Yemen which served to aggravate still further attempts to achieve Arab unity. Since 1911, Yemen had been ruled by a monarchy headed by the Imam Yahya and his descendants. In 1962, the grandson of Yahya was to have ascended the throne. The rule of the Imams had not been popular, however, for they were highly autocratic and often repressive. The military particularly chafed under the Imam's rule, and revolt broke out within the Yemeni Army. The new Imam had to flee from the capital city of San'a. A civil war followed between the supporters of the Imam, known as the Royalists, and the revolutionary forces, known as the Republicans. The United Arab Republic sided with the Republicans and supplied them with both military equipment and troops. The monarchy of Saudi Arabia, however, sided with the Imam and sent military supplies to the Royalist forces.

The civil war in Yemen ebbed and flowed throughout the next five years until the defeat of the Arab armies in the June War of 1967. Throughout those five years, relations between the United Arab Republic and Saudi Arabia remained strained and demonstrated clearly the friction felt between what have been labeled the "moderate" Arab states of Lebanon, Saudi Arabia, Jordan, and Kuwait, and the "radical" Arab states including the United Arab Republic, Syria, Algeria, and Iraq, which considered themselves "revolutionary" and "socialist."

What of the Palestinian Refugees?

Following the Arab-Israeli conflict of 1948, the United Nations attempted to ascertain just how many Palestinian Arabs had been forced to flee their homes and now lived outside the newly formed state of Israel. According to the United Nations' documents released in December 1949, after the U.N. Economic Survey Mission for the Middle East had completed its report, an estimated 726,000 Palestinians had been made refugees. Of that total, over 650,000 persons were in need. This meant they did not have adequate shelter, clothing, and food.

The total number arrived at by the Mission excluded another 200,000 persons who while needy had not been forced to flee from their homes. Many of these people lived in the Gaza Strip or along the Israeli-Jordanian border. While they had not lost their homes, their lands now lay within the state of Israel. The Israelis refused to let them cross over the armistice line to tend their fields, and they were thus deprived of their livelihood. The number also included Bedouins who had once roamed freely through lands now sealed off by barbed wire barriers. Over one-half of the refugees moved eastward into Jordan, while another estimated 200,000 crowded into Gaza, a narrow strip of land lying south of the new state of Israel along the Mediterranean coast. The remainder of the refugees were almost evenly divided between Syria and Lebanon.

The United Nations Relief and Works Agency, which was created by the United Nations and began operations in 1950, took on the major

Dikwaneh refugee camp, on the outskirts of Beirut, capital of Lebanon.

responsibility of feeding and providing shelter for the refugees. Aided by funds from member nations, UNRWA set about supplying the most immediate needs of the refugees on a budget which totaled approximately 35 million dollars a year. This meant that a total of seven to ten cents per day was spent on each refugee or about $40 per refugee per year.

While UNRWA took primary responsibility for the refugees, there were numerous international and church-related groups also working to provide assistance and relief. The Near East Christian Council composed of churches in the Middle East created a special committee for refugee work. The Pro-Secretary of State at the Vatican, Monsignor Montini, now Pope Paul VI, worked to create a special agency which would provide aid. It became known as the Pontifical Mission for Palestine, and most of its funds were raised by the Catholic Near East Welfare Association in the United States. Over 100 million dollars has been channeled to the refugees by the Pontifical Mission. A number of Protestant churches in the United States created the Church World Services through which to channel funds and supplies. The Lutheran World Federation contributed approximately $300,000 yearly to provide food, clothing, and medicine. In the United States, a voluntary corporation known as American Middle East Rehabilitation was chartered in 1948 for the purpose of providing medical assistance to the Palestinian refugees. During the years between 1948 to 1962, AMER contributed to refugee relief work drugs and medical supplies worth over $11 million.

Central Coordinating Council

To coordinate the efforts of these private voluntary agencies, a Central Coordinating Council was created. Through it, requests for aid were channeled to the member organization best equipped to meet the need. But what had begun in 1948 as temporary measures to meet the most immediate needs of the displaced refugees slowly became ongoing programs as the years passed. Repeatedly the United Nations passed resolutions calling on the state of Israel to allow the return of the refugees or to provide compensation to them, and each year Israel refused to settle these claims pending its recognition by the Arab nations. Each passing year saw the number of refugees increased by about 30,000 persons due to a high birth rate. The attention of UNRWA and the private agencies then began to turn towards the education of this younger generation of refugees.

By 1967, UNRWA had registered a total of over 1.3 million refugees. Of this total, however, almost 200,000 were no longer receiving aid except in the form of medical services or education. UNRWA was operating 54 refugee camps, of which 25 were located in Jordan, eight in the Gaza Strip, 15 in Lebanon, and six in Syria. Almost two-thirds of the refugees registered were between the ages of one and twenty-five. Rather than having been alleviated, the problems of the refugees were becoming more acute.

For the Palestinians forced to remain in the refugee camps, day followed dreary day. The major hope which the parents nurtured was that one day their sons and daughters would be able to obtain an education which would allow them to find work outside the camps. Even in the early 1950's, higher education had been a goal of many Palestinians. Some who had completed their secondary education before the 1948 war were able to go on to obtain a university education in Egypt. Following the Egyptian Revolution in 1952, Cairo University opened its doors to the Palestinians and allowed them to attend courses on a tuition-free basis. Among the students attending the university was Yassir Arafat, who later became one of the leaders of the Palestine National Liberation Movement, now known more commonly as *Al-Fatah*. Arafat was chairman of the Palestine Student Federation at Cairo University from 1952 to 1956, and during the invasion of Suez in 1957, he fought with the Egyptians at Port Said.

The exchange of ideas between Palestinian students at Cairo University, as well as those of Palestinians elsewhere in the Middle East wherever they worked or studied, laid the groundwork for the Palestinian liberation movement. The first official group of *Al-Fatah* was formed in 1958, and initially its work revolved around the publication of a newspaper called *Our Palestine,* published in Beirut. The newspaper urged Palestinians to unite in the cause of liberation. The first military operations of *Al-Fatah,* however, were not carried out until 1965.

The Arab governments recognized that the small but growing Palestinian movement had the potential to create difficult situations, particularly if it should launch attacks against Israel. In 1964, therefore, Arab leaders at a summit meeting established the Palestine Liberation Organization as the official and recognized instrument for voicing the aspirations of the Palestinians. The PLO as a political organ was allowed to organize conventional military units which in turn comprised the Palestine Liberation Army. These units were attached to the regular armies of the Arab countries surrounding Israel, but they were cautioned not to engage in commando operations against Israel for fear such attacks might start another war for which the Arab states were ill-prepared.

At the same time in Syria small groups known as *fedayeen,* or "men of sacrifice," were organizing and, as early as July 1964, engaged in commando operations along the Syrian-Israeli border. By the fall of 1966, these attacks had grown into a "resistance-retaliation" cycle of major proportions. Whenever Syrian *fedayeen* carried out a guerrilla attack within Israel's borders, Israeli troops would respond by crossing into Syrian territory and carrying out a similar attack. Numerous incidents, including the shelling of a patrol car, a train derailment, a water pipeline explosion, and a clash with Syrian army patrols, were reported by Israel to the United Nations Mixed Armistice Commission, whose job it was to see that the borders between Israel and the Arab states remained peaceful.

In response to these attacks, Israeli troops crossed into Jordan on the morning of November 13, 1966, and totally destroyed the village of As-Sammu. The Israelis claimed that the tiny village had been a base from which the *fedayeen* had staged many of their attacks. Six days later, a United Nations fact-finding team announced that 18 villagers had been killed, 134 wounded, and 127 buildings destroyed.

It is not difficult to understand Israel's need to retaliate against such attacks. With a population of 2.7 million persons and an army of only 300,000 men, each death or injury slowly gnaws away at Israel's most vital resource: its people. What is difficult to understand, however, is that Israel's answer to attacks on its borders has often been massive reprisals aimed at the civilian population, and thoroughly out of proportion to the act which elicited the retaliating response. Also, frequently the reprisals have been made, not against those who carried out the initial attacks as in the case of the *fedayeen,* but rather against the neighboring Arab state from which such attacks were believed to have been launched. After 1966, Jordan and Lebanon frequently had to pay the price for commando operations carried out by the *fedayeen,* over which they had little control.

The incident at As-Sammu stunned the Arab world. The Foreign Minister of Jordan sharply criticized not only Syria for allowing such raids to take place, but also the United Arab Republic for not defending Jordan. He urged that the U.A.R. move its troops out of Yemen and into the Sinai, close to the southern flank of Israel. On the heels of the attack on As-Sammu, the U.A.R. instead signed a defense pact with Syria.

At this point, relations between Jordan and the surrounding Arab states, with the exception of Saudi Arabia, were not particularly cordial. In July 1966, King Hussein had suspended his support of the Palestine Liberation Organization, even though over two-thirds of Jordan's population was Palestinian in origin. Following As-Sammu, Syria and the PLO openly urged the Palestinians in Jordan to revolt against the King. Negotiations to bring Saudi Arabian and Iraqi troops into Jordan to assist in its defense broke down in December, and clashes broke out between Syrians and Jordanians along their mutual border.

In Cairo, President Nasser was having his own problems. Embroiled in the revolution taking place in Yemen, the U.A.R. was finding the Yemeni war costly in terms of money and manpower. Relations with Saudi Arabia were also strained by the war. United States-U.A.R. relations had reached their lowest point in years. In September 1965, the U.S. Congress had amended the Agricultural Assistance Act to exclude the U.A.R., ". . . unless the President determines that such sale is in the national interest." President Johnson was showing no inclination to renew such food shipments to the U.A.R. An austerity program had been put into effect in Egypt, and Nasser, who desperately needed grain to feed his burgeoning population, accused the United States of waging a war of hunger against the U.A.R.

Though relations between the U.A.R. and Syria did improve to the point where a trade and technical cooperation agreement was signed in July 1966, relations with Saudi Arabia and Jordan continued to deteriorate. Refusing to withdraw Egyptian troops from Yemen, even though faced with a serious financial crisis, Nasser found his country on the verge of bankruptcy by December 1966.

Prelude to War

In January 1967, Syrian commandos resumed their raids on Israel's eastern border. In February, Israel issued a warning to the Syrians that if attacks continued, they could expect a reprisal similar to that directed at As-Sammu. A month passed, and then on April 7, 1967, Syria fired on a tractor in the demilitarized zone south of Galilee. Israel answered by sending jets to destroy artillery installations in Syria, and Syrian and Israeli aircraft engaged in a dogfight over Damascus which resulted in the downing of six Syrian jets.

Syrian attacks continued, and on May 11th, Israeli Prime Minister Levi Eshkol warned that unless the *fedayeen* were contained, drastic measures would be taken by Israel. Two days later he declared that Israel would stop all Arab attempts at sabotage, would keep the Gulf of Aqaba open, and would resist any attempts on the part of the Arabs to divert the Jordan River's waters. He also warned that ". . . we shall choose the time, the place, and the means to counter aggression."

Meanwhile, the Soviets, ever ready to drive a wedge into the Middle East which would further alienate the Arab states from the West, warned the Syrians and Nasser that Israel had massed troops along the Syrian border. These reports were believed by the Arabs, even though reports by United Nations observers and U.S. officials contradicted the Soviet claim. Statements which served only to inflame the already tense situation were made by all parties concerned, but on May 16th what had appeared to be a war of words began to look as if it would become a war of weapons. The U.A.R. announced a state of emergency for its armed forces, and at 10:00 p.m. that night the commander of the U.N. Emergency Forces stationed in the Sinai was notified that Egyptian troops were being brought into the Sinai, and that the U.A.R. was requesting that the U.N. forces be withdrawn immediately. A request was also made to remove the forces from Sharm el Sheikh, a position that had since 1957 insured Israel's ships free passage through the Straits of Tiran.

Though the initial request was not made through the proper channels, and Secretary General U Thant tried in vain to have the request rescinded, on May 18th in the late afternoon he announced that he had no choice but to order the withdrawal of the U.N. forces. Earlier that morning, an Israeli representative had met with U Thant and presented his government's view that the Egyptians had no right to request unilaterally withdrawal of the U.N. forces. In the terms agreed to after the Suez Crisis of 1956, however, this right to unilateral withdrawal had been one of the stipulations, since the troops were all stationed on Egyptian soil. The Secretary General suggested to the Israeli representative that the U.N. troops now be stationed on Israeli soil, but he was informed that this would be unacceptable to Israel.

President Nasser had now placed himself in a difficult situation. His prestige, which had been waning during the past few months, in part because of the financial crisis he faced in Egypt, now began to rise. On May 19th, Egyptian troops replaced the U.N. forces along the Sinai border with Israel. The following day, twelve Arab nations declared that an attack against one of them would be considered an attack against them all. This announcement appeared to be another small victory for Nasser, who was responsible for the Arab Command, whose task it was to defend and protect the Arab states from Israeli attacks.

On May 22nd, Egyptian troops took over the surveillance post at Sharm el Sheikh. Nasser was faced with the choice of backing down from the strong stand he had thus far taken, by continuing to allow Israeli shipping to pass through the Straits of Tiran, or of closing the Straits. He chose the latter course of action and closed the Gulf of Aqaba to Israeli ships and ships of other nations which carried strategic cargo to Israel. The United Nations Secretary General immediately flew to Cairo for discussions with Nasser, who had also begun to mobilize the U.A.R.'s armed forces. Nasser assured U Thant that the Arab mobilization was only for defensive purposes and that the U.A.R. would not be the aggressor. On May 23rd, President Johnson made a speech committing the United States to the support of the territorial integrity of all the states in the area, and he asked that each nation do all it could to assist in resisting aggression in the area.

A Syrian tank, captured by the Israelis in June 1967, on its way to Tel Aviv.

It was the closing of the Gulf of Aqaba more than any other single event which led to the June War. President Nasser in announcing the closing had stated that ". . . sovereignty over the gulf's entrance is not negotiable." Israel responded in a statement issued by Prime Minister Eshkol that the U.A.R. would be committing an act of aggression against Israel if it interfered with shipping through the Straits of Tiran. Eshkol called on the great powers to maintain Israel's rights of "innocent passage."

In response to Israel's plea, the international community increased its diplomatic efforts in the hope of breaking the deadlock before war erupted. Members of the United Nations and the United States appealed to all parties involved to permit a diplomatic settlement. While some progress was being made through such channels, an attempt to gain support for a declaration by maritime powers, which would call for the right of "innocent passage" through the Gulf, failed.

Finally, on May 30th, Israel's Foreign Minister, Abba Eban, declared that Israel would use force to open the Gulf of Aqaba if diplomatic efforts failed, and he indicated that Israel would do it alone, if necessary. Israel had become increasingly impatient and alarmed over the lack of progress being made. On June 1st, Moshe Dayan, who had conducted the Suez campaign in 1956, was named Minister of Defense. Pressure within Israel to attack Egypt was mounting and on June 4th, General Dayan announced that Israel did not want foreign troops to fight for her, and that a diplomatic solution did not seem possible. Israel saw herself as a small nation which could not withstand an attack by all the Arab armies. Her only hope of survival was an offensive attack. With the developments of the past few weeks and the failure of the West to act quickly and vigorously in her defense, Israel now felt very much alone.

World tension over the events in the Middle East grew, and on June 4th, the U.A.R. announced that its vice president would visit the United States to discuss the situation with President Johnson and consider alternate solutions to the impasse. Many believed that the discussions would involve a *quid pro quo* agreement, with Egypt promising to open the Straits of Tiran to Israel in return for the wheat which had recently been denied. But the U.A.R.'s vice president never reached the United States.

The Six-Day War

Early on the morning of June 5th, the Israeli Air Force attacked Cairo, and destroyed the Egyptian Air Force which was still on the ground. Less than an hour later, the airport at Damascus came under attack, and Jerusalem was reporting artillery attacks. Almost immediately thereafter, the "hot line" between Moscow and Washington was activated for the first time in its history. Shortly after the exchange between the Kremlin and the White House, the State Department issued a statement that the United States was ". . . neutral in thought, word, and deed."

ISRAEL AND OCCUPIED TERRITORY

(Since June 10, 1967)

Israeli occupied

LEBANON

SYRIA

Haifa

ISRAEL

Amman

Jerusalem

Gaza

JORDAN

SUEZ CANAL

Suez

Elat
Al 'Aqabah

EGYPT

SAUDI
ARABIA

POPULATION OF ISRAEL (1971)
Jews—2,561,000
Arabs—404,000
Arabs in occupied terr.—1,000,000

The United Nations Security Council, which had gone immediately into emergency session, found itself deadlocked over a call for a cease-fire, since the Arab states demanded full withdrawal of Israeli forces. The United States and Britain opposed this, because it would leave the U.A.R. still in control of the Straits of Tiran.

The following day, the U.A.R. announced the closure of the Suez Canal because of obstructions caused during the intitial bombing and the danger to ships trying to pass through. In the Security Council, a resolution was passed unanimously calling for a cessation of military activity. The resolution did not, however, call for a withdrawal of forces from occupied territories, a customary element in United Nations resolutions dealing with conflict situations. The same day, Jordan accepted a cease-fire with the Israelis. Already thousands of refugees were crossing what remained of the Allenby Bridge into eastern Jordan. They fled because the West Bank of the Jordan was rapidly becoming Israeli-occupied territory.

Arab reaction to the preemptive Israeli strike was a mixture of disbelief, anger, and frustration. They did not believe the Israeli Armed Forces capable of the military accuracy shown during the first thirty six hours of fighting and were convinced that the West had assisted Israel in its military efforts. However, on June 7th, a Pentagon official disclosed that the Israeli planes had attacked Egypt from the sea in order to avoid Egyptian radar.

On the same day, the U.N. Security Council again called for an immediate cease-fire. The cease-fire, to which Jordan had agreed, had been broken by the Israelis, who continued to advance their positions in the West Bank area. Jordan complained, but Israel's Foreign Minister Abba Eban insisted that until the U.A.R. and Syria stopped fighting, Israel could not end her attack on Jordan.

On June 8th, an American communications ship, the *U.S.S. Liberty,* was strafed and torpedoed by Israeli aircraft. Again the "hot line" was used to alert the Russians to this new development.

The following day, cease-fire agreements were reached with the U.A.R. and Syria. President Nasser, in the face of this defeat, resigned the presidency. The next day, however, the Egyptian National Assembly reconsidered his resignation and returned to Nasser full powers as President, when it became apparent that he had the full support of the Egyptian people.

On June 10th, though Syria had agreed to a cease-fire, United Nations observers reported sighting Israeli armored and ground forces advancing into Syria. El Qantara, an important position on the Suez Canal, also fell to the Israeli forces that day, thus solidifying their position in the Sinai. On that day, the June War of 1967 technically came to an end.

Some results of the June War were apparent immediately. Israel now occupied all of the Sinai Peninsula, the Gaza Strip, the entire West Bank of the Jordan River, and Syria's Golan Heights. This meant that a total of 1.7 million Arabs were now under Israeli military control. The most severely crowded of the occupied areas was the Gaza Strip where 430,000 Arabs lived, 70 percent of whom had been made refugees in the 1948 war. Another 566,000 refugees from the 1948 war remained in Israeli-occupied Jordan.

Thousands of people living in the areas that came under attack in June 1967 fled before cease-fire agreements could be reached. An estimated 245,000 fled from the West Bank to the East Bank, which remained in Jordanian hands. Over 115,000 people fled from the Golan Heights eastward into Syria, and over 60,000 persons from Gaza and the Sinai Peninsula fled across the Suez Canal into the U.A.R. Of these, more than 400,000 refugees, 145,000 were made homeless for the second time in their lives.

Immediately following the June War, the United Nations Security Council passed a resolution calling on Israel to facilitate the return of those who had fled when hostilities began. Israel agreed to do so, but of the more than 200,000 persons who had left the West Bank, only 15,000 had been allowed to return by January 1, 1968.

On June 28, 1967, Israel announced its unilateral annexation of the "Old City" of Jerusalem which, it said, would bring about an integration of the city. Less than a week later, the United Nations General Assembly passed, by a 99 to 0 vote, a resolution condemning the Israeli annexation of Jerusalem. The United States abstained from the voting. In fact, the

The Six Day War of 1967 — An Arab woman flees across the ruins of Allenby Bridge.

Israelis had begun their annexation of Jerusalem by the end of the first week of occupation, during which time 135 houses in the Muslim Quarter of the city were destroyed leaving 650 persons homeless. The following week a similar incident took place near the Wailing Wall, the last remaining segment of what had once been the original Temple.

The Israelis rejected the resolution to cease annexation. Pakistan then submitted another resolution, this time to the Security Council, calling for Israel to rescind its annexation and asking the Security Council to take the steps necessary to insure withdrawal. The Pakistani resolution was passed unanimously, with the United States once again abstaining.

On August 1st, a conference of thirteen Arab Foreign Ministers met in Khartoum. In attendance was Ahmed Shukairy, the leader of the Palestine Liberation Organization. Shukairy at this meeting called for Arab resistance within Israeli-occupied territories and asked all the Arab nations to take a strong anti-Western stance. A week later, the first of several Arab strikes closed most of the businesses in the Old City of Jerusalem in protest against the annexation of Jerusalem.

At the end of August, an Arab summit meeting was again held in Khartoum. Though the conference was a closed one, reports leaked from the meeting suggested that the Arab states would seek a political solution to the Palestine issue. As the weeks passed, however, little progress was made in the United Nations towards a negotiated settlement.

Intransigence on the part of both the Arabs and the Israelis had been

Jordanian Jerusalem was unilaterally annexed by Israel in 1967.

building throughout the summer. Israel stated that its conditions for
peace talks were recognition of Israel's statehood, sovereignty, and international rights. Further, she would not accept third-party negotiations
nor would she withdraw from occupied territories until direct negotiations had resulted in a peace treaty. The Arabs, on the other hand, refused to recognize Israel, would not participate in direct negotiations
which would imply recognition of her statehood, and insisted on the return of all occupied land.

Formula For Peace

Finally, on November 22, 1967, the Security Council passed a reso-

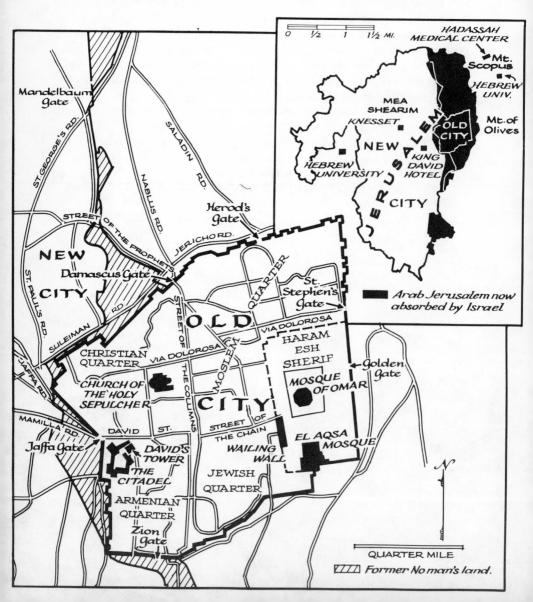

lution which, it was felt, contained the principles necessary to reach a just and lasting peace in the Middle East. The resolution included the following principles:

1. Withdrawal of Israeli armed forces from territories occupied in the recent conflict;
2. Termination of all claims or states of belligerency and respect for and acknowledgement of the sovereignty, territorial integrity, and political independence of every State in the area and their right to live in peace within secure and recognized boundaries free from threats or acts of force;
3. The need for guaranteeing freedom of navigation through international waterways in the area;
4. The need for achieving a just settlement of the refugee problem;
5. The need for guaranteeing the territorial inviolability and political independence of every State in the area, through measures including the establishment of demilitarized zones.

The resolution also called for the appointment of a Special Representative of the United Nations to establish and maintain contacts with the states concerned. Secretary General U Thant named Swedish diplomat Gunnar Jarring to fulfill this difficult assignment.

Jordan and the United Arab Republic immediately accepted the November 22nd resolution as a specific basis for settling the dispute. Syria rejected it. Israel finally accepted it, but with the stipulation that the resolution would be used only as a *guideline* for direct talks between itself and the Arab states. This disparity in interpretation between the Israeli government and the Arab governments led in turn to a prolonged delay in the mission of Gunnar Jarring and to the peace talks which he tried to initiate.

Epilogue

The years since the UN resolution of November 22, 1967, have seen the Arab-Israeli conflict become even more complicated. Scarcely a day has gone by without the situation appearing in the world's newspapers. In the years since 1967, various peace plans have been proposed, but none have been accepted by both sides. Neither direct nor indirect talks have taken place, and the plans of Gunnar Jarring, William Rogers, and others remain in the limbo of good intentions.

The *fedayeen* almost toppled the government of Jordan in 1970, but the civil war that followed the troubles saw them eliminated as a serious threat to King Hussein's regime. They are continuing their campaign for a free Palestine by violent means, such as airplane hijackings and terrorism. It would be impossible in a study guide of this size to cover in detail the recent incidences of violence, but it would seem that they have created greater roadblocks in the path to peace in the Near East.

The political impasse that has existed in the years since the June War has contributed to the amount of wasted lives and energies. The world, and the Near East in particular, cannot afford to let much more time pass before solutions are found to the grave problems facing both Arabs and Israelis. All must work towards the time when the Holy Land will at last be a place of peace and conciliation.

CHAPTER II

Country Profiles

Egyptian Arab Republic

POPULATION: 32.5 million
CAPITAL: Cairo
INDEPENDENCE: Gained nominal independence in 1922 but maintained a strong British presence until 1956.

Geography and People

The Egyptian Arab Republic is situated in the northeastern plateau of Africa. It is bounded on the north by the Mediterranean Sea, on the east by Israel and the Red Sea, on the south by the Sudan, and on the west by Libya. Though the country is approximately 380,000 square miles in size, only about four percent of the land is inhabited. The country is primarily desert with the exception of the Nile Valley, which stretches from the Sudan northward through Egypt to the Mediterranean Sea. It is in this valley where most of the arable land is located, and it is here that most of Egypt's populace has settled.

Egypt generally enjoys a warm, arid climate, though humidity in the river valley becomes quite high during the months between August and December when the Nile floods. Temperatures in the summer range from 70 to 110 degrees F., while in the winter months the climate ranges from 40 to 65 degrees F.

To the west of the Nile Valley lies the Libyan, or Western, Desert. Numerous oases can be found here, most of which have sufficient water to support farming. To the east of the Nile River Valley lies the Arabian, or Eastern, Desert. This area is exceedingly arid and consequently is sparsely populated. The only section of Egypt which receives any appreciable rainfall is the land near the Mediterranean Sea, in the vicinity of Alexandria, where about eight inches of rain falls each year.

Egypt's large population is both a great resource and a liability. There is room for much industrial expansion in the country, and a large labor force could be employed. However, the entire population lives on such a small percentage of the country's total land area that the popula-

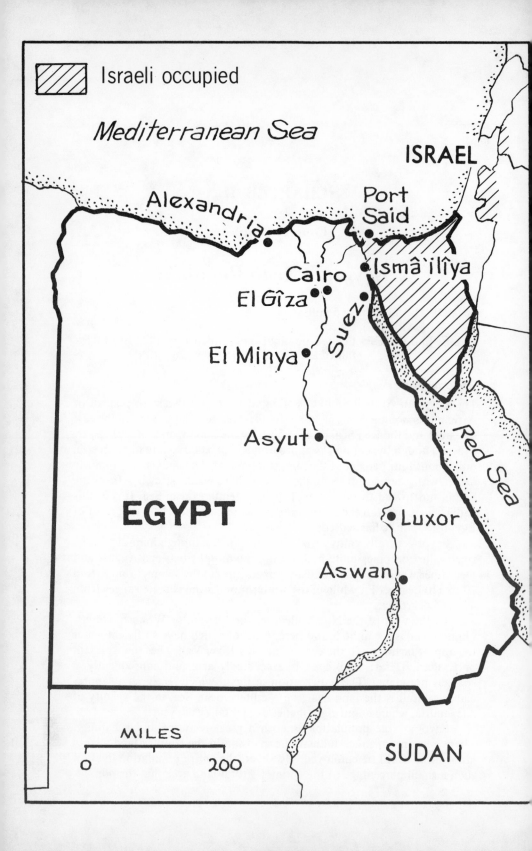

tion density is more than 2,370 persons per square mile. Life expectancy in Egypt has risen to 55 years of age, as diseases have been brought under control. This fact, coupled with an annual population increase of three percent, seriously threatens the country's economic stability.

The population of Egypt is a mixture of the inhabitants who have lived in the Nile River Valley for over 5,000 years and of the Arabs who entered the country in the seventh century A.D. during the Muslim conquests. Over 90 percent of the population are followers of Islam's Sunni sect. The largest religious minority is the Coptic Orthodox Church which claims over three million adherents. This Church traces its origins to St. Mark, who supposedly proselytized Egypt during the first century A.D. Other religions represented in the country include the Greek Orthodox Church, the Coptic and Greek Catholic Churches, the Armenian Apostolic Church, the Armenian Catholics, the Maronites, and the Roman Catholics.

Arabic is the spoken language, though in the Western Desert there are a few Berber-speaking villages. Both English and French are also spoken among the more educated Egyptians.

In 1952, following the Egyptian Revolution, a ten-year plan was inaugurated whereby 400 schools were to be built annually in Egypt. Primary education is offered and is free and compulsory, and there are many secondary and technical schools. Almost five million students are enrolled below the college level.

Egypt's capital, Cairo, boasts one of the oldest universities of the world, Al-Azhar, which was founded in 970 A.D. There are also five other universities in the country, with almost 150,000 students. Education is a primary concern, and the number of teacher training institutions is rapidly approaching 75.

History

Egypt's history is the longest of any nation in the world and dates back over 5,000 years. Egyptian civilization can be traced through the paintings and inscriptions found in its many monuments. The oldest of these are the Step Pyramid and the Pyramids at Giza, which were built over 2,900 years before the birth of Christ. Information about the Middle and New Kingdoms of Egypt can be found on the walls of the temples at Karnak and Luxor and in the tombs of the Valley of the Kings which is directly across the Nile River from Luxor.

Like much of the Middle East, Egypt came under Muslim domination in the seventh century A.D. and was administered as a province of the Muslim Empire. In 969, however, Egypt was conquered by the Fatimids, Shi'ite Muslims who believed the leadership of the Empire should be in the hands of a direct descendant of the Prophet Muhammad's daughter, Fatimah. The Fatimid rule in Egypt lasted two hundred years, during which time it was repeatedly threatened by the Crusaders. In 1172,

Salah al-Din, a Kurdish leader of northern Syria, brought Egypt and most of the area which had been held by the Crusaders under his control. Upon Salah al-Din's death, however, Egypt reverted to the control of the Ayyubids, another Egyptian dynasty, until 250 years later when the Mamluks took control.

The Mamluks were originally slaves that had acted as bodyguards to the ruling Caliph of the Ayyubids. When the last of that dynasty died, the Mamluks took over and retained control of Egypt and Syria until 1517 when the Ottoman Sultan, Selim I, defeated them in a battle at Cairo. For the next three hundred years, Egypt remained under Ottoman control, but the Mamluks continued to govern it as a province.

The modern history of Egypt may well begin in 1798, when Napoleon Bonaparte invaded the country in the hope of destroying British commercial trade both in the Middle East and India. Napoleon never gained effective control of Egypt, and in 1801, his army was forced to surrender to a combination of British and Turkish troops. During those three brief years, however, the idea of controlling Egypt at some future date was firmly implanted in the minds of the French.

After Napoleon's ouster, a power struggle ensued, and in 1805, Muhammad Ali, an Albanian officer in the Turkish army, was recognized as the Governor of Egypt by the Ottoman Sultan. During his rule which lasted until 1849, Muhammad Ali did much to bring about governmental reform in the country. In 1833, his son Ibrahim invaded and conquered Syria where he ruled until 1840 when the country was invaded, conquered, and won back by the Ottoman forces. During the rule of Muhammad Ali and his son, in Egypt and Syria respectively, important educational programs were begun. Numerous European educators, especially the French, were allowed to enter both countries and set up schools.

Muhammad Ali also granted a concession to the English to build an overland railroad from Alexandria through Cairo to the Gulf of Suez. This railroad from Alexandria provided a route for passengers, mail, and small merchandise to the Red Sea, and it reduced the length of passage from England to India from five to one and a half months. Bulky goods, however, still had to travel around the African Cape, and the French proposed a plan to build a canal which would link the Mediterranean and the Red Sea. Muhammad Ali refused to grant a concession for such a canal, for he feared that it would jeopardize Egypt's independent status.

Muhammad Ali's son Said, who succeeded him, did grant such a concession to Ferdinand de Lesseps in 1854, but work was not begun on the canal until 1859, owing to strong British objections and to their refusal to buy 80,000 shares in the canal which had been set aside for them. Said's successor, Ismail, bought up the British shares plus others that had gone unsubscribed, and these gave Egypt the controlling interest in the canal.

In 1866, Ismail was appointed Khedive, and one of his first endeavors was to extend his domination further into the Sudan. Coupled with extensive building programs both in Egypt and the Sudan, this proved extremely costly. Also, as Khedive, Ismail's personal expenses, which were by no means small, were included in the expenses of the state. By 1875, Egypt's economy was seriously threatened, and in order to avoid the collapse of his country, Ismail sold his shares in the Suez Canal to England for four million pounds. It was too late for Ismail to set the country on a sound financial basis, however, and in 1876, Egypt was declared bankrupt. Its fiscal administration, as well as the supervision of the Suez Canal, were placed under international control.

By the early 1880's, a strong nationalistic movement had taken root among members of Egypt's army and its more educated citizenry. Fearing continued foreign influence and domination, members of the army forced Ismail's successor, Tawfik, to grant concessions which would lead to stronger control of the government by Egyptians. This caused consternation among both the French and the British, who felt such a change would jeopardize their shipping rights and their control of fiscal matters in Egypt. In July 1882, the British landed forces at Ismailia, the city at the southern end of the Suez Canal, and took control of Cairo with the stated aim that they were there to help set Egypt's internal affairs in order, and once this was done, they would withdraw.

Such was not the case, however, for Egypt faced several problems including impending bankruptcy, rebellion in the Sudan and French hostility towards British control of the country. The office of the Khedive was retained by the British, but actually it was the British Consul General who ran Egyptian national affairs until the end of World War I. A legislative assembly was introduced into the governmental structure in 1913 by the British with the hope that it would provide a forum where the more vocal Egyptian nationalists could be heard, but where they would not threaten British rule.

Britain continued to control the country as a protectorate until 1922, when in response to promises made to Arab leaders prior to World War I, Egypt was declared an independent state. In March 1922, Fuad, Tawfik's brother, was made King of Egypt, and a constitution was drafted to provide for a parliamentary monarchy. The British refused to withdraw entirely from Egypt, and stipulations made at the time of its independence allowed the British to remain in the country for the next thirty years. These stipulations included the insurance that Britain would be responsible for Egypt's defense and that it would help with the management of the Sudan.

Although Egypt provided Britain with a base of operations in the Mediterranean during World War II, tension between the two countries mounted after the war when negotiations broke down over the questions of the Sudan and of a continued presence of British troops in the Suez Canal Zone. These feelings were further aggravated by the British withdrawal from Palestine and the War of 1948, in which Egyptian troops were defeated by Israel. King Farouk, who had come to power in 1937, and who had at first enjoyed general popularity, now found his position as ruler seriously threatened by the army and a faction of the population which represented growing anti-British sentiment.

Finally on July 23, 1952, a *coup d'état* by a group of young army officers ousted King Farouk. One of the officers, General Muhammad Neguib, became Commander-in-Chief and head of the military junta which took over Egypt. Real power was vested in the Revolutionary Command Council composed of nine of the *coup's* leaders. The Constitution was abolished, and all political parties were dissolved pending a three-year transition period. At the end of that period, representative government was to be restored. On June 18, 1953, Egypt was declared a republic, and Neguib took over as head of state. The following year a power struggle took place between Neguib and Colonel Nasser, another of the army leaders of the *coup,* and by the end of 1954, Colonel Nasser emerged as leader and acting head of state.

An Anglo-Egyptian treaty was signed in October 1954, under the terms of which British troops would be removed from the Suez Canal area within twenty months. By June 1956, this had been effected. Earlier that same year, the United States and Britain had offered Egypt financial assistance to be used for construction of the Aswan High Dam in southern Egypt. In July 1956, both nations withdrew their offers stating that the strain of building such a dam would be too much for Egypt's economy and would place the country in serious financial trouble. Following the retraction of these offers and the withdrawal of the British from the Suez Canal Zone, President Nasser announced the nationalization of the

The Pyramids of Giza, a few miles outside of Cairo, Egypt, were built nearly 5000 years ago as massive tombs for the early pharaohs. They are a great tourist attraction.

Suez Canal Company. He defended his action by explaining that the revenue from the Canal would be used to finance the Aswan Dam Project.

By October, France and Britain, who held the major controlling interest in the Suez Canal Company, and Israel, whose future imports were threatened by the seizure of the Canal, had worked out an agreement that resulted in the invasion of Suez by the Israelis in late October 1956. French and English troops were also supposed to attack Egypt, but they did not land at Port Said until November 2nd, by which time the United Nations General Assembly had called for a cease-fire. Several months passed until all the troops which had participated in the invasion were withdrawn in March 1958.

One of Nasser's professed aims was to bring about greater unity among the Arab states. In 1945, Egypt had been one of the founders of the Arab League. In February 1958, a formal merger of Syria and Egypt took place, and the United Arab Republic was formed with Nasser acting as President. In March of the same year, a loose federation between Egypt and Yemen was also made for political and military purposes. The union with Syria lasted until September 1961, when a *coup* took place in Syria as a result of increasing discontent over Nasser's policies. With the severing of ties between Syria and Egypt, the agreements with Yemen were also dissolved.

Other attempts at union among the Arab states included a closer alignment of Egypt, Syria, and Iraq in 1963, and later between Iraq and Egypt in 1964, but both failed. Meanwhile, relations between Egypt and Saudi Arabia were being strained by Egypt's intervention in the war in Yemen on the side of the revolutionaries. Saudi Arabia favored the royalists, and both countries sent military aid to Yemen.

Temporary Arab unity was brought about in the spring of 1967, when Nasser ordered the United Nations Emergency Forces to leave the Sinai. Subsequently, he closed the Straits of Tiran and cut off the Israeli port of Eilat. These actions drew praise from throughout the Arab world. The resounding defeat which Egypt suffered during the June War did not affect Nasser's power as much as might have been expected. On June 9, 1967, he offered to resign as President of the U.A.R., but demonstrations of popular support the following day were so great he remained in office.

The June War placed a real strain on Egypt's budget, and the cost of replacing military equipment forced Egypt to adopt an austerity budget which included rationing of food. Even with increased aid from the U.S.S.R. and from Kuwait and Saudi Arabia, Egypt has not been able to recuperate financially. The increased aid from the Soviet Union has served to keep the Middle East, and particularly Egypt, in the focus of the international community's concern. Introduction of SAM missiles along the country's eastern border led to intensified efforts on the part of the Western powers to try to reach a solution to the problems of conflict between Israel and the neighboring Arab states. Israeli raids deep into

Egypt and Egyptian commando attacks on Israeli positions in occupied Sinai aggravated the situation.

In the summer of 1970, the U.S. Secretary of State, William Rogers, offered proposals for a settlement, but they have not been implemented. A ninety-day cease-fire was agreed upon in August, 1970, and although subsequent renewals have elapsed, it continues to be observed.

The sudden death of President Nasser, on September 28, 1970, caused great consternation throughout the Arab world. Nasser was succeeded by the Vice President, Anwar Sadat, who has followed his predecessor's policies. A loose federation between Egypt, Syria, and Libya was announced in late 1971, and the name "United Arab Republic" was changed to "Egyptian Arab Republic." On October 4, 1971, President Sadat was named President of the new "Federation of Arab Republics." Federation headquarters are in Cairo. Because of some differences of opinion among the three partners, not much has resulted from the union. Separate diplomatic representatives have been maintained by each, but economic and social cooperation is foreseen.

During the summer of 1972, President Sadat ordered the withdrawal of all Soviet technicians and military advisers. This sudden action ended actual Soviet presence in Egypt and may have resulted from the U.S.S.R.'s hesitation to deliver offensive weapons to Egypt.

Economy

Egypt has always had an agriculturally based economy, even though there are only six million *feddans* of arable land in the entire country. (One *feddan* = 1.038 acres). When the military regime came to power in 1952, 64.5 percent of the total arable land was in the hands of 5.8 percent of the population. Land reform programs were begun immediately, and individual landowners could henceforth own a limit of 200 *feddans* of land. This amount was lowered to 100 *feddans* in 1961.

The redistribution of land was accompanied by improved productivity. A Ministry of Agrarian Reform was set up, which was responsible for initiating rent controls, regulation of land tenure, and the building of cooperatives at the same time the land reforms were being carried out. Even with these reforms in 1965, 49.3 percent of the land was still in the hands of only 5.4 percent of the people.

The general scarcity of arable land, coupled with an annual birth rate which is estimated at three percent, has caused Egypt's government great concern. One major project which was undertaken to relieve the economic strains of a rapidly increasing population is the High Dam project at Aswan. The Dam, which was completed in 1971, cost over one billion dollars. It allows for the cultivation of an additional two million acres of land and provides up to ten times more electrical power than was generated before in Egypt. This will, of course, result in significant industrial development.

Despite five-year plans aimed at development of manufacturing and light industry, agriculture brings the highest percentage of foreign exchange into Egypt. Over fifty percent of the world's long-staple cotton is grown in Egypt, but because of uncertain market conditions, restrictions have been placed on the planting of cotton, and only one-third of a farmer's land may be planted with this crop. Steps are also being taken to increase the production of rice and sugar, both products which are continually in demand in the world's markets.

Oil, too, is beginning to play an important part in Egypt's economy. Despite the fact that oil fields in the Sinai, which had been in production before June 1967, have been taken over by the Israelis who now occupy the area, Egypt's production of oil from offshore wells in the Gulf of Suez was, by May 1968, higher than pre-war productions. Two other fields, one at El Alamein and the other in the Qattara Depressions, are now being exploited, and it is hoped that Egypt will soon become a major oil exporter.

Egypt's second largest source of income was the Suez Canal which has been closed since June 1967. This has caused a major financial setback to the Egyptians, for receipts from the Canal in 1966 alone totaled over $200 million. Tourism too was affected by the June War, and many restrictions were placed on travelers to Egypt. These have eased a great deal, however, and construction of hotels and tourist accommodations has been increasing.

Iraq

POPULATION: 9.5 million
CAPITAL: Baghdad
INDEPENDENCE: October 3, 1932 (formerly a British Mandate from
1923 to 1932)

Geography and People

Iraq has a land area of approximately 170,000 square miles and is about
two-thirds the size of the state of Texas. Its most important geographical
feature is the twin river system of the Tigris and Euphrates. Both rivers
rise in the southern mountains of Turkey and flow through Iraq from the
northwest to the southeast. They meet just north of the city of Basra. The
land lying in the valley between the Tigris and Euphrates rivers forms the
eastern portion of the arable arc of land known as the "Fertile Crescent,"
which begins in Israel and Jordan and stretches to the north and east
through Lebanon and Syria to Iraq. This area receives the largest amount
of rainfall of the Middle Eastern countries, with the exception of Yemen
and southern Sudan.

Another important geographical feature of Iraq is the Zagros mountain range, which forms a natural border in the northeastern section of
the country dividing it from Iran and Turkey. Over one-third of Iraq's
southwestern land area is desert. While the land between the two major
rivers receives between ten and twenty inches of rain each year, water for
irrigation comes primarily from flooding. These flood plains experience a
reasonably moderate winter, but the summer is often hot and humid with
temperatures reaching 110 degrees F.

About 90 percent of Iraq's inhabitants are Muslims representing
both the Sunni and Shi'ite sects of Islam. The Sunnis, or the orthodox
Muslims, trace their Islamic heritage back to Abu Bakr, the first *Caliph*
or successor to the Prophet Muhammad. Members of the Shi'ite sect, on
the other hand, believe that the *Imam*, or religious leader of Islam, must
be a direct descendant of Muhammad. Iraq's largest ethnic minority, the
Kurds, live in the Zagros mountain region and are followers of Sunni
Islam. The population living in central and southern Iraq is Arab in origin and is almost evenly divided between Shi'ite and Sunni Muslims.

The remaining ten percent of the population is made up of Christians of various sects, including Uniate Catholics, who are in communion
with the Pope in Rome, Orthodox Christians, Assyrian Christians, and

various Protestant sects such as Presbyterians, Seventh-Day Adventists, and members of the United Church of Christ. Christian Iraqis are to be found in the area surrounding Mosul, and in Baghdad. There are also members of the Jewish faith and followers of Baha'i living in Iraq. The Jewish community, which once numbered about 250,000, has dwindled to 2,500 or less since the establishment of Israel.

Arabic is the official language of Iraq; Kurdish is used officially in the Kurdish area. There are other languages in use, however, especially in northern Iraq where Persian and Turkish are also spoken.

Though once the center of Islamic civilization, Iraq suffered an intellectual decline after the sack of Baghdad by the Mongols in 1258. Throughout the four centuries of Turkish domination, education was restricted mainly to the religious schools of the mosques. Students at these schools concentrated their studies primarily on the tenets of Islam and its holy book, the *Qur'an*. Since World War I, there has been a dramatic change in Iraq's educational system. In 1920, there were 89 schools in Iraq with a total enrollment of 8,000 students. Today, however, there are almost 5,000 primary schools with a total enrollment of over a million students. The number of secondary schools have also increased proportionately. Education is compulsory on the primary level and is free for all, including those in colleges and universities. Emphasis has also been placed on providing more technical, vocational, and teacher training.

History

Prior to the Muslim conquest of Iraq in the seventh century A.D., this area was the site of several flouishing civilizations, including the Sumerian, the Babylonian, and the Parthian. Baghdad, which became the religious center of Islam and the capital of the Abbassid Caliphate in the eighth century, has a rich history as a center for learning and the arts. Both Arab and Jewish scholarship flourished in the city between 800 and 1200 A.D.

Early in the sixteenth century, the area was conquered by the Turks and became part of the vast Ottoman Empire. Throughout the reign of the Ottomans, Baghdad was relegated to the position of a frontier outpost, and the people of Iraq suffered greatly under the Turkish rule which imposed heavy taxation and which severely limited individual freedom. This rule in Iraq was brought to an end following World War I and the break-up of the Ottoman Empire. When the war ended, many Iraqis felt that they were ready for independence. At the San Remo Conference held in 1920, however, the Allied Powers granted the British a Mandate for Iraq. The Mandate system was a new concept in international affairs, which authorized the nation granted a Mandate to administer the governmental affairs of countries considered not yet ready for total independence by the League of Nations.

The British were aware of the Iraqis' desire for statehood. In an effort to make it appear that the country's independence was imminent, they requested Emir Faisal ibn Hussein to act as king. It soon became evident that, though King Faisal appeared to be ruling Iraq, it was the British who retained actual control of the country. This resulted in demonstrations against the British led by Iraqi nationalists. Finally, on October 2, 1922, the British signed a treaty promising that Iraq would gain its independence within ten years.

Steps toward formal independence were taken as early as March 1924, when legislation known as the Organic Law was passed. The Organic Law provided for a form of government in Iraq, which would include a hereditary monarchy with a representative body centered in a parliament. Even with this concession to self-government, the British continued to maintain a powerful presence in Iraq.

On October 3, 1932, Iraq was granted formal independence. The following year King Faisal I died and was succeeded by his son, Ghazi. The new king was young and inexperienced and was able to do little to alleviate the problems facing the newly independent country during his six-year reign. Ghazi died in an accident in 1939, and because his son was too young to succeed him, an uncle, Abd al-Ilah, served as regent until 1953. Abd al-Ilah maintained strong ties with the British throughout the period of his regency, and this pro-British attitude caused much dissent among Iraqi nationalists. Several *coups d'état* were attempted during this period, but each was quelled. By the time King Faisal II ascended the throne in 1953, there were also strong anti-Western feelings in the country brought about by the creation of Israel in 1948. This feeling intensified during and after the Suez Crisis in 1956 and threatened to topple the monarchy.

King Faisal II, in an effort to satisfy the strong Arab nationalist feelings of his subjects, concluded an agreement on March 19, 1958, with his cousin, King Hussein of Jordan. The agreement called for Jordan and Iraq to form an Arab Federation which would benefit each country in the areas of defense, foreign policy, and education. The effort to placate Iraqi nationalism came too late, however, and on July 14, 1958, a revolution led by the army took place which successfully brought to an end the monarchy in Iraq. King Faisal II and his prime minister were killed, and control of the country passed into the hands of Lieutenant General Abd al Karim Qasim.

Qasim immediately called for the formation of a Republic Council of Sovereignty to replace the monarchy. The Council was to exercise presidential powers and was to be responsible for the appointment of a Cabinet which would include Qasim as Prime Minister. In an effort to reverse the pro-Western stance taken by the former monarchy, Qasim entered into economic agreements with the U.S.S.R. and other Eastern-bloc nations, which allowed Iraq to purchase a variety of Soviet-made military equipment. Iraq also withdrew from the Baghdad Pact, a defense agreement made by Iran, Iraq, Turkey, and Pakistan, aimed at preventing Soviet encroachment into Southwest Asia. Following Iraq's withdrawal from the Baghdad Pact, the United States terminated all technical and military assistance to Iraq.

In March 1961, the Kurds of northeastern Iraq led by Mustafa Barzani rebelled against Qasim's regime. The Kurds, who are not Arab in origin, chafed under Iraqi rule and demanded that they be allowed autonomous status. During the next three years the Kurds engaged in a see-saw battle with Iraqi troops in the Zagros mountain region. Neither side, however, was able to win a decisive battle.

Qasim's cooperation with the U.S.S.R. and the growing influence of Iraq's Communist party eventually led to unrest both in the army and among the educated middle class who feared the growing power of the Russians in Iraq. On February 8, 1963, Qasim was killed during an army *coup d'état,* and there followed a short period during which the Socialist Ba'ath party dominated Iraq's political scene. The Ba'ath party had been founded in Syria in 1941, and one of its main aims was to promote Arab unity. In Iraq there were two branches of the party. One branch was pro-Egyptian and favored greater Arab unity, while the other branch favored complete independence with only loose ties to other Arab states. The Ba'ath party was unable to consolidate its position of leadership following the February *coup,* and it was ousted from power in November 1963 and replaced by the less radical Arab Socialist Union.

Abd as-Salam Arif, who had led the military revolt against Qasim, assumed full control of power on November 18, 1963. One of the first problems which faced him was to bring about a settlement in the long-festering dispute with the Kurds. Early in 1964, negotiations for peace began, and a cease-fire was signed in February. During the negotiations

Shi'ite sect Golden Mosque in the sacred city of Kadamain, a suburb of Baghdad, Iraq.

that followed, the government of Iraq agreed to recognize the national aims of the Kurds in the new provisional constitution, which was in the process of being drafted. The Kurds were to be allowed proportional representation in Iraq's Parliament and Cabinet, and they were to be given regulatory powers over municipal affairs within their own district.

A provisional constitution was adopted in May 1964. The powers of the presidency were to be vested in a three-man Sovereignty Council, while legislative and executive powers were to be exercised by a Cabinet, functioning by approval of the Sovereignty Council. However, no provisions were made for an independent legislative authority, such as the U.S. Congress. Nor did the new constitution grant the Kurds the limited concessions they had been promised, and problems with the Kurds continued in Iraq.

In April 1966, Abd as-Salam Arif was accidentally killed in a helicopter crash and was succeeded by his brother, Abdel Rahman Arif. The June War of 1967 and the defeat of the Arabs considerably weakened the new President's position, and he was deposed in a military *coup* on July 17, 1968. At present, Iraq's government is headed by a Revolutionary Command Council with Major General Ahmed Hassan al-Bakr acting as President.

Apparently there are elements within Iraq who are unhappy with the present regime and would like to see it deposed. The most notable example of internal dissent is evidenced in the spy trials held in Iraq during January and February 1969. In the six months following the trials, over fifty persons were executed for treason and plotting against the state.

The period since 1969 has seen increased stabilization of the political scene as well as nationalization of much foreign-controlled industry, a notable example of which is the Iraq Petroleum Company. Cooperation with the U.S.S.R. has also grown, and a significant amount of Iraqi oil is destined for Soviet use.

Economy

The major single source of revenue in Iraq is oil, which accounts for almost 95 percent of total Iraqi exports. Oil was discovered in Iraq in 1927, and by 1934 it was being exported by the Iraq Petroleum Company through pipelines leading to the Mediterranean ports of Haifa and Tripoli. In 1952, foreign oil companies, having producing wells in Iraq, agreed to pay the state one-half of the profits realized from their operations in Iraq. By 1968, this source of income to the state totaled over $550 million.

The main oil field in Iraq is located in Kirkuk which is in the north-central part of the country. There are also fields near the city of Mosul and in the vicinity of Basra in the southeast. Oil from Basra is exported through the Persian Gulf and amounts to about one-third of the total oil exported from Iraq. The northern fields piped their oil through Syria to the Lebanese port of Tripoli and to the Syrian port of Baniyas. The piping of oil to seaports on the Mediterranean made Iraq heavily dependent on the good will of the Syrian government, and conflicts arose between the two countries concerning the Iraq Petroleum Company's pipelines to the coast. Occasionally the governments of Iraq and Syria failed to reach agreement on transit fees, and this resulted in Syria's refusal to allow Iraqi oil to be shipped to Mediterranean ports. However, both countries have cooperated following the nationalization of the Iraq Petroleum Company.

Only about one-sixth of the arable land in Iraq is now in use. This amounts to less than three percent of the entire country. In part, this underdevelopment stems from inadequate flood control devices on the Tigris and Euphrates rivers. Because most of Iraq is a flat plateau, especially in the area surrounding the two rivers, much of the land which could be cultivated is inundated when the rivers flood, and water levels may reach up to thirty inches in areas located fifty miles from the rivers. Iraq has begun flood control programs which will permit controlled irrigation. Numerous hydroelectric plants are planned. When various projects, such as the building of four major dams and needed barrages, are completed, the amount of usable land will have been increased by almost 80 percent. Much of the money for such projects is being provided by agreements made between Iraq and the U.S.S.R. in 1969 and the years following.

Iraq is capable of feeding its own population, while at the same time it can export dates, wheat, barley, wool, hides, and skins. But, there has been no major industrial expansion in the country. One factor limiting industrial expansion is the shortage of skilled labor and management personnel in Iraq. Recent budgets for Iraq, however, have directed 25 percent to the improvement of education and social services. Twelve percent of the budget is destined for economic affairs, and a like amount is set aside for internal development.

Given the land area of Iraq and its agricultural potential, one may say that the country is underdeveloped. Wise use of the money received from oil production, increased agricultural production, expansion of light industry, and a stable political situation, however, could soon make this country one of the fastest-developing nations in the Middle East.

Israel

POPULATION: 3.1 million
CAPITAL: Tel Aviv / Jerusalem
INDEPENDENCE: May 14, 1948 (formerly part of the state of Palestine under British Mandate from 1923 to 1948)

Geography and People

Israel is bordered on the north by Lebanon, on the east by the Syrian Arab Republic and Jordan, on the south by the Gulf of Aqaba and Egypt, and on the west by the Mediterranean Sea. It is about the size of the state of New Jersey and has a total land area of approximately 7,900 square miles. The northern section of the country is hilly and enjoys good rainfall, as does the narrow central coastal plain. The climate of Israel varies from mild in the north to very dry and hot in the Negev Desert, which constitutes almost 50 percent of Israel's total land area. There is little rainfall from May to September, but along the coastal plains the summers can be quite uncomfortable because of high humidity. Winters are damp and chilly in the northern and central section of the country, but snow is rare.

When the June War of 1967 ended, Israeli military forces occupied additional territories including Egypt's Sinai Peninsula, the Golan Heights of Syria, the Jordanian territory on the West Bank of the Jordan River, and the Gaza Strip. These lands are still under occupation, and almost no progress has been made towards a peace settlement.

Of the 3.1 million people living in Israel proper, 2.6 million are Jews, while the remainder are Arabs. Among the latter, 73 percent are Muslims, 17 percent are Christians, and 10 percent are Druzes and others. The Jews in Israel represent a varied background, since the greater portion of the population migrated to the country from other nations. At present, 43 percent of the Jewish population is native-born, 30 percent immigrated from Europe, America, or the Pacific, 14 percent came from Africa, and 13 percent are from Asia. In addition to its indigenous population of just over 3 million persons, Israel also has political control over nearly one million Arabs living in the occupied territories. These include over 950,000 Muslims, 32,000 Christians, and 6,000 Druzes.

During the period of the British Mandate in Palestine, Arabic was the dominant language, though Jewish immigrants worked hard to learn

MILES

0   25

LEBANON

SYRIA

Haifa

*Sea of
Galilee*

Nazareth

Tiberias

ISRAEL

Jordan R.

Tel Aviv-
Yafo

Jerusalem

Ashdod

*Dead
Sea*

Beersheba

JORDAN

EGYPT

Elat

Israeli occupied

Hebrew. English was the second language. Since 1948, Hebrew has become the official language of the country, with Arabic and English used as second languages.

Education plays an extemely important role in Israel's life and receives the budget's second highest appropriation after defense. Many Jews who immigrated to Israel from Eastern Europe were well educated and formed a cadre of teachers for less educated immigrants and children born both during the Mandate and after Israel proclaimed its statehood. The result has been that Israel has the most advanced educational system in the region. There are now over 1,500 primary schools in Israel serving almost 400,000 students, and nearly 200 secondary schools, with an enrollment of over 60,000 students. There are also numerous vocational and agricultural schools, as well as many teacher training institutions and seven colleges and universities.

For the most part Arabs in Israel and in the occupied territories attend separate schools provided by the Israeli government. There are almost 175 primary schools and ten secondary schools serving Arab students. There are also one teacher training institute, one agricultural school, and four vocational schools.

While education in Israel is free and compulsory on the primary level, students on a secondary level are required to pay tuition.

History

The modern state of Israel was born out of desire on the part of world Jewry to create a homeland where Jews could live freely without repression or persecution. Largely through the efforts of Eastern European Jews and particularly through the work of Theodor Herzl, a movement known as Zionism developed in the late 1800's. The goal of the movement was to urge Jews from throughout the world to consider colonizing a territory, preferably in the Holy Land where eventually a Jewish state could be established.

To enact such a plan, a coordinating agency was needed, and the World Zionist Organization was formed in 1897 to raise funds and to promote the movement of Jews to Palestine. The World Zionist Organization also worked in the political sphere to convince major world powers, such as Britain, that a homeland for the Jews should be established in Palestine. The early Zionist leaders were successful in this work, and in 1917 Britain released a document known as the *Balfour Declaration*, which stated that the British government viewed favorably the establishment of a Jewish homeland in Palestine.

Jewish emigration to Palestine rose steadily throughout the early years of the twentieth century. Many of these emigrants came from the ghettos of Eastern Europe and the Russian Pale. Some, though not familiar with agricultural techniques, settled on collective farms, known as *kibbutzim*, and spent their early years in Palestine adjusting to an agrarian way of life. Others, unwilling to give up their urban way of life, settled in Jerusalem, Tel Aviv, and other Palestinian communities.

At the end of World War I, British troops occupied Palestine. Many Palestinian Arabs who had hoped for independence following the war viewed the British occupation and the talk of a Palestine Mandate with alarm. The Arabs were aware that the British government had publicly stated that it was in favor of the establishment of a Jewish homeland in Palestine. This left open the question of what would happen to the Arabs in Palestine. When the announcement was made in 1920 that Britain had been awarded the Mandate for Palestine, Arab-inspired riots broke out in Jerusalem. A year later, before the Mandate became effective, more serious rioting took place in Jaffa.

Throughout the next decade the situation in Palestine was an uneasy one, but it was not until 1933 that the situation changed dramatically. In that year, Nazi Germany began intensifying its pogroms and persecutions of the German Jews. As the situation in Germany became more intolerable, emigration from Germany accelerated, and many German Jews sought asylum in Palestine. The Arabs saw the balance of population beginning to shift in Palestine, and they viewed the increasingly large number of Jews as a real threat to Arab hopes for self-determination.

Between 1933 and 1936, sporadic rioting by the Arabs took place throughout Palestine. It was motivated in part by the hope that the British would enforce quotas on the number of Jews allowed to enter Palestine. The early years of World War II brought a temporary cessation to the troubles which afflicted all of Palestine, as attention was now focused on defeating the Axis powers. By 1945, however, internal dissent again racked the area.

Many plans had been set forth throughout the British Mandate concerning the future of Palestine, but all had been rejected either by the Arabs or the Zionists. Finally, in 1947, Britain decided to place the entire problem in the hands of the United Nations. Britain also announced its intention to withdraw from Palestine by May 14, 1948, and during the year that the United Nations worked to find a satisfactory solution to the problem, Palestine itself struggled through a period of near-anarchy.

On May 14, 1948, the British completed their withdrawal from Palestine, and at midnight Jewish leaders proclaimed the establishment of the state of Israel. War, which had been imminent between the Jews and the Arabs, broke out on May 15th. All the Arab states surrounding Palestine entered into the war, but Jewish forces proved superior. Eventually, cease-fire agreements were signed with each of the Arab states, and Israel, having obtained recognition from many of the major powers and the United Nations, consolidated its position as a new nation.

Following the war of 1948, immigration to Israel rose sharply, and within the next four years almost 600,000 Jews from throughout the world came to Israel. One of the new nation's first tasks, therefore, was to resettle these new citizens in homes and find employment for them. The administration of this project fell to the Jewish Agency, which had been created in 1929 as a means of ensuring the economic and social development of Jews coming to Palestine during the British Mandate. Provision for the creation of the Jewish Agency had been included in Article Four of the Palestine Mandate. When the Agency was set up, its chief goals were to encourage Jewish immigration, to recover land in Palestine as Jewish public property, and to promote the use of Hebrew and Jewish culture. Since the resettlement of immigrants from all over the world fell within these goals, the Jewish Agency continued to function in these areas after the 1948 war. The Agency also provided much of the money needed for resettlement through its own fund-raising efforts carried on primarily outside Israel. Even today the Jewish Agency continues to function in these same areas through power given it by public laws enacted in 1952 and an agreement made between the Agency and the Israeli government in 1954.

The governmental structures of the new state were built along Western lines and included a unicameral Parliament, a President, and a Cabinet led by a Prime Minister. The country's first President was Chaim Weizmann, and its first Prime Minister was David ben-Gurion. The Parliament was to be known as the *Knesset*. Elections to the first *Knesset* took place in January 1949. They resulted in a body of 120 members elected for four-year terms through proportional representation. One problem which has been encountered in elections to the *Knesset* is that there are numerous political parties in Israel, and no single party has been strong enough to gain a clear-cut majority. At present, for instance,

View of Tel Aviv, Israel, a city that rose from sand dunes in less than one hundred years.

there are at least twelve different political parties represented in the *Knesset*. The most powerful of these is a coalition of three labor parties known as the Israel Labour Party.

The President is elected by the *Knesset* for a five-year term. After consulting the parties represented in the *Knesset*, he chooses a member of that body to act as Prime Minister and to form a Cabinet. Though Cabinet members need not be members of the *Knesset*, the Cabinet is responsible to the *Knesset* and must resign if a motion of nonconfidence is passed against it.

Israel does not yet have an official constitution. Laws have been passed which will eventually form the constitution, however. In 1949, a Transition Law was passed which described in a general way the powers of the *Knesset*, the President, and the Cabinet. This Transition Law has since been superseded by specific Fundamental Laws including those dealing with the *Knesset* (1958), Israel Lands (1960), and the President (1964). The Fundamental Law of Government has been introduced to the *Knesset*, and the Fundamental Law of Human Rights is in preparation. These fundamental laws will eventually form Israel's constitution.

Israel's history is inextricably bound up in its relationship to the Arab states which surround it and in three wars which have been fought in the Middle East since Israel's proclamation of statehood.

Economics

Israel has faced severe financial problems since it became a state in 1948. Nonetheless, great economic progress has been made by the state. This is due in part to good planning by the Israeli government. Even with this excellent planning, however, such progress would have been impossible without an exceptionally large flow of capital into the country. Foreign currency receipts have actually totalled nearly two billion dollars in some years. About half of this money comes from the export of goods and services, while the other half represents economic aid in the form of private purchases of Israel Development Bonds and private gifts, reparation payments by West Germany, and agreements and loans made with other nations.

Early in its statehood, Israel's agricultural ventures played an extremely important role both in the country's economy and in the resettlement of immigrants coming from Europe, Asia, and North Africa. Within twenty years, however, agricultural production accounted for less than nine percent of the national income, while manufacturing and mining contributed nearly 25 percent. The primary agricultural export is citrus fruit. Other exports include polished diamonds, textiles, and clothing.

The Jewish National Fund is directly responsible for land development in Israel, and nine-tenths of the land now under cultivation in Israel is owned either by the state or by the Jewish National Fund. Reclamation of the land has been a primary goal since 1948 and has involved the settlement of immigrants on collective farms and large-scale irrigation and soil research projects. Full development of current water resources in Israel, however, can provide only enough water to irrigate 40 percent of the land which could be cultivated. Like the Arab countries surrounding it, Israel is searching for usable water, and this has led to a continuing dispute between Jordan and Israel over the diversion of water from the Jordan River.

One major budgetary problem which Israel has had to face is the exceedingly large amount of money it must spend on defense. Almost 40 percent of the national budget is devoted to maintaining an army, buying armaments, and the development of weapons within Israel. The continuing conflict in the Middle East has placed a real burden on Israel. Funds which should have been used for development have had to be diverted instead to the defense of the state. Israel's potential for growth has also been hampered by the need to remain constantly on the alert to attacks on its borders by Arab guerrillas. The resettlement of an increased number of immigrants from the U.S.S.R. has also proved a financial strain on the economy of the nation.

If solutions could be found to the problem of Israel's recognition by the Arab states, the problem of the Arabs made refugees in the 1948 and 1967 wars, and the problem created by the occupation of Arab lands in 1967, the peoples of the entire Middle East would be free to redirect their attention towards development and may in years to come, be willing to share with each other the fruits of their labor.

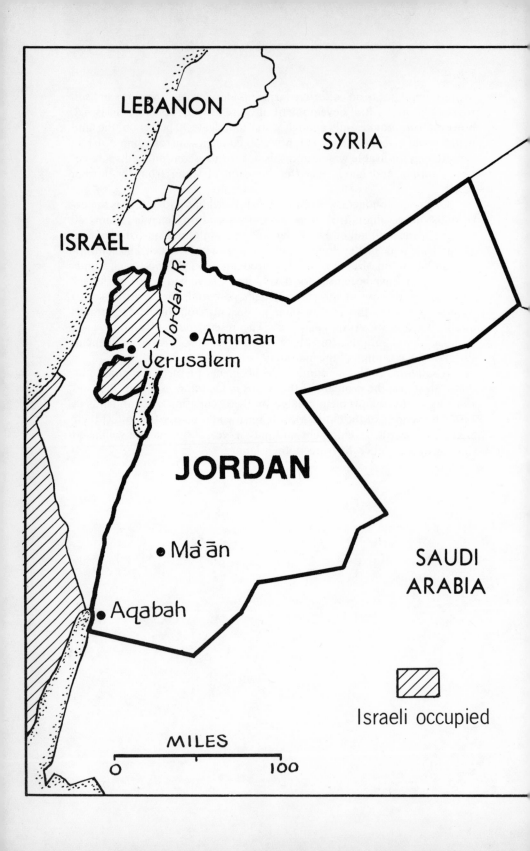

LEBANON

SYRIA

ISRAEL

Jordan R.

• Amman

Jerusalem

JORDAN

SAUDI
ARABIA

• Maʿān

• Aqabah

Israeli occupied

MILES

0   100

Jordan

POPULATION: 2.32 million
CAPITAL: Amman
INDEPENDENCE: May 25, 1946 (formerly under British control from
1918 to 1946)

Geography and People

Jordan is a little larger than the state of Indiana and occupies approximately 38,000 square miles. Its eastern boundaries were arbitrarily drawn by the British following World War I and reflect the lack of natural topographical boundaries such as mountain ranges or bodies of water. The western boundary of Jordan is the result of solidification of armistice demarcation lines agreed to by Israel and Jordan following the 1948 Arab-Israeli war. Jordan is bounded on the north by the Syrian Arab Republic and on the east by Iraq and Saudi Arabia.

The most important geographical feature of the country is the Jordan River valley. The Jordan rises just inside the borders of Syria and Lebanon and flows southward through approximately 100 miles of Jordanian territory before emptying into the Dead Sea. The West Bank of the Jordan was densely populated prior to the June War of 1967, primarily because of the advanced agricultural development which had taken place there. It is estimated that at least one-half of Jordan's total population lived in the West Bank area prior to 1967, but the June War caused almost 350,000 people to flee across the river to the East Bank, which remains under Jordanian control. The 2,000 square miles which comprised Jordan's West Bank are at present under Israeli military occupation.

To the east of the Jordan River valley lies the northwestern corner of the Arabian plateau. This plateau extends throughout eastern Jordan and into Syria, Iraq, and Saudi Arabia. It comprises over two-thirds of Jordan's land area and drops in elevation as it extends to the south and east. Lack of rainfall causes the plateau to be either semidesert or desert and thus capable of sustaining only nomadic life. The western section of Jordan receives between fifteen and twenty five inches of rainfall each year. While the summer temperatures may often reach 120 degrees F. in this area, the winters are relatively cold, and frost and snow are to be expected in the hillier portions of the country.

The Jordanian populace is primarily Arab in origin. Arabic is the official language, though English is also widely spoken. Over 80 percent of the Jordanians are followers of the Sunni sect of Islam. The remainder of the populace is primarily Christian and includes Greek Orthodox, Uniate and Roman Catholics, Episcopalians, Lutherans, Presbyterians and other Protestant sects. About one-half of the 1.5 million Palestinian Arabs, who have been made refugees by the three Arab-Israeli wars, live in Jordan proper and its occupied West Bank.

Education is one of Jordan's major concerns, and primary education is free and compulsory. Primary education consists of a six-year elementary and a three-year preparatory cycle. Before the June War, there were over 2,000 schools operating in Jordan, with over 280,000 students enrolled on a primary level and over 23,000 students enrolled on a secondary level. Over 600 of these government schools are now in the territory controlled by Israel.

There are three types of schools in Jordan: government schools, privately operated schools, and schools operated by the United Nations Relief and Works Agency. The latter schools provide education for Palestinian refugee children. In 1966/67, UNRWA was responsible for a total of 198 schools with an attendance of over 82,000 students. In the year following the war, however, only 115 UNRWA schools were open with an attendance of 57,608 students. Likewise, 136 of the 295 pre-June War private schools were forced to close for a variety of reasons.

The University of Jordan in Amman is rapidly becoming a fine institution of higher learning. The absence of a university in the West Bank has proved to be a real disadvantage for the students under Israeli occupation, for many are forced to leave home permanently in order to further their education.

History

Though Jordan has seldom in its long history been an independent state, it has figured prominently in the political history of the Near East and the religious history of the world. Amman, the present capital of Jordan, dates back to the twelfth century B.C. when it was the capital of the Ammonites. The area which comprises the present state of Jordan is situated in the middle of the coveted land bridge that links the continents of Europe, Asia, and Africa. As such, it came under the control of many of the powerful civilizations which arose in the Middle East, including the Egyptians, the Assyrians, and the Persians. Late in the fourth century B.C., the territory was captured by Alexander the Great, and it remained part of the Greek Empire until 30 B.C., when the Romans defeated the Greeks and conquered the entire eastern Mediterranean. The Roman

Empire continued to dominate the area until the Empire was divided. Then the Byzantine, or Eastern Roman, Empire retained responsibility for the area.

In 636 A.D., the Muslims swept out of Arabia northward into the area, where they defeated the Byzantine Emperor Heraclius and claimed the land in the name of Islam. For four hundred years it remained part of the Islamic Empire, but in 1099 the Christians of Western Europe launched their Crusades against the Muslims in an effort to regain the Holy Places of Christianity from the "infidels." The First Crusade was successful in recapturing the city of Jerusalem from the Arabs, and subsequently a tiny Christian kingdom of Jerusalem was established. Less than a hundred years later in 1187, Salah al-Din, a Kurd from northern Syria, defeated the Crusaders and went on to take control of Egypt. The area remained under his successors' control until 1516 when it was captured by the Ottoman Turks.

What is now Jordan remained under Turkish domination until the end of World War I. During the war through an exchange of correspondence between Sharif Hussein of Mecca, and Sir Henry McMahon, the British Agent in Cairo, an agreement was reached which would allow certain Arab lands independence following the war in exchange for Arab assistance in defeating the Turks. At the war's end, Britain did help to establish boundaries which would encompass an area called Transjordan. Hussein's son, Abdullah, was recognized as the *de facto* ruler, and Transjordan was not included in either Britain's Mandate for Palestine or its Mandate for Iraq. Nominally, Transjordan was an independent state though it maintained a strong British presence until May 1946, when it became formally independent.

During the 1948 Arab-Israeli war, Transjordanian troops advanced into the area on the West Bank of the Jordan River which in the partition plan for Palestine had been destined to become part of Arab Palestine. The troops remained stationed there throughout the truce period, and towards the end of the year, Palestinian leaders and Abdullah agreed to form a union of Arab Palestine and Transjordan. Abdullah was then proclaimed King of All Palestine. In April 1949, the country's name was changed to Jordan, and Abdullah signed the formal armistice agreement with Israel on April 3rd. A year later Abdullah formally annexed Arab Palestine. This move was seen by other Arab states as critical, both because Arab Palestine now ceased to exist and because it implied that the King was willing to accept, as permanent, the armistice lines which had been drawn with Israel. Also, it implied a *de facto* recognition of Israel.

Abdullah's actions plus his willingness to relocate the refugees of the 1948 war caused much friction between Jordan and its neighboring Arab states. Many Arabs, both within and outside the country, were also upset by the Jordanian king's hopes of seeing Syria, Jordan, and Iraq united into what could be called a "Greater Syria." Abdullah's brother, Faisal, occupied the throne in Iraq, and a move to unite the two countries would inevitably lead to a strengthening of the Hashemite dynasty.

In 1951, Abdullah was assassinated as he entered the Al-Aqsa mosque in Jerusalem. The assassins were Jordanians who opposed his plan for a "Greater Syria." Abdullah's grandson Hussein, the present King of Jordan, was with him at the time of the killing, but he managed to escape. Hussein's father, Talal, reigned for only a brief period, but he suffered from a mental disorder, and plans were made to crown Hussein when he reached the age of eighteen.

In January 1952, a new constitution was drawn up in anticipation of the new monarch. It provided that executive power would be vested in the King, who in turn would appoint a Prime Minister and a Council of Ministers. Legislative power would be vested in a bicameral National Assembly, consisting of a Chamber of Deputies and a Senate. The Chamber of Deputies was to be similar to the U.S. House of Representatives, and members were to be elected to four-year terms by secret voting of adult males within the country. The Senate would be composed of members who had had prior service in the government. Senators were to be appointed to four-year terms by the King. In the spring of 1953, Hussein ascended the throne of Jordan.

For the next few years, Jordan continued to maintain a British presence within its borders. The Commander-in-Chief of the Jordanian Armed Forces was, in fact, a British military officer, Sir John Bagot Glubb, known to the Jordanian troops as Glubb Pasha. But, as with

Amman, capital of Jordan, in 1922. Ruins of Roman amphitheater can be seen here.

other Arab countries in the mid-1950's, Jordan wished to show its desire for greater Arab unity and its independence of Western powers. On March 2, 1956, King Hussein dismissed Glubb Pasha from his position as Commander-in-Chief.

Later that year, following the Suez Crisis, tensions between England and Jordan grew. Jordan had been the recipient of economic and military aid from the British since 1946, but it strongly resented the British involvement in the invasion of Suez. In March 1957, bolstered by promises of aid from other Arab states, Jordan abrogated the Anglo-Jordanian treaty, which provided for a British presence in Jordan, and asked that the British withdraw all troops still stationed in Jordan. This was done by early November.

In February 1958, the kings of Iraq and Jordan agreed to a union of their two countries to be known as the Arab Federation. The merger was short-lived, however, for in August it was dissolved following a *coup* in Iraq, in the course of which Hussein's cousin, King Faisal II, was killed and a republic established.

The years between 1958 and 1967 were, if not entirely peaceful, at least relatively stable in Jordan. Much attention was given to internal economic development, and to the prudent use of aid and loans supplied to Jordan by Arab nations and Western powers. There were problems, however. One was the continuing dispute carried on between Jordan, Iraq, Syria, and Israel over the distribution of the Jordan River waters. Another which became acute in 1966 was centered on an argument be-

The same scene of Amman, capital of Jordan, in 1965.

tween Jordan and Syria. Each country charged the other with attempts of subverting its government. A third problem was the growing Palestinian resistance movement, which posed a real threat to Jordan's internal security. Palestinians launched raids into Israel from Jordanian territory. There were countered with retaliatory attacks that took the lives of many Jordanian citizens.

And then came the June War of 1967. Of all the Arab countries which fought in the June War, Jordan paid the greatest price. When the war ended, Jordan's West Bank was occupied by the Israelis, and people from the West Bank had fled across the river into the less-developed eastern portion of Jordan. This meant finding food, shelter, and clothing for these refugees. Jordan had lost its two principal sources of income: agricultural production on the West Bank and revenue from tourism. The results were an immediate and very grave economic situation, coupled with a refugee problem of vast proportions.

Saudi Arabia and Kuwait helped finance Jordan's sagging economy, but as in 1948, there was no work for the refugees. Increasing unrest in both the refugee camps and the overcrowded city of Amman led to expanded guerrilla activity which seriously jeopardized King Hussein's po-

Jerash, Jordan. Ruins of the Roman forum show that this city was once a major center.

sition. The government underwent many changes in an effort to avoid a military or political *coup*.

The four years following the June War were critical for Hussein's government. Cabinets rarely remained in office for more than two or three months. The Palestinian commandos continued constant raids into Israeli-controlled territory, and these forays were followed by reprisal attacks against Jordanian towns and villages. The Jordanian army, a majority of which was of Transjordanian origin, found itself almost helpless before the Palestinian guerrillas. Arms were openly carried on the streets of Amman, the capital, and there were increasingly frequent confrontations between the army and commando groups.

On September 6, 1970, commandos hijacked three passenger jets headed for New York from various European cities. They were flown to a small airfield near Amman, and the passengers were held as hostages. King Hussein found himself powerless to effect their release, even though they were held in a luxury hotel in Amman. Finally, he ordered the commandos back to their refugee camps, and insisted that the army enforce the order. A ten-day civil war followed. This resulted in the breaking of Palestinian commando power in most parts of the country. In January 1971, further operations were directed against the commandos, and the following July more than 2,000 guerrillas were captured in the northern part of the country. Many fled into Israeli-controlled territory and across the border into Syria. Several Arab countries suspended diplomatic relations with Jordan, and Syria and Iraq closed their borders. Nevertheless, Hussein did succeed in eliminating the Palestinian guerrilla groups as threats to his regime.

If Jordan should continue to be divided by the Israeli occupation, its future is at best uncertain.

Economy

Jordan's two major sources of income were seriously impaired by the June War. With the annexation of Jerusalem by the Israelis, Jordan lost a considerable source of revenue through tourism to the Holy Places. The West Bank of the Jordan River, which had been fully developed agriculturally and which provided the principal source of Jordanian exports, was also occupied by the Israeli Army. The loss of income from these two sources caused a serious economic setback in Jordan, and had it not been for emergency financial aid from other Arab nations, principally Saudi Arabia and Kuwait, Jordan might have collapsed completely.

In recent years, concessions have been made to various companies for oil exploration. So far, oil has not been found in sufficient quantities to encourage commercial exploitation. As for mineral wealth, copper, nickel, iron ore, and manganese deposits may well exist, and these could be developed. Prior to 1948, potash was produced near the Dead Sea, but the Palestine Potash Company's factory was destroyed in the fighting that year. Because of the unstable political situation, it has not been rebuilt. Phosphate deposits have been discovered near Amman, and since 1963 phosphates have become one of the major exports of Jordan.

Development of light industry has been gradual, primarily because of a lack of fuel or electrical power. Lack of water to provide such power or to expand agricultural ventures is one of Jordan's biggest problems. The principal sources of water for the country are the Jordan River and the Yarmuk River, which flows into the Jordan at a point just south of Lake Tiberias. This particular area involves the borders of Syria, Israel, and Jordan, and for over twenty years the three countries have been disputing each other's rights to the use of the waters. Israel has diverted waters from the Jordan to be used for irrigation in the Negev Desert. Jordan, on the other hand, is presently completing its East Ghor Canal project, which carries waters from the Yarmuk River forty four miles to the eastern slope of the Jordan valley. Another project involved in the Greater Yarmuk Scheme is the building of a dam on the Wadi Khalid at Mukheiba. Land reclaimed from this project would total about 90,000 acres.

Internal development in Jordan is hindered by three factors: the loss of income from the West Bank, the added economic strain of 300,000 refugees, and political unrest. The solution to these problems rests in great part on the ability to settle the Arab-Israeli conflict.

Kuwait

POPULATION: 733,000
CAPITAL: Kuwait
INDEPENDENCE: June 19, 1961 (formerly a British protectorate from 1914 to 1961)

Geography and People

The state of Kuwait is located in the northeastern corner of the Arabian Peninsula and is bordered on the north and west by Iraq, on the south by Saudi Arabia, and on the east by the Persian Gulf. It is approximately 6,000 square miles in area, though it also holds jointly with Saudi Arabia two neutral zones which include another 2,000 square miles. Kuwait is almost entirely desert without any rivers or streams. The temperatures in the summer months reach highs of 125 degrees F., and during the winter months range between 50 degrees and 60 degrees F. The annual rainfall varies between one and seven inches per year and usually occurs between October and April.

More than half of Kuwait's population lives in the capital, Kuwait. Only about one half of the population is native-born. The remainder came to the country from other Arab states. Many Palestinians also reside in Kuwait. Almost all of the Arabs from other states came there following the discovery of oil in 1934. Sizeable numbers of Iranians and Indians have also settled there.

The native Kuwaitis are Muslims of the Sunni sect. Arabic is the official language of the country, though English is also widely used. In 1966/67, compulsory education was introduced into Kuwait. Education is free from kindergarten through secondary school, and there are now 200 schools throughout the country, with almost 120,000 students. There are also about 80 privately owned schools in the country with an enrollment of over 26,000 pupils. Kuwait also has its own university which opened in 1966 and now has almost 1,500 students attending classes. Prior to 1966, advanced education was sought abroad at universities in Egypt, Britain, and the United States. Over 50 percent of the country is literate even though modern education was not introduced into Kuwait until 1936, when teaching missionaries arrived there from Palestine.

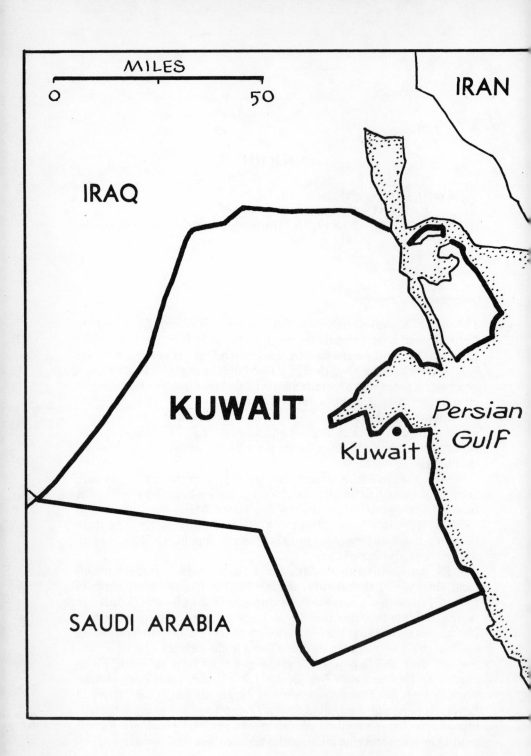

History

Though little is known of the ancient history of Kuwait, there is evidence that the Persian Gulf was a principal trade route from the Arabian Peninsula to India. According to archaeological finds, Kuwait carried on extensive trade with India and was itself primarily a seafaring nation.

The state of Kuwait did not begin to take shape until the early 1700's, when members of the Anaiza tribe migrated to the area from central Arabia. In 1756, the Anaiza appointed a member of the as-Sabah clan of the tribe to act as the primary administrator of their affairs. Thus began the as-Sabah dynasty which is still in power in Kuwait.

Kuwait's ties with the West date back to the beginning of the nineteenth century, when the embryonic state was threatened with attacks by the Wahhabi tribesmen of central Arabia. While the Ottoman Empire technically controlled the area, the British East India Company maintained a supply depot in the town of Kuwait. Protection of the British depot automatically meant protection of the Kuwaitis. In 1899, Britain and Kuwait signed an agreement, according to which Kuwait promised it would not enter into any formal agreements with foreign powers other than Britain. This was done in exchange for British protection on a formal basis.

An oil concession was granted by Sheikh Ahmad as-Sabah in 1934 to the Gulf Oil Corporation and the Anglo-Persian Oil Company. Drilling began in 1936, but World War II broke out before large-scale oil production could begin. After the war, however, production began on a full scale. A previously unknown prosperity resulted. In 1950, Ahmad died, and his successor, Sheikh Abdullah as-Sabah, inaugurated several reforms. Oil revenues were to be used to pay for numerous development projects designed to transform Kuwait into a modern state. These programs included public works, education, health services, and improvement of communications and transportation.

Kuwait's governmental system was largely patriarchal until 1961. In June of that year, however, Kuwait and Britain terminated their agreement of 1899, and Kuwait became a fully independent nation. In December, popular elections were held for the first time, and twenty members were elected to serve in a Constituent Assembly. The Assembly's task was to draft a constitution, which was published in November 1962. The constitution provided for a National Assembly of fifty members, who were to be elected every four years. The National Assembly is the legislative branch of the Kuwaiti government. Executive power rests with the Sheikh, who in turn appoints a Prime Minister and on his advice also selects a Council of Ministers. The National Assembly has the right to request the removal of the Prime Minister, but if the Sheikh honors this request, the National Assembly is automatically dissolved, and new elections must be held. Succession to the throne is limited to the descendants of the first Sheikh, as-Sabah, and an heir apparent must be appointed within a year after a new ruler comes to power.

One of the first crises faced by the nation following its independence was a claim by Iraq that the territory comprising Kuwait came under Iraqi sovereignty. Members of the Arab League, meeting in July 1961, agreed to defend Kuwait's independence, and several Arab states sent troops to fill the void left by the withdrawal of British troops. It was not until October 1963 that Iraq announced that it had given up all claims to the area. Subsequently, the two states reached an agreement by which Iraq promised to supply much needed water.

Kuwait's recent history has evolved principally around internal development though it has also acted as mediator in various disputes between Arab nations. Located as it is, far from the continuing Arab-Israeli conflict, Kuwait has not been involved in the military aspects of the struggle. The present Sheikh, Sabah as-Salim as-Sabah, who ascended the throne in November 1965, has provided much monetary assistance to the Palestinian refugees and also to Jordan and Egypt, both of which badly needed aid following the June War. Kuwait also joined in the oil embargo against the United States and Great Britain, which took place following the 1967 war, but it has since resumed trade with both nations.

Economy

Kuwait's economy is based almost entirely on oil and the by-products of oil such as natural gas. The country contains almost 20 percent of the world's known oil reserves, and today is the fourth largest producer of oil in the world. Income is derived either directly from the sale of oil, or indirectly from oil revenues and royalties paid to the country by those companies who have been granted concessions to drill there. These payments amount to almost one billion dollars annually, or about 98 percent of the nation's income. Oil has brought an unprecedented prosperity and has provided Kuwaitis with the second highest per capita income in the Middle East, almost $4,000.

Arable land in Kuwait is practically nonexistent, and the country must depend almost entirely on imported food. Lack of water to reclaim the land and to provide adequate irrigation once it has been reclaimed is a major problem. Construction has begun on the Shatt-al-Arab irrigation project, however, and when completed will ensure that 120 million gallons of water will be pumped to Kuwait each day from southern Iraq. Of this water, 70 million gallons will be used for agricultural purposes. Underground deposits of water have been found at Al Shigaia which will do much to help meet the country's water needs. Some work has been done on experimental farming but it is quite minimal. A survey to determine if Kuwait's soil can be made productive is also underway.

About one-tenth of the country's meat supply is provided by Bedouin tribes. Poultry farming has met with some initial success, and the industry is growing. Also, there are sufficient fish in the waters of the Persian Gulf to meet local consumption needs. The Persian Gulf supplies another source of income through pearl fishing, which was, until the discovery of oil, one of the major sources of income for Kuwait. Pearls are still taken from the Gulf and exported throughout the world.

Kuwait's success story as a nation is indeed amazing. It has been transformed from a state where in 1951 the per capita income was $21 to a nation whose per capita expenditure on education and health programs is one of the highest in the world. Oil is responsible for the transformation by providing the nation with a great amount of revenue. Equally important, however, has been the vision of the country's leadership and its willingness to use revenue to improve the lives of all its citizens.

The national museum in Kuwait contains many ancient archaeological discoveries.

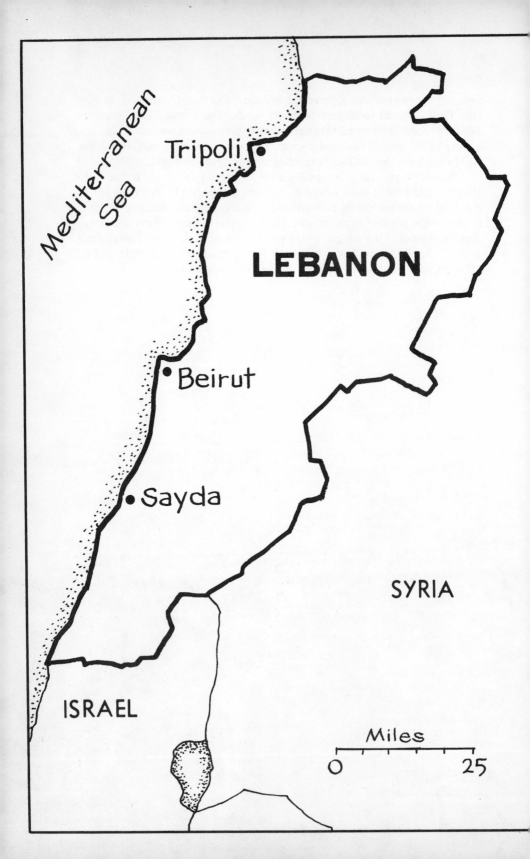

Republic of Lebanon

POPULATION: 2.8 million
CAPITAL: Beirut
INDEPENDENCE: November 22, 1941 (formerly a French Mandate
from 1923 to 1941)

Georgraphy and People

Lebanon is located at the eastern end of the Mediterranean Sea and is bordered on the south by Israel and on the north and west by Syria. It is the smallest state in the Middle East and has a total land area of about 4,000 square miles. Along the Mediterranean coast the land forms a narrow coastal plain. The Lebanon mountain range which reaches heights of over 10,000 feet rises immediately to the east of the coastal plain. Eastward, beyond these mountains, lies the Biqa Valley, which is approximately seventy five miles long and averages nine miles in width. The Litani, Lebanon's only river of any size, flows through the Biqa Valley from north to south, but just before it reaches Israel's border, it turns abruptly west and empties into the Mediterranean. Eastward from the Biqa Valley, there is a second mountain range known as the Anti-Lebanon Mountains, which forms the border between Lebanon and Syria.

It is estimated that 27 percent of Lebanon's land is at present under cultivation. Another six percent of the land is covered with forests while the remaining land is either barren, mountainous, or occupied by towns and cities. The climate of coastal Lebanon resembles that of southern California, and though temperatures rarely exceed 90 degrees F., the area is extremely humid. The winter months are generally rainy, and along the coast the average rainfall is 38 inches, while in the mountains precipitation may reach as high as 50 inches in one season. Snow is common in the mountains along the coast. As a result, Lebanon has many fine ski resorts.

Religion has had a strong influence on the country's political and cultural development. Since shortly after the time of Christ there has been a strong Christian community in Lebanon. These early Christians settled primarily in the Lebanon Mountains, east of the present city of Beirut. When the Muslims came out of Arabia in the seventh century and conquered most of the Middle East, Lebanon continued to maintain its Christian character in the mountain region, which provided a refuge for those unwilling to accept Islam. Despite the fact that the Muslims were hindered in spreading Islam throughout the region because of the terrain, many Arabian Muslims settled in the area. By the ninth century, there were settlements of Shi'ite Muslims in southern Lebanon, as well as followers of the Druze religion, which combines concepts found in Islam and Christianity. Members of the Sunni sect of Islam settled to the north of Beirut in the area surrounding Tripoli. Many Greek Orthodox Christians settled in the Biqa Valley.

Though no formal census has been taken in Lebanon since 1932, it is estimated that Christians number about one half of the population. Muslims, almost evenly divided between Sunni and Shi'ite, make up the majority of the remainder. There are also about 90,000 Druzes.

Lebanon is also known as an "exporter of men." It is estimated that over one million Lebanese have either emigrated or permanently reside in foreign countries. Almost 500,000 native-born Lebanese live in the United States and almost 600,000 in South America.

During the French Mandate in Lebanon most of its educational institutions were privately run schools sponsored by foreign missionaries. When the Mandate ended, the Lebanese themselves concentrated on the development of public education. The Lebanese government is now responsible for most primary schools, and free primary education was introduced into Lebanon in 1960. Private institutions still carry the heaviest responsibility for secondary schools and higher education.

There are over a half million students in over 2,500 schools. There are also four universities in Lebanon, as well as several teacher training institutes. Because of the heavy emphasis on education by foreign missionaries during the French Mandate and later by the Lebanese government, almost 87 percent of the country's population is literate.

History

Lebanon is believed to have been continually inhabited for almost 6,000 years. From its coastal regions, the highly civilized Phoenicians plied their trade throughout the Mediterranean. The Phoenicians were also responsible in part for supplying the cedar and the architectural expertise, used by Solomon in building his palace and the first Hebrew Temple in Jerusalem. In the eleventh century B.C., the Phoenicians developed an alphabet, from which the Hebrew, Greek, Roman, and other western alphabets have been derived. The ruins of the temples at Byblos and Baalbeck stand as reminders of the area's occupation by the Romans, while its mosques and churches reflect the influence of the Arab Muslims, Crusaders, and Ottoman Turks, all of whom held power over the area at different times.

Under the rule of the Ottoman Empire, Lebanon held privileged status. In 1864, it became an autonomous province ruled by a non-Lebanese Ottoman Christian, who was in turn aided by an elected administrative council. Following World War I and the defeat of the Turks, however, Lebanon was occupied by both British and French forces. Despite its privileged status under the Ottomans, Lebanon had throughout history been considered an integral part of Syria. Therefore, when in April 1920, France was granted a Mandate for Syria, the territory included Lebanon. Following the awarding of the Mandate, France divided the area into two major portions: Syria and the Greater State of Lebanon. In so doing, they added much Syrian territory to Lebanon, including the cities of Tripoli, Sidon (Sayda) and Tyre.

This somewhat arbitary division of the area by France was to have long-lasting repercussions, for there were many Sunni Muslims living in the areas which had been added to Lebanon. Their sympathies were with Syria and its growing nationalistic movement. The Sunnis resented their incorporation into Lebanon and called for either a return to the old Turkish boundaries or the complete incorporation of Lebanon into Syria. On the whole, the Maronite Christians favored a separate Lebanon which would include the newly added Syrian territory.

In November 1941, Lebanon was proclaimed a free and sovereign state. French officials and military personnel remained in Lebanon throughout the war, however, and they soon came in conflict with Lebanese nationalists with respect to transfer of administration within the country. In 1943, the government passed legislation which removed from the constitution certain provisions, which the Lebanese felt were inconsistent with their goal of independence. The French then arrested the President and suspended the constitution. International pressure led to the release of the President, and the French began preparations to withdraw from the country. Their withdrawal was completed in 1946.

The governmental structure of Lebanon, provided by its constitution, calls for a parliamentary republic with a unicameral legislature known as the Chamber of Deputies. The 99 member chamber reflects the religious make-up of the country. Voting in the country is divided along these religious, sectarian lines. The Maronites being in the majority, not only exercise considerable political influence, but also have a dominant voice in the selection of the country's President. Traditionally, through an agreement reached in 1944, the President of Lebanon is a Maronite Christian, and the Prime Minister is a Muslim of the Sunni sect. The Chamber of Deputies elects by a two-thirds vote the President, who serves a six-year term. The President, in turn, selects a Cabinet of Ministers, headed by a Prime Minister. This Cabinet is directly responsible to the Chamber of Deputies.

While the Lebanese government has remained relatively stable since the state gained its independence, the country has faced a number of problems, many of which were often closely related to the continuing antagonism between Syria and Lebanon. In September 1952, for instance, President al-Khuri was forced to resign after nearly nine years in office.

His resignation was brought about by economic unrest directly related to Syria. The two countries for some years had strong economic ties. Syria supplied most of Lebanon's agricultural products, while at the same time it was the recipient for most of Lebanon's industrial goods. These economic arrangements were ruptured in 1950, when the Lebanese government refused a Syrian proposal that there be full economic and financial union between the two states. By 1952, the results of this refusal were being felt in trade deficits, higher living costs, and growing unemployment.

President al-Khuri was replaced by Camille Chamoun, who introduced a number of reforms including granting the franchise to women, reforming voting laws, and reorganizing the judicial structure of the country. Economic agreements with Syria remained on a provisional basis for the next few years, but talks held in 1956 concerning mutual defense stalemated when Lebanon refused to allow Syria control of Syrian troops, should they be sent into Lebanon. During the mid-1950's, Lebanon adopted a neutral stance in the international sphere and refused to enter into an alliance of Arab states which would exclude Iraq. It also adopted an impartial attitude towards trade agreements and signed com-

The presence of snow in Lebanon makes it an important tourist center during the winter.

mercial treaties with several Eastern-bloc countries, although American aid for the improvement of its international airport was accepted.

There were disturbances in Lebanon in 1956 following the Suez Crisis. These were caused by Lebanese who felt the government's refusal to break off diplomatic ties with England and France showed pro-Western rather than pro-Arab tendencies. Then, in 1957, the government entered into talks with the United States concerning financial, military, and economic aid, provided under the Eisenhower Doctrine. Again there were protests that the government was too pro-Western. Elections were held in June 1957, and though they were marked with serious disturbances caused by anti-Western Lebanese, the government was returned to power. These disturbances continued throughout the year, and by December the northern part of Lebanon had been declared a military sector. In March 1958, the government announced its refusal to join in either the United Arab Republic or the Arab Federation. This announcement angered many of the Muslims in Lebanon, especially in the areas of Tripoli and Sidon, where sympathy for Syria and a greater desire for Arab unity were still strong.

In May 1958, serious disorders broke out in Tripoli and quickly spread throughout Lebanon. By July, the country was in a state of undeclared civil war with Muslims venting their anger against the country's Christians. On July 14, 1958, President Chamoun requested that the United States send its marines into Lebanon under terms agreed to in the Eisenhower Doctrine. By the end of the following week, over 10,000 American troops had landed in Lebanon. In part, the disruptions within the country had been triggered by an accusation that President Chamoun had attempted to amend the constitution so that he could seek reelection. This had angered many who felt the government was already too pro-Western.

On July 31, 1958, elections were held, and General Fuad Chehab was elected President by the Chamber of Deputies. Tensions eased in the country despite the continuing presence of American marines. Following the adoption of a U.N. resolution by the General Assembly, the United States agreed to withdraw, and the last contingent of troops left Lebanon in October.

Throughout the continuing conflict between the Arab states and Israel, Lebanon had tried to maintain its ties with the West, while at the same time defending its position as an Arab state. However, since December 1968, Lebanon has been shaken by several events directly related to the dispute, which have threatened her security as a sovereign state. In December 1968, Israeli commando troops attacked Beirut International Airport and blew up thirteen commercial airplanes of Middle East Airlines, the Lebanese national carrier. This was done in retaliation for an Arab terrorist raid on an El Al plane in Athens in which one man was killed and another wounded. Israel maintained that it retaliated so severely against Lebanon because Arab terrorists were being trained within the Lebanese borders.

The months that followed the raid saw stepped-up commando activities by Arab guerrillas operating out of southern Lebanon, which became known as "Fatahland," after the commandos of the Al-Fatah organization. The government was placed in the difficult position of trying to suppress these activities without precipitating an insurrection by Palestinian refugees and Lebanese who were sympathetic to the guerrillas. This sympathy was particularly high in the city of Tripoli, and in October 1969, guerrillas occupied several towns on the Syrian-Lebanese border and sparked rioting in Tripoli in an effort to obtain concessions to use Lebanese territory from which to launch raids into Israel.

After the commandos were driven from Jordan in 1971, they intensified their activities in south Lebanon. Israel massively retaliated several times, and many innocent Lebanese civilians have been killed. In May 1972, Japanese terrorists, trained by Palestinian commandos in Lebanon, killed and injured scores of civilians at Lod Airport, Tel Aviv. Although the Lebanese government denied responsibility, this action provoked additional incursions of Israeli troops into southern Lebanon. Massive Israeli retaliatory raids have continued. In March 1973, Israel launched another major attack against refugee camps in the vicinity of Tripoli. Lebanon remains in a delicate position and faces further retaliatory raids on private citizens or the possible take-over of its southern territory by the Israelis. Open conflict between Lebanese troops and Palestinians broke out in May 1973.

Economy

About 40 percent of Lebanon's population is engaged in some type of agricultural activity, and one-fourth of the country is under cultivation. Another 15 percent is deemed cultivable. Fruit production is the most important agricultural venture, and apples, citrus fruits, and bananas are all exported in quantity. Lebanon also produces a variety of vegetables, but it is heavily dependent on other countries for the import of cereal grains and flour.

Other sources of revenue for the small nation include light industry, which provides about 12 percent of the national income, though only three percent of the total population is engaged in industrial activities. Also, though Lebanon does not itself produce oil commercially, it has become important to Middle Eastern oil interests because of its geographic location. Two important oil pipelines cross the country. One links the oil fields of Kirkuk in Iraq with the Mediterranean port of Tripoli; the other stretches from Saudi Arabia through Syria to the port of Sidon and is known as the "Tapline," an abbreviation for Trans Arabian Pipeline. The continued use of both pipelines is, of course, heavily dependent on the good will of Syria, which has in the past refused to repair damages to both pipelines caused by guerrillas.

Tourism has been a profit-making industry as Lebanon has lovely beaches, skiing in the mountains, and many important historical sites, including the ancient ruins at Byblos, Tyre, Sidon, and Baalbeck. This source of income has been jeopardized, however, by continuing conflict and reprisal raids both in southern Lebanon and along the Syrian-Lebanese border.

The Lebanese economy is strongly supported by the importance of Beirut as a center of trade and commerce. Lebanon is a free market, and over half of all Lebanese trade is transit traffic destined for other countries. There are at present over eighty officially recognized banks in Beirut alone, many representing branches of major international banks. Most Arab businesses have some connection with Beirut banks.

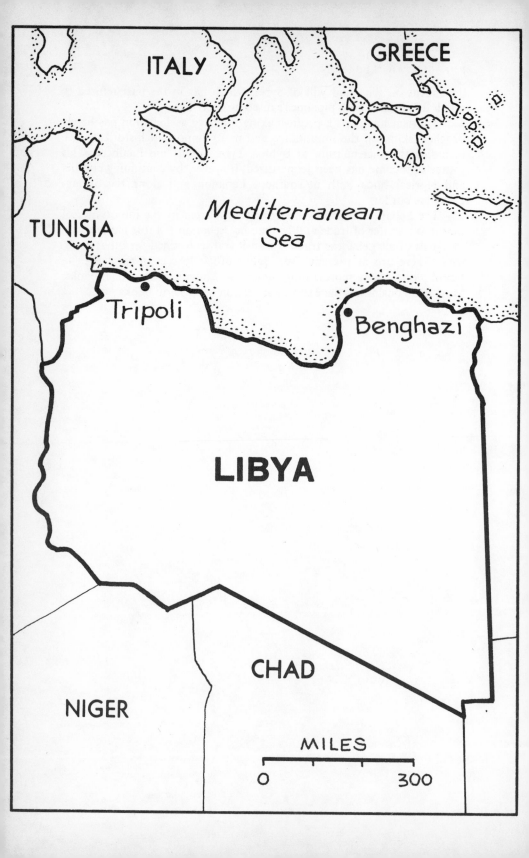

Libyan Arab Republic

POPULATION: 1.9 million
CAPITAL: Tripoli and Benghazi
INDEPENDENCE: December 24, 1951 (Gained from the Italians who controlled the country from 1931 to 1951)

Geography and People

The Libyan Arab Republic is located on the north-central coast of Africa on the Mediterranean Sea. It is bounded on the east by the Egyptian Arab Republic, on the southeast by the Sudan, on the south by Niger and Chad, and on the west by Tunisia and Algeria. The total land area equals 680,000 square miles, and Libya is roughly one-fifth the size of the United States.

The only areas in Libya which are not desert lie along the Mediterranean coastline and include two low mountain ranges located in the northwest and northeast sections of the country. There is also an area several hundred miles south of the coast in the region of the Fezzan where cultivation is possible through the use of several large oases. Approximately four percent of the total land area is arable, with another four percent capable of use as grazing land.

Rainfall is sporadic, and the climate is generally arid. Temperatures vary widely, and while the northern part of the country often experiences cold raw winters, summers in the same area may bring temperatures as high as 115 degrees F. Libya is noted for its *ghibil,* a very hot dry wind which rises in the south, usually during the spring or fall, and can cause temperatures in the northern part of the country to rise as much as forty degrees in a few hours.

It is estimated that nearly 75 percent of all Libyans live in urban areas while about eight percent are considered nomadic and the remaining 17 percent are semi-nomadic. The country's population is a racial mixture of Berbers, who are closely identified with the inhabitants of the countries to the west of Libya, and Arabs, who are descended from the Arabians who invaded the country in the seventh century. The people of the country are almost all followers of the Sunni sect of Islam. Until recent years, about three percent of the population was Christian, for the most part Italian Roman Catholics living in the area of Tripoli. Beginning in 1970, these Italians, most of whom had been born in Libya, were expelled from the country. Few, if any, remain.

Arabic, which was brought to the region by the Arab invaders, is the official language. Though Libyans were encouraged to send their children to school during the Italian occupation of Libya, instruction was primarily in Italian, and most Libyans refused to enroll their children in schools for fear their Muslim traditions would be jeopardized. Because of this, when Italian occupation ended in 1951, over 90 percent of the population was illiterate. At present, all education including the university is free, and elementary education is compulsory for boys and girls.

There are over 1,400 educational institutions in Libya, 1,200 of which are primary schools with an enrollment of over 300,000 students. The rest are preparatory, secondary, technical, and vocational schools. There are also 23 teacher training institutes. Libya has its own university, with campuses in Tripoli and Benghazi.

History

The modern history of Libya begins with its reoccupation by the Ottoman Empire in 1835. Libya had originally been brought under Turkish rule in the middle of the sixteenth century, when the North African coast was invaded by the Turks and divided into three Regencies, which correspond to modern-day Algeria, Tunisia, and Libya. The rise of a professional army known as the Janissaries, however, seriously threatened the Turkish administration in Libya.

The Janissaries became so powerful within Libya that they elected their own ruler known as the Dey. The Dey rivaled the Turkish Pasha sent to Libya by Constantinople. In 1711, an officer in the Janissaries, named Ahmed Karamanli, was selected Dey, and through maneuvers which included killing the former Dey and the Turkish Pasha, he succeeded in wresting complete control of the Turkish territory from Constantinople. Libya gained a semi-autonomous status, and Karamanli established a dynastic government which lasted until 1835.

During the 1700's, the area's revenue came from piracy, which had become a way of life along the North African coast. Tribute was also exacted from major maritime powers through agreements allowing ships to pass Libya's coast unmolested in return for money or goods. Piracy was outlawed by the international community in the early 1800's, however, and with the loss of its most important source of revenue, the Karamanli dynasty suffered a loss of power and prestige. When the government, in an effort to raise revenue within Libya, imposed heavy taxes on both Muslims and Jews in the country, revolt broke out.

Weakened by this internal dissent, Libya was an easy prey for the Turks, and in 1835, it was once again brought under Ottoman control. Like other provinces in the Ottoman Empire, Libya suffered under corrupt government and suppression for the next eighty years. Then at the end of September 1911, Italy declared war on the Turks and four days later landed troops in the city of Tripoli. The Libyans and the Turks withdrew to the inhospitable regions of the interior, and though the Italians were able to secure the cities along the coast, it took a year of intensive fighting before they got a peace treaty from Turkey on October 18, 1912.

Italy was unable to gain full control of Libya for another twenty years, however, for the Libyans continued the struggle begun in 1911. The struggle was particularly intense in the eastern province of Cyrenaica, where no effective Italian colonization ever took place. During World War I, Turkey and her German allies supplied arms to the Libyans of Cyrenaica. Thus, they continued their fight against the Italians. After the war, the battle continued for yet another decade, with various sections of Libya slowly yielding ground until at last, in 1931, the country was forced to recognize Italian rule. By 1940, there were 110,000 Italians in Libya.

Libya is divided into three major provinces: Tripolitania, in the northwest, Fezzan, in the southwest, and Cyrenaica, which includes the entire eastern half of the country. These provinces have existed since Roman times, but during the North African campaign in World War II, they took on renewed significance. After the Allies' victory over German Field Marshall Rommel in 1943, the British occupied Tripolitania and Cyrenaica, while the French controlled Fezzan.

The major powers were unable to reach an agreement concerning Libya's future after the peace treaty with Italy was ratified in the fall of 1947. The matter was then referred to the United Nations, which passed a resolution calling for Libya's independence, to become effective no later than January 1, 1952. A former resistance leader from the province of Cyrenaica, Sayyid Muhammad Idris, was elected by the National Constituent Assembly to be Libya's first king. It was also decided that Libya would be ruled by a federal monarchy with a representative government and that special provincial legislatures would be set up to administer local affairs in each of the three provinces. Representation to the federal government was to include a bicameral legislature, consisting of a Chamber of Deputies and a Senate. Members to the Chamber of Deputies were elected by popular vote to a four-year term. The Senate consisted of 24 members appointed by the King to eight-year terms.

Since its independence on December 24, 1951, Libya has faced serious internal problems. One of the major ones has been a rivalry between the provinces of Tripolitania and Cyrenaica. Tripolitania, which is heavily populated and had a large Italian community, cooperated more or less with the Italians during their occupation of Libya. Cyrenaica, on the other hand, resisted Italian colonization until 1937, and this, coupled with their strong attachment to King Idris, who had helped lead their resistance, has caused ill-feelings between the two provinces.

Libya's history since 1951 has, to a large degree, revolved around its

need to place itself on a sound economic footing in the community of nations. In 1953, an agreement was reached with England, which allowed
the British to build military and air bases in Libya in exchange for hard
currency to be used for economic development and to meet budget deficits. A similar agreement was signed with the United States in 1954,
and this resulted in Wheelus Air Force Base, outside of Tripoli.

In the winter of 1955, concessions were granted to several American
oil companies allowing them the right to explore. In June 1959, oil was
discovered, and with the revenue obtained from the oil, Libya at last
began to move towards a sound economy, based on internal development. The government also signed several other agreements including
provisions for military arms, the exchange of foodstuffs, and trade agreements with Turkey, Egypt, and Italy.

Minor jealousies continued to prevail within the Libyan federated
government. In April 1963, the newly appointed Prime Minister, Dr.
Fekini, who had been Ambassador to the United States, introduced legislation calling for an end to the federated system and for the creation of a
united kingdom. The councils, which had formerly administered local affairs in the three provinces, would be abolished. The legislation also
called for enfranchisement of women. Executive power was now placed
in the hands of the Council of Ministers. The legislative changes were accepted on April 27, 1963, and Libya became a united state.

By the early 1960's, there was a growing feeling that the military
agreements which had been signed with the United States and Britain
ought to be dissolved. In part this was because Libya, as a member of the
Arab League, identified strongly with the League's feelings that con-

A seaside view of Tripoli, Libya.

tinued aid by both powers to Israel was a manifestation of imperialism. Initially, these bases had supplied Libya with financial, economic, and military aid. Now, however, the oil industry was providing the country with adequate revenue, and the government felt it could safely afford to let the treaties lapse. In 1964, Libya announced it had no intention of renewing or extending these agreements.

In 1967, Abd al-Hamri al Bakkush took office as Libya's Prime Minister. He worked hard to foster the alignment of Libya with other Arab nations and to reform the government and particularly the Council of Ministers, which he felt was not truly responsive to the people's needs. Ten months later, Bakkush resigned as Prime Minister, evidently at the insistence of King Idris who felt that changes were coming too rapidly and that they threatened the old order.

On September 1, 1969, while King Idris was out of the country on vacation, a small group of younger officers in the Libyan Armed Forces led a *coup* and deposed the monarch. The government was taken over by a Revolutionary Command Council, with the power of both the Presidency and the control of the Armed Forces vested in the hands of Colonel Mu'ammar al-Qadhaffi. The new government promptly announced its intentions of a total "Libyanization" of the country. This policy went so far as to abolish all street signs in foreign languages. Thousands of Italians were forced to leave the country after their possessions were confiscated and their residence permits recalled. Many of these refugees were sent to camps in southern Italy and Sicily until they could be reintegrated into Italian life. Roman Catholic churches and schools were also taken over by the government.

Because of Libya's great income from oil, Colonel al-Qadhaffi has had increased influence in Middle Eastern politics through subsidies granted to Egypt and other countries which suffer financially as a result of the 1967 war with Israel. An avowed enemy of Israel, al-Qadhaffi has sent Libyan troops to aid the Palestinian commando movement. His support of projects in Uganda in Africa was dependent upon that nation's rejection of all Israeli aid. This resulted in an actual rupture of diplomatic relations between Uganda and Israel. Libya's conflict with Israel has intensified for several reasons, including open support of Palestinian guerrilla activities, the burying with honor of the commandos responsible for the killing of Israeli athletes at the Munich Olympic games in 1972, and the downing of an off-course Libyan jetliner with over 100 civilians on board in February 1973.

On September 1, 1971, Libya joined Egypt and Syria in the "Federation of Arab Republics," the headquarters of which is in Cairo. Libya retains its sovereignty, as do the other two members of the Federation.

Economy

Like many countries in the Middle East which gained their independence during or after World War II, Libya had no sound economic base, on which to build when it gained independence in 1951. Prior to 1951, Libya had been occupied by Italy, and its economy was heavily dependent on investment and aid brought to the country by the Italians. Throughout the early years of its statehood, Libya continued to depend heavily on financing from abroad, but with the discovery of oil in 1959, the Libyan economy began to undergo a transformation.

Between October 1961 and February 1968, five major pipelines were opened from various oil-producing areas to ports on the Mediterranean Sea. Libya, as an oil exporter, has distinct advantages over oil-producing countries near the Persian Gulf since it has easy access to the Western European market. The closure of the Suez Canal after the June War of 1967 has also been distinctively advantageous to Libya, for the countries on the Persian Gulf have been forced either to ship oil around Africa or to seek new markets. At present, Libya is producing over 3.5 million barrels of oil a day, and it is now the third largest exporter of oil in the world.

Before the discovery of oil, Libya's economy was based on agriculture, even though only four percent of its total land area was under cultivation. Libya still exports ground nuts and esparto grass, which is used in the production of paper currency. Goats and sheep are raised, and sponges are found off its coastline. Since 1951, there has been a population shift to the urban areas of Libya, which has meant that a large portion of the population is no longer engaged in farming. This shift, in turn, has made it necessary for Libya to increase her food imports.

In 1962, only one year after the exportation of oil by Libya had begun, the balance of trade was such that the value of Libyan exports exceeded the value of its imports. In that year, the government approved a $500 million program of development, which was to be extended over a five-year period. The plan included agricultural expansion, increased building programs, and improved education. A similar plan was scheduled to go into effect in the spring of 1968, but Libya's economy was slowed down considerably by the June War of 1967, since oil production dropped during that summer due to agreements made by several Arab states to place an embargo on oil exports to Western Europe. This temporary setback forced the postponement of the new five-year plan, based on spending the anticipated $3.2 billion from oil revenues. The oil embargo was lifted in September 1967, however, and the plan was put into effect in late 1968. It includes the building of 5,000 housing compound units, hospitals, 135 water supply projects, electric power plants, road construction, and an education program, which will include building two new universities, each with a capacity for 10,000 students.

Libya has managed in two decades to move from a country, whose economy was based almost entirely on aid supplied by agreements with other nations, to a state with a viable economy, permitting considerable expansion and development. Its future growth will depend on actions taken by the Revolutionary Command Council.

Saudi Arabia

POPULATION: 7.7 million
CAPITAL: Riyadh   DIPLOMATIC CAPITAL: Jiddah
INDEPENDENCE: Unified kingdom established September 23, 1932

Geography and People

The Kingdom of Saudi Arabi occupies most of the Arabian Peninsula and is approximately 830,000 square miles in size. It is bound on the west by the Red Sea, on the north by Iraq and Jordan, on the east by the Persian Gulf, Kuwait, and the Trucial States, and on the south by Yemen and Southern Yemen. The Hejaz mountain range rises along the coast bordering the Red Sea. To the east, beyond these mountains, the land slopes downward to a steppe, which receives only two to four inches of rainfall a year. Most of the southern part of the kingdom is desert, which is too arid to support life, and is known as the "Empty Quarter."

Though it is estimated that 15 percent of Saudi Arabia's land is arable, only one percent is presently under cultivation. Crop growing takes place primarily in the southwest region, where there is an annual rainfall of about twelve inches. There is also farming in the Qatif and al-Hasa oases in the Eastern province. Water is obtained there from artesian wells.

Since a large portion of Saudi Arabia's population is either nomadic or widely scattered throughout the country in small villages, it is difficult to obtain an accurate population count. No nationwide census has yet been undertaken, but varying estimates judge the country to have between five and eight million inhabitants. The population is primarily descended from indigenous Arab tribes, who have lived in the Arabian Peninsula for centuries.

Most of the Saudi Arabians are members of the Sunni sect of Islam, though there are large numbers of Shi'ite Muslims living in the Eastern province of the country. It is in Saudi Arabia that Islam was born, and two of the faith's most important centers, Mecca and Medina, are located near the Red Sea in the central section of the country. The official language of Saudi Arabia is Arabic.

About 25 percent of the estimated total population is literate, but during the past two decades an intensive program to improve education has been undertaken. The program is all-encompassing and aims to provide free education to all of the country's citizens. Enrollment figures indicate that almost 300,000 pupils are attending about 1,500 primary schools, while some 50,000 students attend 375 intermediary, secondary, and technical schools. In 1957, the University of Riyadh was opened, and a second university was recently established in Jiddah.

History

In ancient times, Arabia played a major role in the trade and commerce which took place between the countries of the Mediterranean and India. Arabia was crisscrossed with caravan routes, traveled by merchants bringing silk, spices, and ivory from the East to the area which is now Jordan. Southern Arabia was a principal source of frankincense and myrrh, and caravan routes extended northward along its western coast to the city of Damascus.

One of the most notable episodes in Arabia's early history was the birth and rise of the third great monotheistic religion of the world, Islam.

The Prophet Muhammad was born in the city of Mecca about 570 A.D., and there he first preached his message: "There is no god but God, and Muhammad is a messenger of God." The people of Mecca rejected Muhammad and his preaching and forced him and his disciples to flee to the city of Medina, where he continued to spread his teaching, while carrying on sporadic battles with the Meccans. Finally, in 630, he successfully subdued the people of Mecca and converted them. His followers spread the faith of Islam northward out of the Arabian Peninsula.

The spread of Islam was rapid, and less than 100 years after Muhammad's death, the Muslims had conquered the entire Middle East, North Africa, and Spain, and had moved westward into Central Asia. Control of the Islamic Empire moved out of Arabia in 750, when the office of Caliph, the successor to Muhammad, was seized by the Ummayads who made their capital in Damascus. For the next thousand years, Arabia remained a vast land area inhabited by numerous tribes, but with no strong central government.

The modern history of Saudi Arabia begins in 1902, when Abd al-Aziz al-Saud, now popularly known as Ibn Saud, returned to Arabia from exile in Kuwait. He managed to capture Riyadh, which had been held by his family during the mid-1800's, but which had been subsequently taken by the Rashids, a powerful clan. After recapturing Riyadh, Ibn Saud began to consolidate his control over land held by other tribes. In 1913, he drove the Turks out of al-Hasa, the area along the Persian Gulf, and in 1921, he captured Hayil, a city northwest of Riyadh.

Meanwhile, in 1919, Ibn Saud became irritated by claims of the Sharif of Mecca, Hussein, who maintained that he had primacy over the entire Hejaz area containing the holy cities of Islam, Mecca and Medina. Ibn Saud sent forces to the Hejaz, but it was not until 1925, that he could claim control of both cities. In January 1926, Ibn Saud proclaimed himself King of the Hejaz. For the next four years he worked to consolidate his control over lands he had conquered in central and eastern Arabia, and in 1932, he declared himself King of Saudi Arabia.

The following year, the King granted oil concessions to several American oil companies. Exploration began almost immediately, and in 1938 the first commercial strike of oil was made. The export of oil became the single most important source of revenue for the kingdom, but during World War II oil exports ceased, and the number of Muslims who traveled to Mecca to participate in the annual pilgrimage to the Islamic Holy Places dropped alarmingly. With both the export of oil and the pilgrimages interrupted, the country suffered a serious financial setback which was countered only by grants and loans to the kingdom by Britain and the United States.

Ibn Saud died in 1953, and his son, Saud, ascended the throne. A Council of Ministers was formed which in consultation with the King exercised both executive and legislative authority. While the Council of

Ministers determines national protection, civil rights are based on the *Shari'ah,* or "law" of Islam, based on the *Qur'an* and the teachings of the Prophet Muhammad.

From 1953 to 1958, and from December 1960 to October 1962, King Saud exercised direct rule and presided over the Council of Ministers. The brief lapse of his authority from 1958 to 1960 is explained by a financial crisis which forced the King to relinquish his power to his younger brother, Prince Faisal, whose task it was to save the country from bankruptcy.

Though oil-rich, the country was in severe financial straits by 1958, partially because the royal family had almost absolute control of all oil revenues. Faisal, on the advice of the International Monetary Fund, instituted major financial reforms including curbs on the expenditures of the royal family. In slightly less than two years, the Prince was able to bring about much fiscal reform, but he was unable to eliminate waste entirely.

King Saud resumed his direct control of governmental affairs in December 1960. He continued to follow the fiscal policy set by his brother, but pressures from within the country calling for more representative government, plus external pressures caused by Saudi Arabian involvement in Yemen's civil war, proved too much. Saud once again turned over the throne to his younger brother in 1962. He made one more brief attempt to assert his leadership but failed, and in November 1964, Faisal was proclaimed King of Saudi Arabia.

Since 1964, there have been great strides in social reforms in Saudi Arabia, particularly in the areas of education, medical services, and agriculture. Faisal continued the involvement in the Yemen civil war, how-

Dhahran, Saudi Arabia. This beautiful mosque was built by the Saudi government for the Saudi Arabian employees of the Arabian American Oil Company headquartered in this city.

ever, and this caused a break in diplomatic relations with Egypt, which backed the revolutionary forces in Yemen. Saudi Arabia was supplying military aid to the conservative, or royalist, forces trying to maintain a monarchy in the small state.

Relations between Saudi Arabia and Egypt remained tense because of the situation in Yemen and because Saudi Arabia refused to participate in various plans for greater Arab unity. Following the June War of 1967, the situation changed. Egypt had suffered a severe financial setback with the loss of its air force and the closure of the Suez Canal. Following the war, Saudi Arabia agreed to provide Jordan and Egypt with over $150 million in aid to help restore the losses suffered during the war. Saudi Arabia also convinced the other oil-producing states in the region that they should end the embargo on oil placed on the countries of Western Europe after the war. The King pointed out that the embargo hurt the Middle East far more than it did the Western powers. Oil shipments were resumed in September 1967.

In July 1970, Saudi Arabia officially recognized the Republic of Yemen and agreed to cease all support of the royalist faction. Relations with Southern Yemen, formerly Aden and now called the People's Democratic Republic of Yemen, are not good, and there have been several border clashes.

Saudi Arabia is still the most conservative Arab country, and the traditional Muslim customs and laws are observed and strictly enforced.

Economy

Oil is the single greatest source of revenue in Saudi Arabia, and it accounts for 80 percent of the government's revenue and one half of the national income. Current oil production exceeds three million barrels a day, from which the government realizes an annual income of more than $950 million. Approximately half of recent budgets has been earmarked for development, and one of the most ambitious projects underway is an improved network of highways. About one fourth of the budget was set aside for defense, even though Saudi Arabia has been involved in actual combat situations only on a limited scale.

Though only one percent of the land in Saudi Arabia is presently under cultivation, a hydrological survey is being made. Indications are that there exist vast aquifers (water-bearing formations) underlying many sections of the country. If this water can be reclaimed, prospects are good that agricultural production could be expanded rapidly. At present, the principal crop is dates, but this is supplemented by wheat, corn, rice, grapes, coffee, and tomatoes. The country is still largely dependent on the import of staple food items, mostly from the United States, Britain, and Lebanon.

The discovery of oil brought about a shift in Saudi Arabia's population from the rural towns and villages to the cities, which were built near the oil-bearing areas. This necessitated an enlarged building program. Today construction is the second most important industry in the country.

Another important source of revenue in Saudi Arabia is the annual pilgrimage to Mecca made by followers of Islam from throughout the world. Thousands of Muslims journey to Mecca to fulfill the *hajj*, or pilgrimage, which is one of the five basic obligations of the Muslim faith. Each year, over 300,000 pilgrims come to Mecca from abroad. No accurate estimate of how much money is spent during the *hajj* can be made.

Though limited by its terrain which is primarily desert and by its widespread population much of which is still nomadic or semi-nomadic, the Kingdom of Saudi Arabia has made great strides both in development and as a major Middle Eastern power.

Sudan

POPULATION: 15.7 million (estimated)
CAPITAL: Khartoum
INDEPENDENCE: January 1, 1956 (formerly under British and Egyptian administration from 1888 to 1956)

Geography and People

The Sudan is bordered by Egypt to the north, the Red Sea and Ethiopia to the east, Kenya, Uganda, and Zaire to the south, and the Central African Republic, Chad, and Libya to the west. It is about 967,500 square miles in size and occupies one-tenth of the continent of Africa. Just as the Nile River is the most important geographical factor in Egypt, so it is also in the Sudan. Near Khartoum, the White Nile, which rises in the lake districts of Kenya and Tanzania, joins the Blue Nile, which rises in Ethiopia. Here it starts its long journey northward through the Sudan and Egypt to the Mediterranean.

The distinctive land features of the Sudan can be seen as one moves from its southern border, which is primarily tropical rain forest, north along the White Nile and the swamplands which surround it. Beyond these papyrus swamps, as they are called, lie rolling plains that are covered with grass and scrub and are used for cattle grazing. Near Khartoum, these plains have only enough vegetation to feed sheep and a few cattle. From Khartoum northward to the Egyptian border, cultivation can take place only along the Nile itself. To the east of the river lies the Nubian Desert and to the west, the Libyan Desert.

The climate in the Sudan can be easily related to its distinctive land features. Rainfall is heaviest in the south where wet and humid summers are to be expected. Khartoum, on the other hand, receives an average rainfall of only about five inches per year, while the northern section of the country has a desert climate with almost no precipitation, extremely hot summers and cool dry winters.

The people of the Sudan also reflect the geographic differences of the country. For the most part, the population in the north is descended from Semitic tribes who have inhabited the area for over two thousand years. In the southern Sudan, however, the population is mostly Negroid, because of the area's affinity to sub-Saharan Africa. In the central part of the country, the population reflects the intermarriage of the Semitic

SUDAN   139

tribesmen of the north with the Negroes of the Nubian area to the south. Arabic is the major language spoken in northern and central Sudan. To the south, there are dialects of the East African languages.

Just as the Sudanese in the northern and central regions speak Arabic, so too most of these people are followers of Islam. It is estimated that there are approximately eleven million Muslims. Those living in the southern Sudan are followers of more primitive religions, such as animism. There are also small communities of Christians living throughout the country, and these include members of the Coptic and Greek Orthodox Churches, the Evangelical Church, the Episcopal Church, and the Maronite, Greek, and Roman Catholic Churches. Foreign missionary activity has been concentrated in the south.

These differences in race, language, and religion have caused some major political and social problems in the Sudan. Often, repressive action has been taken by the government in power against the people living in southern Sudan, and the result has been that these people have at times felt more closely akin to the neighboring African countries to the south.

As in the rest of the Middle East, education plays an important role in the Sudan. In 1898, only two primary schools existed in the country. Today, well over a half million students are enrolled in primary and intermediate schools. About 150,000 students attend governmental and private secondary schools. There are also about a hundred Muslim religious schools. Great stress has also been placed on technical education, since there is a real need for skilled laborers, and several such institutions have been opened. Almost 4,000 students attend the University College in Khartoum, where there is also a branch of the University of Cairo. Teacher training is being stressed, and at present eleven institutions designed to train teachers on the elementary and intermediate level are in operation.

History

Because of the Nile River, the Sudan's history has been closely associated with that of Egypt throughout the ages. This is particularly true in terms of events which have taken place during the last two centuries. In the early 1800's, Muhammad Ali, the Pasha of Egypt under Ottoman control, had dreams of creating an empire independent of the Turks. Though unable to expand his dominion northward out of Egypt, with the exception of a brief period when he controlled Syria, Muhammad Ali did gain control of the entire Nile Valley including the Sudan in 1821. The Sudan was at first administered as a province with a centralized government located in Khartoum. Later the government was decentralized along tribal lines. This resulted in poor communications and poorer administration. But this was only one of the problems the Sudan faced under Egyptian rule.

A far more serious problem was the slave trade, which flourished in the southern section of the Sudan. Slavery had long been accepted in the social structure of the country, but Muhammad Ali's successors gave trading rights to ruthless men, who relentlessly hunted down potential slaves with arms. Those who refused enslavement were often mercilessly slain. One of Muhammad Ali's successors, the Khedive Ismail, enlisted the help of the British General Charles Gordon in an effort to end such practices. Gordon's extreme measures in dealing with offenders, however, soon alienated large sections of the Sudanese populace.

In 1883, the British occupied Egypt and took effective control of the Egyptian Government. Then, in 1885, a religious fanatic, Muhammad Ahmed Abdullah, who had proclaimed himself *Mahdi,* a type of religious and temporal leader, precipitated a religious rebellion in the Sudan. He called on the Sudanese to oust the Egyptians and British from the country and to work for a religious reformation of Islam. The rebellion at first appeared to be minor, but it soon became apparent that it was turning into a full-scale uprising. When it became clear in Cairo that the *Mahdi* was gaining great support from the Sudanese and that he intended to wipe out all vestiges of foreign control in the Sudan, the British decided to withdraw all Egyptian troops from the Sudan. General Charles Gordon was again sent to Khartoum, this time to evacuate the Egyptian forces there. While he was in the city, it was placed under siege by the *Mahdi.* The siege lasted many months and considerably weakened the Egyptian troops. Finally, the *Mahdi's* forces stormed Khartoum. Gordon and the Egyptian troops were massacred.

The *Mahdi* himself died the following year. For the next thirteen years, the Sudan remained independent under his successor, Khalifa Abdullahi. Finally, fearing French influence in the Sudan, the British prevailed upon the Egyptians to recapture the country. Anglo-Egyptian forces commanded by General Herbert Kitchener, were able to subdue the Sudan in 1898. Control was nominal, for an Anglo-Egyptian agreement, known as the Condominium, was soon reached, and this in fact placed the Sudan under British colonial control. Administration of the country was placed in the hands of a Governor General, holding all civil and military powers, and from 1899 to 1924, the Sudan's Governor General was always British.

In 1924, the Egyptians stationed in the Sudan were evacuated, and the British were left in complete control of the country. This angered many educated Sudanese who felt strong ties with the Egyptians and shared a common language and religion with them. While in the Sudan, the Egyptians had acted as intermediaries between the Sudanese and the British, and it was felt that a valuable ally was lost when they left the country. Demonstrations against the British took place, but these were quickly suppressed. Reacting against the strong feelings of the Sudanese and fearing that the more educated would try to seize control of the government, Britain instituted a policy known as "Indirect Rule." Power was again placed in the hands of the tribal chieftains. This served to decentralize the government and thus eliminate all governmental structures employing educated or nationalistic Sudanese.

At the same time, repressive measures were instigated against the three southern provinces of the Sudan. This "Southern Policy" involved the removal from the provinces of all Muslims and Arabic-speaking people. The goal of this policy was to clear from the area all religious, cultural, and linguistic differences which might influence the southern Sudanese. The British hoped that such actions would keep the southern provinces from becoming infected with the spirit of the nationalism found in the north. At the same time, they hoped this alienation would lead those in the south to band together with other British-controlled central African territories.

In 1938, a Graduates' General Congress was formed by the educated nationalistic Sudanese whose desire for statehood was becoming more intense. The Congress in 1942 drew up and submitted to the British a *Memorandum* which stated demands for closer unification of the northern and southern sections of the country. The *Memorandum* also called for a greater share in administration of the government on the part of the

Khartoum University College in the capital of Sudan.

Sudanese and a demand for self-government when the war ended. Though the British refused to accept the *Memorandum,* they were aware of its possible impact and began to work towards the development of a more modern system of government. In 1948, a Legislative Assembly was allowed.

Eventually, the Graduates' Congress split into two factions: one favoring union with Egypt; the other calling for complete independence. The fate of the Sudan was in great part, however, decided by the Egyptian Revolution in 1952. The Egyptian military regime, led by Generals Neguib and Nasser, offered the Sudanese the right of self-determination, and in February 1953, the British and the Egyptians signed an agreement which granted the Sudan a three-year period of self-government under international supervision. Both Egypt and Britain began evacuating their nationals from the Sudan.

In January 1954, following the first national elections, Ismail al-Azhari became the first Sudanese Prime Minister. There was at the time much speculation concerning whether or not the Sudan would choose to join in a union with Egypt or declare itself independent. It soon became clear that Azhari favored independence. There was one major problem facing his government, however, and that was the problem of the southern provinces. The British had been very effective in their "Southern Policy," and in August 1955, nearly 300 northern Sudanese were killed during a mutiny of southern troops. The mutiny was quelled, but those representing the southern provinces in the Parliament insisted that before they would vote for independence, they wanted it made clear that they preferred a federated government, and that when independence was obtained, this would be considered in formulating the Sudan's government structures. Agreement was reached on this issue, and on January 1, 1956, the Sudan became an independent state.

Almost immediately the country was faced with severe financial problems, caused by difficulty in selling the Sudan's major cash crop, cotton. This, combined with factionalism and discord in the Parliament, led to a bloodless *coup* in November 1958. General Ibrahim Abboud took over the government and set up a Supreme Council of Armed Forces. The military regime did much to balance the Sudan's budget, but it continued to encounter many difficulties with the southern provinces. Rather than dealing with these problems in a political way, Abboud instituted suppressive military control in the south. The more educated saw this as once again dividing the country, and in reaction to these measures, a general civilian strike took place in October 1964. The strike brought the country to a standstill and finally forced Abboud to submit his resignation.

A transitional government was established with Sir-al-Khatim al Khalifa as Prime Minister. In March 1965, discussions were held about what kind of government the southern provinces would accept, but no agreement was reached. In June of the same year, the first general elections to be held since 1958 took place. The new government that was formed was made up of the Umma and the National Unionist Parties, but with the Umma's Muhammad Ahmed Mahgoub as Prime Minister. The new coalition had to face the troubles with the southern provinces, but in July of the same year, serious fighting broke out. For the next seven years, clashes accelerated in frequency, and the provinces were in actual revolt.

Except for nine months, Mahgoub remained in power until May 25, 1969, when army officers and some civilians led a bloodless *coup*. Colonel Jaafar Numeiry presided over the newly established Revolutionary Council. All political parties and organizations were dissolved, as well as the Constituent Assembly. Once again, the Sudan began close cooperation with Egypt, and Numeiry has announced his intention of eventually joining Egypt, Syria, and Libya in the Federation of Arab Republics.

Despite several brief attempted *coups,* Numeiry has remained in power. In the spring of 1972, peace was made with the rebels in the southern provinces. According to the compromise, the south will be ruled by an autonomous regional council of ministers, and the Vice President of the central government will be a southerner. Following the assassination of the American ambassador and his aide and the Belgian *chargé d'affaires* by terrorists in March 1973, President Numeiry outlawed Palestinian guerrilla organizations.

The Sudan must still face the problems of placing the country on a sound economic footing and of completing the formation of a permanent constitution, which will guarantee a permanency of government.

Economy

The economy of the Sudan is based almost entirely on agriculture, and it is estimated that almost 85 percent of the populace is engaged in farming activities. In the south, cultivation is primarily dependent on rainfall, while in the central and northern regions irrigation from the Nile is employed. The primary cash crop is cotton, and it accounts for almost 50 percent of the Sudan's agricultural exports. Heavy dependence on cotton has led to many financial problems, because a drought or a drop in prices on the world market directly affects the Sudan's economic balance.

Other exports include livestock and hides, peanuts, and gum Arabic, of which the Sudan produces 80 to 90 percent of the world's supply. Efforts are being made to introduce citrus crops into the central region of the country and coffee, tea, and tobacco into the southern provinces. The mining of minerals and light industry at present play only a small part in the Sudan's economy. Major concessions have been made to foreign investors, however, and it is hoped that such concessions will soon attract foreign investment to the Sudan.

The June War of 1967 and the subsequent closing of the Suez Canal greatly strained the Sudanese economy. Almost 50 percent of the Sudan's imports and exports had until that time passed through the canal. With its closure, import costs rose steadily, resulting in increased cost of consumer goods and a generally higher cost-of-living index. Following the war, the Sudanese severed diplomatic relations with the United States. This resulted in the loss of foreign aid and loans from America, but increased cooperation with the Soviet-bloc countries brought much needed economic assistance. In 1972, President Numeiry expelled most Soviet advisers because of suspected subversive activity. Diplomatic relations were reestablished with the United States. Increased American aid is expected.

Syrian Arab Republic

POPULATION: 6.1 million
CAPITAL: Damascus
INDEPENDENCE: April 17, 1946 (formerly a French Mandate from 1930 to 1946)

Geography and People

Syria is roughly the size of North Dakota and includes a land area of almost 72,000 square miles. It is bounded on the north by Turkey; on the east by Iraq; on the south by Jordan; and on the west by Israel, Lebanon, and the Mediterranean Sea. Its primary topographical features are the Anti-Lebanon and Alawite mountain ranges, both of which parallel the Mediterranean and extend from the border of Israel northwards into Turkey, the Euphrates River Valley, the Jabal Druze, a hilly area caused by lava flows located in the southwest, and a vast semidesert plateau covering the entire eastern section of the country.

In the summer the days are hot and dry, except along the seacoast where there is much humidity. Temperatures may reach as high as 110 degrees F. during the day. Precipitation ranges from 30 to 40 inches in the desert-like plateau area. The winter season is rainy, and the weather is generally quite cold, although temperatures usually stay above freezing. Syria is one of the few Arab countries with adequate arable land for its population. At least one fourth of the land can be cultivated, while another one third is good for seasonal pasturage.

The population of Syria is ethnically mixed. While the majority of its people are of Arab descent, there are also large numbers of Kurds, Armenians, and people of Turkish descent living in the northwest. The population is approximately 85 percent Muslim, most of whom are followers of Islam's Sunni sect. The largest religious minority in the country is the Alawite community, which combines tenets of Christianity and Islam with pre-Christian fertility rites. There are over 400,000 Alawites in Syria. Other religious minorities include 172,000 Greek Orthodox, 100,000 Syrian Orthodox, 117,000 Druzes, and a smaller number of Greek, Armenian, Syrian, Roman, and Maronite Catholics. There are also several different Protestant denominations represented in Syria.

Arabic is spoken throughout the country, but Kurdish is widely spoken in the northern part of Syria. Armenian can be heard in most of the large urban areas.

Heavy emphasis has been placed on schooling in Syria. Education is free in governmental schools through the secondary level. Legislation has also been introduced to make schooling through the primary level compulsory for all children. It is estimated that over 40 percent of the Syrian population can read and write. About 800,000 students are enrolled in primary level schools; almost 200,000 in secondary schools. Over 30,000 students are enrolled at the university level. Most of these students attend Damascus University, which opened in 1923. A second university was opened at Aleppo in 1960. Syria also has over 30 technical institutes.

History

The area which is now Syria has always played a significant role in history because of its geographical position as a land bridge from the Mediterranean to Asia. Historically, the area referred to as Syria comprised not only the present state, but also Lebanon, Israel, and part of Jordan. It was not until the French Mandate that the present boundaries of Syria were drawn. Through the ages it has been dominated by numerous powers including the Babylonians, the Greeks, the Romans, the Byzantines, the Egyptians, the Crusaders, the Mongols, and the Turks. Damascus is one of the oldest continually inhabited cities in the world and was first settled about 2500 B.C. The city reached its zenith when,

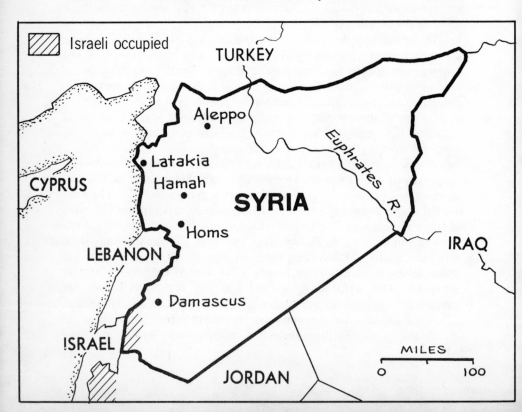

under Muslim rule in 661 A.D., it was chosen as the capital of the Omayyad Empire, which at that time extended from India to Spain. In 750, however, the Abbasid dynasty gained control of the Islamic Empire and transferred the capital to Baghdad.

The history of Syria for the next 350 years is one of a pawn in power plays made by surrounding nations. Egypt occupied Syria in 878, but northern Syria fell into the hands of the Byzantine Empire in 997. In 1075, Damascus fell to the Turks, and in 1098 the Crusaders captured Antioch. The country was again occupied by Egypt under the Mamluks from 1250 to 1517, although during this subjugation the area was victim of assaults by the Mongols. When it at last fell to the Turks in 1517, Syria had already experienced an economic and political decline due to plagues, warfare, and periodic famine.

Turkey's rule was marked by further internal division and poor administration, which Syria endured until the end of World War I with only one brief respite. Between 1833 and 1840, it was once again captured by Egypt — this time under the rule of Muhammad Ali. His son Ibrahim administered the country and for a short time brought about a centralized and stable government. He also permitted both French and American missionaries to come to the area and to establish schools. Inadvertently, these schools did much to foster Arab nationalism through a revitalization of interest in Arabic literature and culture, and by the late 1800's Syria had a growing nationalistic movement.

In 1840, Turkey regained control of Syria and retained it until the end of World War I. During the war the Syrians had held great hope for their future independence, fostered by an exchange of letters between the British and the Arab leader, Sharif Hussein. This correspondence had promised independence for most of the Arab territories in the Middle East in exchange for their help in defeating the Turks. Following the war, however, the coastal areas of Syria were put under French administration, while the interior was ruled by Amir Faisal, a son of Hussein.

In March 1920, a Kingdom of Greater Syria was announced by Syrian nationalists. This kingdom was to include Lebanon and Palestine also. Less than a month after the announcement, however, the French were given the Mandate for all of Syria, except Palestine, at the San Remo Conference. In July, Damascus was occupied by the French, and King Faisal fled the country.

It soon became apparent that the Syrians' desire for independence was stronger than the French had realized. In an effort to stabilize its rule and to ward off further dissent among Arab nationalists in the mandated territory, France divided Syria into four units in 1925. Lebanon, which had always been considered a province of Syria, was enlarged and given a separate government. Also, two districts were carved out of the territory. One was Latakia, which lay along the Mediterranean coast in the northern section of Syria, and the other was Jabal Druze in the west. The fourth unit was the Syrian Republic, which included the area surrounding Damascus.

For the next twenty years, French rule in Syria was marked by unrest, demands for independence, and occasional riots. A constitution was drawn up in 1929 by a Constituent Assembly, but it was rejected by the French because it stated that the territories of Latakia and Jabal Druze were integral parts of Syria and would revert to the Syrian Republic after independence. In 1930, the French High Commissioner himself issued a new constitution without any reference to the two areas.

In 1936, a Franco-Syrian treaty was signed. Syria's right to self-rule was recognized, and it stated that, following its independence, there would be a three-year period of adjustment at the end of which the French would withdraw entirely. The treaty was not ratified, however, within the given time period, and riots led by Syrian nationalists broke out in 1941. France, under German occupation in Europe, could do little, but the leader of France's Free Government recognized Syria's independent status in September 1941. Still the French remained in Syria. An Arab nationalist, Shukri Kuwatly, was elected President in 1943, and slowly the French began to transfer control of the country into Syrian hands. It was only after further riots broke out in May 1945, and after the British moved into Syria, that the French sped up their withdrawal. By April 1946, both French and British forces had moved from Syria. The nation formally proclaimed its independence on April 17, 1946.

Among the countries of the Near East, Syria has perhaps suffered most from an unstable political situation since its independence in 1946. In 1949, following the first Arab-Israeli war, Syria experienced three military *coups d'état*. For the next five years it was ruled by the military under the leadership of Lieutenant Colonel Shishakli. During his administration, the Chamber of Deputies was dissolved, all political parties were abolished, and a new constitution was announced. Shishakli was opposed throughout his regime by those hostile to military rule, however, and the unrest led to the collapse of the military regime in Syria early in 1954. Shishakli fled the country, and new elections for the Chamber of Deputies were held in September 1954.

There also existed in Syria two different schools of thought as to how the country should relate to other Arab states. There were those who favored union with Iraq, even though such a move might prove to strengthen the Hashemite dynasty, and there were those who favored union with Egypt. In August 1955, Shukri Kuwatly became President. His sympathies lay in the direction of union with Egypt, and shortly after his appointment, Syria and Egypt signed an agreement which created a joint military command with headquarters in Damascus.

Two years later, the Syrian National Assembly voted in favor of a resolution calling for a formal union with Egypt. The union combined Syria and Egypt into one state which, though geographically separated, would be one in economic, military, and diplomatic policies. Each state was to have a regional government, but President Nasser was to be head of the new union. It was to be known as the United Arab Republic, and on February 21, 1958, the two states formally merged. In July 1960, the first meeting of a single National Assembly comprised of 400 Egyptians and 200 Syrians took place in Cairo.

The Ba'athists, who made up Syria's largest political party and who were strongly socialistic in ideology, had originally urged the merger of the two states. After two years, however, the members felt that rapid economic development, which they had thought would follow such a merger had not taken place. Not only they, but other Syrians as well, began to view the merger with growing dissatisfaction. On September 28, 1961, a military *coup* took place. The new government quickly seceded from the United Arab Republic and cancelled all former agreements. New elections were held, a provisional constitution was put into effect, and a new Constituent Assembly was elected to begin work on a new constitution. Though the Ba'ath party was very influential in the new regime, it did not control it.

The Ba'athists finally did gain control of Syria, following a seizure of the government by a military junta on March 8, 1963. Once again, the problem of union with Egypt arose, but this time the Ba'athists carried out a purge to rid the military and the government of any pro-Egyptian elements. Now, instead of favoring union with Egypt, the government favored union with Iraq, by that time also dominated by the Ba'athists. In November 1963, however, a *coup* took place in Iraq, and the Iraqi Ba'athists were forced out of power.

Meanwhile, the Syrian Ba'athists had begun a policy of nationalization of the country's resources. In the spring of 1963, all banks and many textile plants were seized. The following year all mineral resources, including the undeveloped petroleum industry were nationalized, and early in January 1965, nearly all of Syria's light industry was also brought under government control. These moves, coupled with an amended land reform bill that limited possession of land to between 15 and 55 *hectares* (1 *hectare* equals about 2½ acres), caused much unrest. Demonstrations and strikes followed.

On February 23, 1966, yet another military *coup* took place, this time putting into power a military junta made up of the more radical members of the Ba'athist party. The Prime Minister of the new government was Dr. Yusuf Zeayen. Almost immediately, he entered into an economic agreement with the U.S.S.R. under the terms of which Syria was provided with almost 150 million dollars for the construction of a dam on the Euphrates. Zeayen also signed a military defense agreement with the United Arab Republic in November 1966.

Border incidents were common occurrences between Syria and Israel throughout the 1960's, but in the winter and spring of 1967, the activity increased until war broke out on June 5, 1967. After heavy fighting, Israeli troops moved into Syria in the Golan Heights area. When the cease-fire was finally signed, the Israelis had come within forty miles of Damascus. Syria has since rejected all compromises or possible solutions to the problems it faces with Israel, including the November 22, 1967, U.N. resolution.

The military is still in power, Dr. Nureddin al-Atassi, of the Ba'athist left, headed the government between 1965 and late 1970. In March 1971, General Hafez al-Assad became President. Several trade agreements have been made with both Soviet-bloc countries and the Peoples' Republic of China. This has led to speculation about where Syria is turning.

Syria's relations with Jordan and Lebanon have been strained by the presence of *fedayeen* from Syria in both countries. The Syrian group, known as Sa'iqah, has grown considerably. Through 1969 and early 1970, these *fedayeen* launched attacks on Israel from both Lebanese and Jordanian territory. Israeli reprisals against both countries followed. As a result of Jordan's expulsion of the commandos, Syria broke relations, engaged in border skirmishes, and closed its airspace to all Jordan-bound planes.

Some examples of the famous inlaid wood mosaics of Syria.

Economics

Agriculture is the primary source of income for over 60 percent of Syria's population. Until 1963 much of the arable land in Syria was owned by a few wealthy families. Since then the land has been more evenly distributed through a land reform program. When the land reform program was being realized, the government took steps to nationalize the financial and industrial activities of the country. These two reform programs caused an economic slowdown, which can be expected when such moves are not coupled with massive foreign investment. The result was that the country faced a real balance-of-payments problem by late 1966. This is only now being remedied.

Syria's major crop is cotton, and it accounts for 40 percent of all agricultural exports. One third of it is sold to Eastern-bloc countries. Cotton is also Syria's single largest source of foreign exchange earnings. Cereal grains, particularly wheat, are the second largest export. Other exports include fruit, vegetables, textiles, wool, and meat. Syria's agricultural economy suffered severely from a drought which lasted from 1958 until 1961. Another drought in 1967, coupled with the Israeli conflict that year, put an additional drain on the economy.

Oil deposits, found in the northeast, may prove to be another valuable source of income. Oil already plays an important part in the economy, however, since two major pipelines across the country. One is from the Kirkuk fields in Iraq and leads to the Syrian port of Baniyas; the other is the Tapline, which brings oil from Saudi Arabia through Syria to the port of Sidon in Lebanon.

Finally, the textile industry provides Syria with another important source of income. Approximately ten percent of its population is employed in the manufacture of textiles.

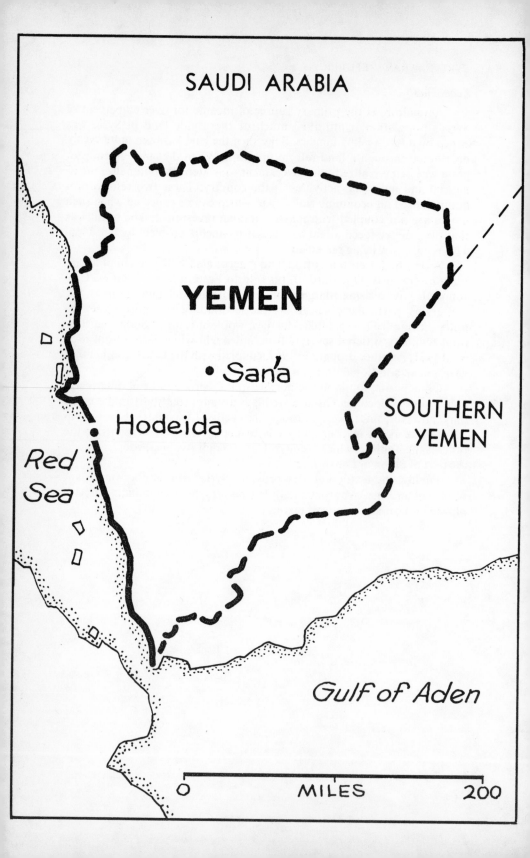

SAUDI ARABIA

YEMEN

• San'a

Hodeida

*Red
Sea*

SOUTHERN
YEMEN

Gulf of Aden

0   MILES   200

Yemen Arab Republic

POPULATION: 5.7 million
CAPITAL: San'a
INDEPENDENCE: 1918

Geography and People

Yemen is located on the southwestern tip of the Arabian Peninsula. It is bordered on the west by the Red Sea, on the south by Southern Yemen, and on the north and east by Saudi Arabia. Its northeastern border is not well delineated, however, for it faces on the Rub al-Khali, or Empty Quarter, which is the vast desert that makes up the greater portion of southern Saudi Arabia. The land area of Yemen is approximately 75,000 square miles.

Yemen's coastal plain bordering the Red Sea is about 375 miles long. This plain, known as the Tihama, is a dry, sandy, semidesert strip reaching inland thirty to forty miles. Rising from the Tihama is a rugged mountain range that reaches heights of 12,000 feet. Here the summers are temperate, and rainfall may average up to 35 inches per year. The winters in the mountainous area are cool and mild, although there is occasional frost and snow.

The population is primarily Arab. There was a sizable Jewish population in Yemen until 1948 when about 50,000 Yemeni Jews migrated to Israel. Both sects of Islam are present in Yemen. Members of the Shi'ite sect reside primarily in the northern, central, and eastern portions of the country; members of the Sunni sect of Islam live in the southern and southwestern portions of the country. The principal language in Yemen is Arabic.

Until the withdrawal of the Ottoman Turks in 1918, the education system in Yemen consisted for the most part in traditional religious institutions devoted to the teachings of Islam. In recent decades high priority has been placed on educational reform, and at present education is compulsory between the ages of seven and seventeen. There are now about 3,000 primary and intermediate schools and 20 secondary schools in Yemen. About 75,000 students are enrolled at the primary level, while over 2,000 students attend secondary schools. Yemen also has six vocational schools, a college of aviation, an agricultural school, and a school designed to teach radio telecommunications. Many Yemeni students also attend colleges and universities abroad.

History

The ancient and powerful kingdom of Sheba was located in Yemen. Its capital was Marib, a city situated in the extreme eastern section of the country near what is now the border of Southern Yemen. It was from Marib that the Queen of Sheba is believed to have traveled northward to meet with the Israelite king, Solomon. Sheba was a kingdom of traders, and their prosperity was based primarily on supplying incense and myrrh to peoples to the north, in the area of modern Jordan.

Located as it is at the tip of the Arabian Peninsula, Yemen has not been invaded with the same frequency as the areas lying to the north of it. It has, however, been occupied by such disparate powers as Ethiopia and Persia, and in the seventh century A.D., it accepted the teachings of Islam brought to it by the Muslims of Central Arabia. Leadership in the country was claimed by descendants of the Himyarite dynasty, who ruled from the time of Christ until the sixth century, and even in the nineteenth century the Imam, or ruler, of Yemen was descended from the Himyarites.

The Ottoman Turks took possession of Yemen in 1517, but they did not fully occupy it until 1872, shortly after the opening of the Suez Canal. With the opening of Suez, Yemen had become strategically more important, for its southern border marked the entry of the Red Sea into the Gulf of Aden. Aden, which is now Southern Yemen, had been occupied by the British in 1839. The British contested Ottoman control of Yemen, because they feared disputes over navigational rights near the Yemen-Aden border.

In 1911, the Imam Yahya led a revolt against the Turks. He was successful in gaining administrative control of the mountainous section of Yemen. With the outbreak of World War I, the Imam supported the Turkish cause. The British, in turn, supported the activities of the Idrisi, a tribe to the north of Yemen whose small state, Asir, had quarreled with Yemen over boundaries between the two states. In 1926, Asir signed a treaty which placed it under the control of Ibn Saud, who was trying to bring all of the Hejaz under his control. The Imam Yahya refused to recognize Ibn Saud's claims and finally provoked him into attacking Yemen. Ibn Saud successfully forced the Imam's troops to withdraw to San'a, however, and in 1934 the Treaty of Ta'if was signed, and Yemen's present borders were established. Meanwhile, the Imam also launched attacks against Aden to provoke the British stationed there.

Yahya continued to rule Yemen in a conservative fashion until 1948. Though a despotic ruler, he did wish to strengthen Yemen's ties with other Arab states, and Yemen was one of the founding members of the Arab League. His absolute reign ended in February 1948 when he was murdered in an attempted *coup d'état*. The attempt failed, however, and Yahya's son, Ahmad, ascended the throne. Ahmad recognized the need for foreign investment to be used for development within Yemen, and he worked hard to attract technical aid and to establish diplomatic relations with major foreign powers. Though he managed to improve Yemen's international relations and attract foreign investment, Ahmad's rule was as absolute and repressive as his father's had been. In April 1955, another *coup* took place which also failed. This time, however, the Imam reacted to the internal pressure by setting up a formal Cabinet in August 1955.

The border dispute with Britain over the Aden-Yemen boundaries continued to erupt sporadically, and in the winter of 1956, Yemeni tribesmen were accused of attacking villages in Aden. Similar incidents were repeated the following winter and again in the spring of 1958.

Following the merger of Egypt and Syria into the United Arab Republic in 1958, Yemen entered into an agreement with the newly formed U.A.R. The agreement resulted in the formation of the Federation of Arab States, the purpose of which was to unify the defense and foreign policies of the three states. The Federation was short-lived, however, and was dissolved following the break between Egypt and Syria in November 1961.

An unsuccessful attempt to murder the Imam Ahmad took place in March 1961. The following September he died of natural causes, and was succeeded by his son, Muhammad Badr. A week later members of the Yemeni army supported by Egyptian troops revolted against the new Imam, destroyed his palace, and forced him to flee San'a. Although Badr made several attempts to regain the capital, he did not succeed. Saudi Arabia provided him with military supplies, but this was no match for the revolutionary army, which continued to receive both troops and military support from Egypt. Those siding with the Imam were known as the Royalists, while the revolutionaries were known as the Republicans.

The new government created by the Republican faction was recognized by both the United States and the U.S.S.R., and it was admitted to the United Nations in 1963 as the Yemen Arab Republic.

Fighting continued, and though an agreement was reached in the winter of 1963, whereby Saudi Arabia promised to cease supplying military aid to the Imam if Egypt's forces were withdrawn, a United Nations Observer Mission to Yemen early in 1964 found that neither side had honored the agreement. Meanwhile, Britain refused to recognize the Republican regime, for it was obvious that one of its aims was to rid the southern tip of the peninsula, including Aden, of all British influence.

Agreements similar to the one signed in 1963 were reached again in 1964 and in 1965, but relations between Egypt and Saudi Arabia were strained in other areas besides Yemen, and no real withdrawal took place. In the meantime, the Republican government published its new constitution in April 1964. The new Prime Minister, Hamud al-Jaifi, sought to align Yemen's policies with those of Egypt, and in July 1964, an agreement was signed which established a joint military command between the two countries financed primarily by Egypt.

The position of Prime Minister was a precarious one, and al-Jaifi was replaced in January 1965 by Lieutenant General Hassan al-Amri, who in turn yielded to a more moderate man, Ahmad Muhammad No'man, in April. As the third Prime Minister in less than a year, No'man worked towards trying to bring about a peace settlement, but his sympathies were not with Egypt, which maintained a certain amount of financial control in Yemen. No'man was forced to resign in July 1965 and was again replaced by the more pro-Egyptian Hassan al-Amri.

In late summer of 1965, President Nasser and King Faisal met at Jiddah and agreed to bring the fighting in Yemen to an end. An interim government was to be set up which would exclude both the Imam Bakr and Yemen's President Abdullah Sallal who had initiated the *coup* against Bakr in 1962. The agreement called for the withdrawal of Egyptian troops and an end to Saudi Arabia's supplying military arms to the Royalist troops.

Again the agreement was not honored, and by the fall of 1966 it was apparent that the Republican government was having internal problems. Prime Minister al-Amri and President Sallal were in disagreement over the future government of Yemen, and al-Amri flew to Egypt to demand troop withdrawals from Yemen and removal of the President. Al-Amri overestimated his position, however, and upon his arrival in Cairo he was arrested and put in jail. Sallal took over the duties of the Prime Minister

San'a, capital of Yemen, from the north. At the right, remains of the ancient wall.

and initiated a purge of the army and the government to remove all who disagreed with his policies.

The war between the Royalists and the Republicans now escalated as did diplomatic moves to settle Yemen's future. Following the Arab-Israeli conflict in June 1967, the Royalists initiated the heaviest fighting in Yemen in over two years. Though initially the Royalists successfully captured some land, Egypt continued its military build-up and soon re-captured the territories taken by the Royalists.

At the Arab Summit Conference held in Khartoum in August 1967, however, the Egyptians proposed once again that efforts be made to implement the agreements for withdrawal, which had been reached in 1965. King Faisal and President Nasser came to terms on the last day of August, and it was agreed that Egyptian troops should be withdrawn from Yemen within three months. President Sallal was to continue in office as head of a transitional government, and a plebiscite was to be held to determine what form the new government in Yemen would take. Nasser had been severely criticized for having over 80,000 troops stationed in Yemen at the time of the June War, and this, coupled with the fact that he was now dependent on Saudi Arabian financial help, were factors leading to his acceptance of the new agreement.

The 80,000 Egyptian troops stationed in Yemen were withdrawn by January 1968. Prior to their removal, President Sallal had been deposed and replaced by a three-man Presidency Council. The withdrawal of Egyptian troops was followed by renewed efforts on the part of the Royalists to regain the capital city of San'a. Republicans maintained that the Royalists were still receiving aid from the Saudi Arabian government but their siege of San'a was unsuccessful and was lifted in mid-April.

In June 1968, the Imam Badr was deposed from his position as leader of the Royalist forces and was succeeded by his son, Muhammad ibn Hussein. This led to dissension among the Royalists. Saudi Arabia withdrew future support following the failure of the Royalists to capture San'a, and this withdrawal resulted in declining efforts on the part of the Royalists to assert themselves. By August 1969 the Republicans had secured their position and were pursuing a policy which would align them more closely to the Western powers.

The Civil War finally ended in March 1970, when Yemeni and Saudi Arabian representatives met privately in Jiddah. The following month the two countries announced an agreement, which included the appointment of several Royalists to the Yemeni government. The Presidential Council supervises the administration of the country. For several years the chairman has been Abdul Rahman al-Iriani.

Economics

Yemen is primarily an agricultural country. The careful use of land through the terracing of arable ground in the mountains makes the country self-sufficient. Along the dry coastal plain, dates, cereal grains, and cotton are grown. The southern area of the country produces corn and Mocha coffee, which is Yemen's prime export product. The mountain highlands are rain-fed and produce a large assortment of fruits, vegetables, and cereal grains. Nuts, olives, tobacco, and alfalfa are also grown in the mountains.

The raising of livestock is also an important source of income, and Yemen is noted for its Arabian horses. Fishing along the coast provides a livelihood for many inhabitants in that area.

Absorbed by the Civil War which lasted from 1962 to 1970, Yemen has only recently turned to industrial development. It received 42 million dollars in American aid between 1959 and 1967, but following the June War of 1967, this aid was suspended, when diplomatic relations between the two countries were severed. Since 1967, Yemen has received aid from the Soviet Union to be used in road construction. The Peoples' Republic of China has also provided financial assistance. Loans have been received from Algeria and West Germany. Relations were reestablished with the United States in 1972.

Yemen has a wide assortment of natural resources including coal, precious metals, and iron. In 1955, concessions were made to American firms to prospect for both oil and minerals. These concessions were terminated, however, and new concessions were made to another American firm in 1960. So far, no appreciable progress has been made in discovering oil.

CHAPTER III

Judaism, Christianity and Islam

It is a startling fact that over one and a half billion people throughout the world can trace their religious heritage to an area in the Middle East which is not much larger than the state of Texas. Yet three of the seven major religions of the world* arose in such an area. Judaism's roots are planted in the Sinai Desert; Christianity struggled to life in the area surrounding Jerusalem; and Islam's birthplace is Mecca in the Arabian Peninsula.

All three religions share a common belief in monotheism, or the existence of one Supreme Being. Judaism bases its belief on the direct revelation of Yahweh (God) to Abraham and Moses. Christianity, while accepting the historicity and the moral values found in the literature of ancient Israel (notably the Old Testament), adds to these beliefs a faith in the Messiah, the Son of God, Jesus Christ. Islam, the youngest of the three major religions, bases its beliefs on the *Qur'an,* or Holy Book, which is believed to be the direct revelation of *Allah* (God) transmitted to the Prophet Muhammad through the Angel Gabriel.

Yet, though all three religions profess a belief in one Supreme Being, a great deal of misunderstanding exists between the three faiths. The Bishops of the Second Vatican Council of the Roman Catholic Church recognized this and, in an effort to promote a better understanding between all major faiths, issued a *Declaration on the Relationship of the Church to Non-Christian Religions.* Though directed towards Catholics, this *Declaration* can well be applied not only to all Christians but to all men of good will who wish to promote peace. In part the *Declaration* exhorted ". . . through dialogue and collaboration with the followers of other religions, and in witness of Christian faith and life (to) acknowledge, preserve and promote the spiritual and moral goods found among these men (of other faiths) as well as the values in their society and cul-

*The other major religions are Buddhism, Hinduism, Confucianism, and Taoism.

ture." This, of course, cannot be done unless something of the history and growth of each faith is known. Also, to understand the Middle East, one must have some acquaintance of the development of the three religions.

*   *   *

The Ancient Middle East

Religion has always played an important role in man's life. No matter how primitive a people may be, within their view of life there exists the belief in something or someone greater than man himself. There existed in the Middle East three thousand years ago tribes of such peoples, who had progressed from the magic and superstition of the most primitive stages of religious development to the belief in many gods.

This belief in many gods, or polytheism, was partly animistic in nature. Natural objects such as stones and trees and natural phenomena, such as the sun and moon, were believed by men to possess spirits of divine beings. These spirits did not move from place to place, nor was any one spirit considered more powerful than the others. It was man's task to seek out each spirit and to ascertain the area which the spirit controlled. For instance, the spirit of the god with the power to make crops grow or wither may well reside in a certain tree in some field. Once the spirit had been identified, man's next task was to pay proper homage to the god in order to ensure a good crop, victory in battle, or proper grazing land for his cattle or sheep. The homage was often paid by praying magical incantations, by performing fertility rites, or through animal sacrifices.

Another major characteristic of the ancient Middle East which should be considered is the state of almost constant warfare which existed among the peoples inhabiting the area. Many tribes lived in the lands bordering the eastern Mediterranean including the Canaanites, the Moabites, the Ammonites, and the Philistines. Even though most of these tribes had passed from a nomadic existence into a semi-agrarian way of life, constant warfare raged among them. There were skirmishes over pasture land, forays into each other's camps to steal what little wealth there was and to carry off the women, and large-scale battles waged over disputed territory.

Beyond this intertribal strife, there loomed the continual threat of attack from the more advanced and powerful Egyptians to the south and the mighty Assyrians to the east. Both coveted the Sinai Desert and the area of Palestine, which today includes Israel and Jordan, as a buffer zone and as a path to the Mediterranean. This land was constantly under attack, and life was seldom peaceful for the smaller tribes settled there.

It is, then, in this setting that the first major monotheistic religion of the world begins.

Ancient Israelite Religion

Judaism

Its Beginnings

The best recorded history of the birth of Judaism can be found in the first five books of the Old Testament. Though often referred to as the Pentateuch by Christians, for Jews these books have a special name, the *Torah,* or the Law. The *Torah* contains a graphic description of the life of the earliest Israelites, and the story told in its pages is one filled with adventure, hardships, enslavement, and a flight for freedom which ended only after forty years of wandering in the Sinai Desert.

The focal point of the story, however, is the covenant made between Yahweh (God) and the people, represented by Moses, on Mount Sinai. It is to Sinai and to their forefather, Abraham, that the Jews trace the origins of their faith. As a sign of the covenant between Yahweh and Abraham, each Hebrew male child should be circumcised on the eighth day after birth. In return, Yahweh is said to have promised that the descendants of Abraham would be given the rich and fertile land of Canaan.

Tradition tells that before completion of this covenant, Abraham took his family and left Ur, a city-state in Chaldea located near the juncture of the Tigris and Euphrates rivers in what is today Iraq, and made his way west and then south into Canaan. It is to be remembered that at this point in history, borders, as they are in the modern world, did not exist. The land of Canaan generally constituted the area along and north of the Jordan River. For reasons like drought or pestilence, some of these early Israelites migrated farther south and west into Egypt. There they remained and settled in the fertile lands of the Nile Delta region.

In the middle of the 13th century B.C., the Pharaoh Ramses II ascended the throne of Egypt. In an effort to glorify himself, he began a vast building program, and in order to provide the huge labor force needed to build temples and monuments, he rounded up every able-bodied male in Egypt, including the Hebrews, and imposed a *courvet,* or forced labor on them. After Ramses' death, however, the powerful Egyptian state began to crumble as marauders from the north invaded the kingdom. In the midst of the chaos which followed, the Hebrews led by Moses escaped into the Sinai Desert.

The Mosaic Covenant

Three months after the Hebrews had fled from Egypt, Yahweh revealed himself to Moses on Mount Sinai, and the covenant upon which Judaism is based was made. The central point of the covenant is a matter of choice. Yahweh, through Moses, told the Hebrews that he had chosen them to be his people. He promised that if they would follow his laws he would protect them, lead them through the desert, and guide them once they entered Canaan. The people, on their part, swore allegiance to Yahweh. He would be their one and only God.

Thus, central to the Mosaic Covenant is the obligation to observe Yahweh's laws. To make this special relationship concrete, the Hebrews drafted their covenant with Yahweh in the same manner as the ancient Near Eastern peoples solemnized a treaty with a king. This treaty, or covenant, consisted in a preamble, stipulations, curses and blessings to ensure observance, taking of an oath, instructions for keeping a copy for posterity, and an exhortation for periodic public reading. Most of these elements are found in the formulation of the Mosaic Covenant as found in the Old Testament's book of *Exodus,* chapter 20. This section contains the text of the Ten Commandments, or the Decalogue. The laws found in the Ten Commandments are basically "apodictic," which means that they are direct commands. This type of law is different from the ordinary law of the ancient Near Eastern law codes, like the Code of Hammurabi, insofar as those laws were "casuistic," which means they first state a particular case, and then tell what the solution or punishment should be. An example of this is: "If a man murders another man, then he will be put to death."

When the text of the covenant was inscribed on clay tablets, it was deposited in the Ark of the Covenant, which the Israelites carried with them in their wanderings through the Sinai Desert and into Canaan. Yahweh's presence was thought to be associated with the Ark in a special way.

In addition to the Ten Commandments, there were many other laws, which the Hebrews observed. These can be found throughout the *Torah,* and according to Jewish tradition there are 613 laws, of which 248 commands are positive and 365 are prohibitions. These laws covered not only the method of worshiping Yahweh, but also many aspects of the Hebrews' everyday life.

Some of the laws were difficult to observe, like the keeping of the Sabbath. To set aside a full day for rest and worship, in a time when men struggled from day to day merely to eke out an existence, was a real sacrifice. Not only were men, women, and children to rest, but also the sheep, cattle, and oxen. No work was to be performed from sundown on the sixth day until sundown on the seventh day. No food was to be prepared, no lamps lit, no housecleaning done.

Other laws, most of which are still practiced as closely as possible by Orthodox Jews, included strict dietary prohibitions. These included the manner in which certain animals were to be killed and prepared, the kinds of food which could be eaten, and the method in which they were to be served. The meat of the swine was considered unclean, so the Hebrews were not allowed to eat pork. Today these laws may seem inconvenient, but 3,000 years ago it is likely that such laws were necessary to maintain good hygiene. Many of the laws relating to food can be found in the 11th chapter of *Leviticus*.

And so the covenant between Yahweh and the Hebrews was completed, and the Ark of the Covenant which in a special way personified Yahweh was built. During the next forty years, most of the Hebrews, who had fled with Moses out of Egypt died, and it was the second generation of the "Chosen People" who followed Joshua, Moses' successor, across the Jordan River and into the "Promised Land."

Life in Canaan

The first task facing the Hebrews in this new land was to settle down to grow crops, and to raise herds. This was no easy task, since there were several tribes already living in the area who claimed parts of the fertile

Jerusalem, a holy city for three religions — Judaism, Christianity, and Islam.

land as their own. Faced with this reality the Hebrews had no choice but to enter into the pattern of intertribal warfare which existed. Eventually, probably with the help of kinsmen who had remained in Canaan and who had not been in Egypt, the Israelites were able to secure land on which they raised crops and herds. They did not settle in only one area of Canaan. Of the twelve tribes of Israel mentioned in the Old Testament, ten moved northward out of the Jordan River area and settled throughout the land that was to become known as Palestine. The tribes settled in various places and banded together only when one or another was faced with the threat of invasion. This tribal confederation was united around the central sanctuary, where the Ark of the Covenant was kept.

It was the threat of an invasion by the Philistines which finally united the tribes which to that time had been led by different "Judges." This led to the establishment of an Israelite kingdom under Saul in about 1030 B.C. Saul did not live to see the Philistines defeated, although he lived long enough to see them carry away the Ark of the Covenant. It was his successor, David, who managed to rout the Philistines and become the second king of the Hebrews. David's three greatest accomplishments as king were that he recovered the Ark from the Philistines, created a capital for the kingdom, and planned to build a Temple where the Ark would be enshrined. David did not simply locate a place suitable for a capital and proceed to build a city. The people were much too poor to build an entire city, so David, after considering the choice, captured a Canaanite stronghold known as Jerusalem and ordered that this fort-like city become the center and capital of the kingdom. Jerusalem became an extra-tribal, royal city.

In the beginning, David's rule was devoted to securing the borders of the young kingdom. He did this by attacking surrounding tribes and carrying off their wealth. Through these tactics he convinced the surrounding tribes that it was better to live at peace with the Israelites. In his later days, however, David grew lax in governing the kingdom. He took Moabite and Canaanite wives, who brought with them into the kingdom their many gods, or *baals*. And, by the time of David's death, internal dissension in the kingdom, plus the influences of polytheism, threatned to destroy the united kingdom.

The Temple

David's successor, his son Solomon, was not a warrior like his father. Solomon preferred to live in a manner similar to the wealthy tribal chieftains he saw in the tribes surrounding him, and his first interest was to build a grand palace with the Temple which David had planned attached to it. In the Temple, the Ark of the Covenant would rest, and the Israelite people would at last have a place where they could properly worship Yahweh.

It was around this Temple that the religion of the Israelites would devolve for the next four hundred years. Since the Israelites themselves were not at this time craftsmen, Solomon brought in Phoenicians from the land bordering the Mediterranean to plan the Temple. Work was begun on the Temple about 967 B.C., and it was completed thirty years later. It was richly decorated with cedar, cypress, and olive wood covering the walls and floors, but in keeping with Yahweh's command that the Israelites allow no graven images to come between themselves and Yahweh, there were no statues or likenesses of people or animals.

Shortly after Solomon's death, the tribes in the north revolted, tearing the young kingdom in two. The northern tribes banded together forming a kingdom called Israel, and a shrine was built in Bethel to rival the temple in Jerusalem. The southern kingdom, with its capital still in Jerusalem, became known as Judah. Thus ended, after only slightly more than 100 years, the united kingdom which encompassed all of the tribes.

The Prophets

With the placing of the Ark in the Temple, the worship of Yahweh had been centralized. A priesthood had developed which was responsible for offering sacrifice to Yahweh. The worship of the *baals,* brought into Jerusalem by the heathen women who married David and Solomon, posed a real problem. And the Israelites, struggling to live with the code of laws which Yahweh had entrusted to them, often slipped into polytheistic practices which were often more magical than religious.

There were those among the Israelites who said not only the worship of *baals,* but also the hypocritical worship of Yahweh, was evil. These men, known as *nevi'im,* or prophets, roamed throughout Palestine. They warned that evil days would befall the people, if they did not return to the simple, pure religion which the Hebrews had practiced in the Sinai Desert. These men were looked on with a mixture of awe, contempt, and repugnance.

It is not without reason that the proverb "A prophet is without honor save in his own country" had become so familiar. Surely the saying could be applied to these holy men, especially Amos and Jeremiah. Amos was probably born in the southern kingdom of Judah in the eighth century B.C. A pious and simple man, he preached not in Judah but in Israel, and foretold the destruction of the northern kingdom. The people refused to listen to his pleas for reform, and in 722 B.C. Israel was conquered by the Assyrians, and the ten tribes who had settled there were led away into exile or dispersed. This ended their existence as part of the nation.

Other prophets followed Amos, among them Hosea, Isaiah, and Micah. The prophet Jeremiah surely ranks as one of the most courageous. Unafraid of the Temple priests, the King, or the people, Jeremiah preached against the formalistic worship in the Temple and warned of the destruction of both the Temple and Judah. But more importantly, he warned the Israelites that if they broke the covenant they could no longer consider Yahweh their exclusive God, and he intimated that Yahweh would belong to all nations and all peoples.

This surely must have disturbed the people for they believed Yahweh had chosen them exclusively. He belonged to them. And, if they stole away in secret to offer sacrifice to a *baal,* did they not also go to the Temple and offer a greater sacrifice to Yahweh? Still, they did not heed Jeremiah's warnings.

The Babylonian Exile

In 586 B.C., Jeremiah's prediction to the Israelites came to pass, and the Babylonians under Nebuchadnezzar captured Jerusalem, destroyed the Temple, and laid waste the city. Of those who survived the slaughter, only the poor, uneducated, old, and weak were left in what remained of Jerusalem. Most of the influential and educated men and women were marched away into exile in Babylonia. They were well treated in the Exile, especially when we consider that they were a conquered people in an age which did not deal gently with captives. They were allowed to manage their private affairs and continue their worship of Yahweh. Perhaps they were fairly treated because Nebuchadnezzar had waged war against Judah, not to destroy it, but to ensure his hold on Palestine and to guarantee himself a land bridge between Babylonia and the Mediterranean.

It was in Babylonia that the Israelites first became known as Jews. This title of identification probably stems from the fact that they had come from the kingdom of Judah and were more readily identified with the kingdom's name. At any rate, it is the title by which they are identified even today, although the titles Hebrew or Israelite connote their ancestors from the time of Abraham.

The one major problem faced by the Jews during the Exile was the loss of the Temple as a central place of worship and sacrifice. In an effort to preserve their own faith, the Jews began to meet together in small groups in each others' homes. At these meetings, they would pray and discuss their religion. They did not offer sacrifice, since this was a form of worship reserved for the Temple. This meeting together became the forerunner of today's synagogues and became an integral part of the Jewish faith from that time on.

The Return from Exile

In 538 B.C., Cyrus of Persia conquered Babylonia and set the exiled Jews free. Although they had been in Babylonia only about fifty years, many of the Jews preferred the advanced culture and the freedom which they enjoyed there and decided to remain in the country. Many others, however, desired to return to Jerusalem, and when they reached the city, they immediately set about rebuilding the Temple. It was a small crude Temple and had little of the beauty of the Temple of Solomon, but at least sacrificial worship to Yahweh was restored.

The names of two men now fill the pages of Jewish history. The first, Nehemiah, who though a Jew, had held a high position in the Persian court, was appointed governor of Judah. Upon his arrival in Jerusalem, he began to rebuild the fortification wall which surrounded the city. It was a long and arduous task with half of the able-bodied men working on the wall, while the remainder defended them from attack. When the wall was completed, however, it was both stronger and much longer than the one which had encircled Jerusalem during David's time.

The second man was Ezra, a scribe in the Persian court, who in 458 B.C. sought and received permission to lead some of the Jews still in Babylonia back to Judah. Upon his arrival in Jerusalem, he saw the urgent need to revitalize the religious practices of the Jews. With the permission of Nehemiah, Ezra purified the Temple worship and revived the practice of observing the Sabbath. Perhaps more far-reaching, however, was the issuance of an order that all the heathen women who had married Jews must leave the city — taking with them the *baals* and other idols which they worshiped.

A large number of Mosaic documents were collected, and the results of their efforts were the first five books of the Old Testament or the *Torah*. To dramatize the importance of these books, people were sent throughout the Persian kingdom to alert the Jews that on the Jewish New Year's Day, they would be read in the Temple. Thus, in 444 B.C. the *Torah,* as it is today, was presented to the Jews and read aloud in the Temple. From that day forward no additions or changes were made in the books, and the law was codified.

The Midrash

Under the Persians, the common language of the Jews had become Aramaic, a Semitic language understood by most of the educated men living in the area of Palestine and Syria. After the Exile, Aramaic replaced Hebrew as the spoken language of the region. The books of the *Torah* were written in Hebrew and read aloud in Hebrew, however, and many of the Jews had difficulty in understanding what was being read. It was decided that interpreters were needed to read and translate the more difficult passages to those who came to the Temple to hear the *Torah* read.

The interpreters initially merely translated the passages to the Jews. These translations, some literal and some free, were known as *Targumin*. As time passed the scribes took it upon themselves to explain what certain passages meant. The practice became more and more common and slowly there evolved a new institution in Jewish religious life known as the *Midrash,* or "school of exposition." The interpreters not only read the *Torah* to the common folk, but also met together to discuss among themselves the meanings of certain passages. Their discussions, though not recorded in the beginning were memorized. The conclusions about the meanings of certain passages led to the development of an "oral law." This oral law was not binding like the *Torah's* law, but it was considered as an explanation of it. In the early Christian era, the oral law was committed to writing.

The Priesthood

The priesthood which offered sacrifice in the Temple has been mentioned briefly. The history of the priesthood is quite involved, and it was only after the Exile that various functions were assigned to certain Jews. According to custom there were three levels of priesthood. There were those who could minister in the outer precincts of the Temple — preparing the animals for sacrifice and accepting the gifts of the Jews to be used in sacrifice. In the post-Exilic period, only men from the tribe of Levi were allowed to perform these services. The priests who actually performed the sacrifical offerings, however, had to be descendants of Aaron, the brother of Moses. The High·Priest, the only person who could enter the Holy of Holies where the Ark of the Covenant rested, had to be a direct descendant of Zadok, the High Priest at the time of David and Solomon.

At this time, the Jews were not allowed to govern themselves. As a possession of Persia, Judah was governed by a representative of the Persian court, who looked after their temporal needs. Unable to exist as a sovereign state, the Jews slowly began to develop a consciousness of themselves as a people drawn together by a common faith. As a people of faith, they turned for leadership to the priests of the Temple. Though they could not have a king, the Persians did allow the Jews to crown their High Priest. From this point forward for the next five hundred years, the Jews looked to the High Priest as their leader.

The Jews lived for a hundred years under Persian domination until, in 333 B.C., the Empire fell under attack by the Greeks. Alexander the Great, intent on subduing the world and spreading Greek civilization throughout the eastern Mediterranean, took possession of Palestine in 332 B.C. The Greeks soon established settlements throughout the country, and exposed all who lived there to their way of life. Their culture was quite different from that of Palestine, and the Jews looked upon their love of sports, games, drama, fashion, and learning, and their religion of many gods with a mixture of interest and contempt.

With Alexander's death, the Greek Empire was divided into two kingdoms. Ptolemy gained control of Egypt, while the Seleucids retained much of Babylonia and Syria. In 301 B.C., Ptolemy captured Palestine, and the country remained under the domination of the Egyptians for a hundred years. In 198 B.C., however, the Seleucids captured Palestine and incorporated it into the Syrian kingdom. For the next quarter century, the Jews were allowed great freedom. It was during this period that the Greeks had perhaps their most cultural influence on their fellow-countrymen. In 176 B.C., however, a man named Antiochus Epiphanes ascended the throne in Syria. He viewed the Jews with suspicion for, though they had adopted much of the Greek culture, they still clung tenaciously to their own religious practices. Antiochus felt that the Jews' faith was not only a threat to the kingdom but also to a true Hellenization of the kingdom. Thus, he instituted severe religious persecution against the Jews. He forbade worship on the Sabbath, introduced pagan rites into the Temple, and refused to allow the Jews to differentiate between clean and unclean food. Most repugnant to all, however, was his order that in the future sacrifices in the Temple should be offered, not to Yahweh, but to Antiochus himself, and that the sacrifices must be of swine's flesh, an unclean animal in the eyes of the Jews. A statue of Zeus was set up in the Temple in direct contradiction to Yahweh's command that there be no idols.

The more devout Jews, incensed by their loss of religious freedom and the repression practiced by Antiochus, rebelled. There followed a lengthy period of what might be called guerrilla warfare against the Syrian king and his army. Led by a small band of men, known as the Maccabees, the revolt was finally successful, and in 143 B.C., the Syrians were driven out of Palestine, the Temple altar was purified, and again for a short period of time what had been the kingdom of Judah belonged to the Jews.

The Roman Conquest

The short-lived freedom of the Jews in Judah ended in 63 B.C., when Palestine was once more subjected to foreign rule — this time under the Romans. However, the Jews had practically invited conquest. A power struggle within Judah had been going on for some time between the interpreters of the *Torah*, who had come to be called Pharisees, and the members of the priesthood, who were known as Sadducees. The Pharisees, trying to live their faith as Yahweh had transmitted it to them, saw the priests as corrupt, power-hungry men, whose major interest was not a revitalization of the Jewish faith which had suffered from the practices Antiochus had imposed, but rather political power and wealth. The Pharisees struggled to reform both the priesthood and the religious practices of the Jews, but they failed. Finally, in the last desperate attempt to gain power, they tried a political maneuver. They appealed to the Roman general, Pompey, and asked him to refuse to recognize either Hyrcanus, a

Pharisee, or Aristobulus, a Sadducee, both of whom were contesting the position of High Priest. Pompey's response to this request was to march into Judah in 63 B.C. He immediately claimed it in the name of the Roman Empire and renamed the territory Judea.

The occupation by the Romans increased internal strife. The rulers chosen by Rome were despotic, and they exacted exorbitant taxes from the Jews, while they continued to suppress their freedom. Despite this pressure, which might have caused them to band together once again as they had against Antiochus, the Jews continued to squabble over who would control what remained of their religious power.

The Messianic Concept

As the persecutions of the Jews grew worse, written tracts dealing with the coming of a Messiah began to appear. This hope for a deliverer had a long history in Judaism. But it was only during and after the Maccabean period that real expectation grew. The deliverer now began to take on characteristics that were more than human. This was in great part due to Persian influences upon the Jewish religion. The expected Messiah would restore the kingdom lost to the Jews, and under his reign the Jews would prosper and would once again live in peace.

The Temple had been restored to use under Nehemiah upon the Jews' return from exile, but it was only now under the rule of the Roman-appointed king, Herod, that the Temple was being restored to the grandeur of the Temple built by Solomon almost a thousand years earlier. For some Jews, notably the Essenes, this restoration of the Temple augured the fulfillment of the older prophecies.

The Essenes were a sect of Jews who had withdrawn from the fight for religious power carried on by the Pharisees and the Sadducees. They lived outside the cities in small monastic communities. They believed in baptism by immersion, the immortality of the soul, and personal resurrection. They clung with hope to the thought that a Messiah would appear to bind together the Jewish community. John the Baptist, who, if he was not himself an Essene, was strongly influenced by them, appears at this point in history. Thus, his heralding of Jesus as the Messiah becomes more easily understandable.

Jesus plays only a small role in Jewish history. He is acknowledged by some early Jewish writers as a minor prophet, but since no writings can be ascribed to him, the Jews do not tend to view him as more than a minor religious figure in their own tradition.

In 66 A.D., after 130 years of struggle between Rome and the Jews of Judea, the revolt by the Jews became so severe that the Roman legions marched out of Syria into Judea with orders to settle the matter once and for all. The Romans, who had perhaps thought they could subdue the Jews in a matter of weeks, found instead that they were faced with a small, but determined, army of resisters. It took three years of continual fighting to conquer Judea, but even with this task accomplished, Jerusalem still remained in the hands of the Jews. The city was put under siege, and there followed the bloodiest and most appalling event in early Jewish history.

The writings of a Jew, named Josephus, give the clearest account of what happened during the siege. In brief, the city struggled against the Roman troops for more than two years. Thousands of Jews were killed through repeated assaults on the city. Those who did not die by the sword, often suffered the slow agonizing death of starvation. When the siege finally ended with an assault by the Romans, the streets of Jerusalem literally ran with blood. The city was completely destroyed, as was the Temple. The fields were sown with salt so that no crops would grow, and Jerusalem was closed to the Jews. It is estimated that tens of thousands of people died in the siege, and of the Jews who survived most were led into slavery either to Egypt or to Rome.

The Diaspora

The destruction of Jerusalem in 70 A.D. is one of the most important events in Jewish history. It is referred to as the date when the Diaspora, or "dispersion," of the Jews began. In actuality, however, the dispersion of the Jews had begun centuries earlier, when Jews had volun-

Jews praying at the Wailing Wall, the only surviving remains of the Temple.

tarily remained in Babylonia after the exile or had migrated to Alexandria or other Mediterranean cities as merchants and traders. The year 70 A.D. does mark the official date of Rome's closing of the city of Jerusalem to Jews, and the date has a great religious significance to members of the Jewish faith.

The destruction of the Temple and the closing of Jerusalem also brought to an end the sacrificial form of worship to Yahweh by the Jews. The one place officially sanctioned by Yahweh for sacrificial worship had been destroyed. Jews would continue to offer similar sacrificial worship outside Jerusalem, but it would never replace Temple worship, and in the future this and other religious practices associated with Jerusalem would undergo slow, but radical, changes. The synagogue, which had had its beginnings during the Babylonian Exile, would now become the center of religious life, and Judaism itself would become a highly intellectualized religion.

Small numbers of Jews continued to live in Judea despite the Roman victory, and for the next sixty-five years they continued to be a thorn in the side of the Roman Empire. In 113 A.D., and again in 132 A.D., the Jews rebelled. The second revolt, led by Simon bar Kochba, was suppressed only after three years of fighting. The Romans, unwilling to expend their money and energies on this type of warfare, finally resorted to a policy of total destruction of both the Jews and their property. Thus in 135 A.D., not only Jerusalem, but also Judea, was closed to the Jews.

Christianity

Although the full story of the development of Judaism has not been completed, it would seem appropriate at this point to focus on the origins and growth of Christianity in an attempt to show the historical interrelationship between Christianity and Judaism.

The birth of Jesus and his place in Jewish history have been mentioned briefly already. As has been said, the life and ministry of Jesus in Palestine had little influence on the majority of Jews. Considering that today there are over one billion Christians in the world, it may seem unusual that Jesus himself was considered only a minor personality. But the fact remains that Jesus lived a relatively quiet, simple life among the common people of Palestine. He was raised in the Jewish tradition, learned the Jewish law, heard the *Torah* read in the Temple, offered sacrifice to God. How then did the son of a carpenter eventually affect the lives of a billion persons?

Little is known of what transpired in Jesus' life or what his views of Judaism were prior to his entry into public life at the age of thirty. Tradition maintains that even at the age of twelve, when he remained in the Temple after his parents had begun their return trip to Nazareth after celebrating Passover, he was profoundly interested in learning about his faith, Judaism. But what forces shaped his life during the next eighteen years are not recorded in the New Testament, which is the primary source of information on his life and teachings. At the age of thirty, he requested his cousin, John the Baptist, to baptize him in the Jordan River. During the following forty days, Jesus lived alone fasting and praying in the desert, and shortly after that time his public life began at the wedding feast of Cana in Galilee.

It is probable, that during those early years Jesus lived the life of an orthodox Jew, worshiping in the Temple and questioning the formalism of the Pharisees and the piety of the Sadducees. It is also likely that he had contact with Essenes, who lived simple and prayerful lives and who also questioned the religious practices of the contemporary Judaism. And through these exposures, it is likely that Jesus developed a belief that Judaism, as it existed, would have to go through radical changes in order to survive as the true faith of God.

More is known of Jesus' public life following the wedding at Cana.

The gospels of the New Testament relate quite clearly his love for the sick, the poor, and the troubled. Unlike the Pharisees and the Scribes who taught only in the Temple, he went out among his fellow Jews to preach love and to bring solace to those in need. His last days on earth are also discussed at length in the New Testament including the Last Supper at which the Eucharist was instituted, his trial before the Jewish high priest, Caiaphas, who condemned him but had no authority to put him to death, and his trial and subsequent death at the hands of the Roman governor of Judea, Pontius Pilate. The New Testament announces that three days after his death, Jesus was raised from the dead, appeared to his apostles and disciples, and asked them to carry on his work.

Had it not been for the twelve apostles who had been chosen to work with Jesus in spreading his message of love and reform, Christianity might have withered and died in the barren Judean hills. Together with their disciples, these men of deep faith and conviction set forth to bring the Gospel, or "Good News," to the world. The greatest of the disciples was Paul of Tarsus, who as an orthodox Jew was an avowed enemy of Christianity. Originally known as Saul, this man set out from Jerusalem to Damascus to persecute whatever Christians he found there. On the road to Damascus, Saul was thrown from his horse and a blinding light which temporarily impaired his vision surrounded him. From this cloud of light Jesus spoke to Saul and brought about his conversion to Christianity. For the next twenty years, Paul carried the message of Jesus throughout the Near East and on to Turkey, Greece, and Rome. Since he could speak both Aramaic and Greek, he could communicate in a familiar way with most of the people with whom he came in contact. It was perhaps Paul's efforts more than any other's that helped Christianity develop from a sect of the Jewish faith to an entirely separate religion. His efforts to convert first focused on the Jews, but often they rejected him. He would, therefore, speak also to the Gentiles, who did not accept the Jewish faith, and it was among these pagans that Christianity took root and flourished.

One of the steps that led to the final division of Judaism and Christianity was the siege of Jerusalem in 70 A.D. Those who had converted from Judaism refused to support the Jews in Jerusalem in their attempts to hold off the Roman troops, and they left Jerusalem before the actual siege began. The Jewish survivors of the siege never forgave the Christians. This was perhaps the first in a number of incidents which have left their mark on believers of both faiths.

The Spread of Christianity

The Roman Empire at the time of Paul almost completely surrounded the Mediterranean Sea. There was no one fixed religion within the Empire though variations of paganism prevailed, especially in Rome and in Athens. Both the Romans and the Greeks worshiped many gods, and these gods were closely akin to one another. Rome's Jupiter, the mightiest of gods, was apparently equal to Greece's Zeus. This worship of many gods in the beginning was almost a protective covering for the Christians, for what harm could one more minor god do?

However, it soon became apparent, through the dedication and zeal with which the Christians practiced their religious beliefs, that they were not only aliens in an Empire which followed polytheistic religious practices, but that they were also intent on spreading their own faith. At first Christians had been viewed with respect by the Roman intelligentsia, but this respect soon turned to fear that they would subvert the Empire from within. As early as 64 A.D., Christians were being persecuted by the Roman Emperor Nero in the Roman arenas. Flogging, stoning, and death by wild beasts seemed only to strengthen their resolve, so the persecutions became more and more severe.

In the meantime, the Roman Empire was being threatened from without by the Germanic tribes to the north. When Marcus Aurelius ascended the throne of the Roman Empire in 161, it was apparent that the

The Grotto of the Nativity in Bethlehem marks the traditional birthplace of Jesus.

pacifistic creed of the Christians, plus the general dissolution which the Empire was experiencing after two hundred years of ruling the Mediterranean, had weakened the Romans considerably. Persecution of the Christians grew even more severe, and by 303 under the rule of Diocletian, it appeared that Christianity would be completely destroyed.

Yet, at the same period, a Roman general named Constantine was leading his troops to victory under a banner which bore the Christian symbol of the cross. History relates that Constantine saw a fiery cross in the sky on the evening before an important battle, and he was so impressed by its majesty that he had the symbol placed on banners and the shields which his men carried into battle. The next day the Roman troops routed their adversaries, and from that moment forward the cross went before the Roman legionaries into every conflict.

Constantine led the Roman troops against those who threatened the Roman Empire in the western part of the Empire, while Licinius, another Roman general, proved victorious in the eastern part of the Empire. After the death of Diocletian a power struggle ensued in which these two generals ultimately emerged victorious, with Constantine ruling the Western Empire and Licinius ruling the East. This dual rule lasted until 323, when Constantine defeated Licinius in battle and claimed the entire Empire as his to rule.

While still in control of only the western part of the Empire, Constantine had issued the Edict of Milan which granted freedom of worship to the Christians. It was this Edict which turned the tide for Christianity, which a few years later became the official religion of the state. Persecution of the Christians ceased. Where possible, restitution was made to Christians who had suffered under previous emperors. Christians were allowed to worship openly, and paganism was discouraged. It appeared that the infant faith had triumphed.

Ironic as it may seem, it was Constantine, the champion of early Christianity, who inadvertently was responsible for the first major division of that faith. Wishing to preserve Christianity and aware that Rome itself was still paganly oriented, Constantine determined to build a city where Christianity could be exalted. He chose the site of the ancient city of Byzantium, located strategically at the entrance to the Black Sea on a peninsula overlooking the Bosphorus Strait. The new capital, Constantinople, was magnificent in all respects. The architecture of the Roman West and the Oriental East met in the many civic buildings, palaces, and Christian churches of the city. Yet even as East met West and melded in the architectural beauty of the new religious capital of the Roman Empire, an intellectual and cultural meeting of the two heritages never quite took place. As Constantinople was taking shape, differences in interpretation of the teachings of Christianity were developing outside the Roman Empire. They would soon affect the eastern parts of the Empire.

The most notable of these differences was the interpretation put forth by a monk named Arius, who lived in Alexandria, Egypt. He denied the divinity of Christ and maintained that only God was truly divine. Thus, he contested the teaching concerning the Holy Trinity. Constantine, recognizing that such a teaching could seriously damage the faith, called together some 250 bishops at Nicea, in what was to be the first Church Council, to discuss the doctrine put forth by Arius. The Council met in 325, and they judged Arius' teachings to be heresy, that is, a formal denial of a revealed truth of the faith. The heresy became known as Arianism, and though condemned by the Council of Nicea, it had many adherents particularly in the eastern Mediterranean. It was at the Council of Nicea that the Nicene Creed was formulated. This statement is still recognized by most Christian churches today as the official statement of belief.

In 330, Constantine dedicated the city of Constantinople to Christianity, and in so doing, he split the Roman Empire liturgically. The

The altar of the Crucifixion in the Holy Sepulchre in Jerusalem. This is the site of Calvary.

Christians in the West looked to Rome as the center of Christianity and followed its patterns of worship, including the use of Latin in its rites. In Constantinople, however, worship was conducted in Greek, and the Christians of the East looked to the Patriarch, or bishop, of Constantinople as their leader.

Nestorianism and Monophysitism Split the Church

As might be expected, Christianity did not limit itself solely to the West. There is considerable evidence that followers of the Christian tradition also moved eastward into the Persian Empire, which was Rome's strongest rival. It is quite possible that Christians living in Palestine migrated to Persia during the second and third centuries to avoid the persecutions directed against them by the Roman Empire, and that they were welcomed because the Persians felt such great antagonism against Rome.

The Church of the Christians in Persia developed along the lines of an eastern tradition, and although the Patriarch of Antioch, a city in southern Turkey which was the ancient capital of Syria, did maintain some supervision over the Christians in Persia, they managed to build up their own eccleciastical organization independent of Rome. The Christian church in Persia was centered in Baghdad, and its bishop was given the title of Katholikos. It was a vigorous church, disposed to spreading the "Good News." Its missionaries spread out into Assyria, Chaldea, and Kurdistan, and in time each became almost entirely Christian. Not satisfied with proselytizing in the area immediately surrounding Baghdad, however, Christian missionaries also traveled eastward into Samarkand, Southern India, and China, where traces of their success can still be found.

The division between Eastern and Western Christendom became wider when, in 424, a synod of Persian bishops met and declared their independence of Antioch. This decision was influenced by the fact that Christians were still looked upon with distrust by the Persians, who were not Christians and who viewed Christians as an extension of the Roman Empire, where Christianity had by then become the official religion, into Persia. It was, therefore, politic for Christians in Persia to disassociate themselves as completely as possible from Western Christianity and Rome.

It was the heresy of Nestorianism that brought about the first major rift between Eastern and Western Christianity. Nestorius, Bishop of Constantinople, held that there was only a moral union between the two natures of Christ. He also taught that Mary could only be considered the mother of Christ as man. A Church Council, the third in history, was held at Ephesus, and the heresy was condemned. The Persian Church, however, rejected the Council of Ephesus, and in so doing seemed to side with the Nestorians. Whether they actually believed in the doctrine is not quite clear, for they may have refused to attend the Council of Ephesus for reasons motivated by political expediency. At any rate, their refusal to attend the Council resulted in the Persian Christian Church being branded heretical, and by the seventh century they were officially considered separated from the Catholic Church.

The Monophysite heresy split an even larger segment of the Christian Church from its Roman core. Monophysitism, sometimes called Eutychianism after Eutyches, who promulgated the heresy, taught that Christ had only one nature which was single and composite. Again a Council of the Church was called, this time known as the Council of Chalcedon and it condemned the heresy which denied the human nature of Christ. The Council, held in 451, led to the splitting away from Rome of Christian groups including the Armenians, the Copts of Egypt, the Abyssinians, the Syrian Jacobites, and the Malabar Jacobites of India.

The Armenian Church had developed along distinctly national lines and had developed its own rite, even though it professed a perfectly orthodox faith. In 440, however, the Armenian Kingdom had been divided between the Roman and Persian Empires. When Greeks and Persians colonized their respective segments of Armenia, they built their own churches, since they did not accept the Armenian Rite. During the Council of Chalcedon, Armenia was under strong attack by the Persians, and the Armenian bishops were unable to attend the Council. Because of this, they were unwilling to accept the decisions of the Council, and in time, encouraged by the Syrian Jacobites, they rejected the Council.

For a brief period during the Crusades, the Armenian dissident, or "heretical," Church, frequently called the Gregorian Church after St. Gregory the Illuminator, reunited with Rome, but it was a short-lived reunion. Both Gregorian Armenians and Catholic Armenians, who are still affiliated with Rome, have been subject to severe persecution over the centuries. They are now scattered throughout the Middle East.

The Coptic Church was the early Egyptian Church, traditionally founded by St. Mark the Evangelist, who was a disciple of St. Peter. Because of this affinity to the Roman Church, Alexandria was accorded a patriarchate which was next in rank to those in Rome and Antioch, both of which Peter had personally founded. At the time of the Nestorian heresy, St. Cyril, patriarch of Alexandria, defended his See against the heresy. His successor, Dioskoros, however, went so far in defending the faith against Nestorianism that he became a Monophysite, and a segment of the Coptic Church went into heresy. For the most part, those who followed him were native Egyptians. There were also large colonies of Greeks living in the major Egyptian cities, and as was the case with the political bases for the adoption of Nestorianism in Persia, so too, the Egyptian Copts defended Monophysitism, as a sign of their unwillingness to be subject to the Byzantine Emperor at Constantinople. The Abyssinians, or the Ethiopians as they are known today, were drawn into the heretical struggle by reason of their affiliation with the Egyptian Coptic Church and their dependency on the patriarch of Alexandria, Dioskoros. Thus, in effect, the heresy was imposed on them.

The Monophysite heresy did not affect the Syrians as deeply as it had the Egyptians, but the Syrian bishops also rejected the Council of Chalcedon as an expression of political opposition to Constantinople. There was a purge of bishops in Syria by the Emperor Justinian I, but through political intrigue arranged by Justinian's wife Theodora, who favored Monophysitism, a secret consecration of two bishops was arranged in 543. This resulted in the establishment of a Monophysite hierarchy. It is after the bishop named Jacob Baradai that the Monophysite Church in Syria is named. Generally, the Monophysite Church in Syria flourished, but persecutions in the 14th century, coupled with internal dissent and numerous apostasies to Islam, left the membership of the Jacobite Church a small minority in the area of Christianity.

The final group to split from Western Christianity did not break away in the period following the Council of Chalcedon. Rather, the Malabar Jacobites went into schism following a series of mistakes on the part of the European missionaries during the 16th and 17th centuries. Christians of both the Malabar Jacobite Church, which is still in schism from Rome, and Malabar Catholics of the Chaldean Rite, who are in union with Rome, are located on the southwestern coast of India. They maintain that the Gospel was brought to them by the apostle, St. Thom-

The Church of All Nations, built by Roman Catholics from all over the world, stands in the Garden of Gethsemane, the place where Jesus was arrested the night before his death.

as. Originally, these Christians on the Malabar coast were affiliated with the Persian Church centered in Baghdad. The Malabarites may have inherited the heresy of Nestorianism from the Persian Church, but this does not seem to be the case, and in the early 1500's when the Portuguese colonizers arrived in Malabar, the Indians were considered Catholic. It was the colonization policies of the Portuguese which ultimately led to the schism of the Malabarites. The Portuguese insisted on "Latinizing" the Chaldean rite practices of the Malabarites, obstructed the appointments of their bishops, and finally imposed on the Malabar Christians the rule of Portuguese bishops. This imposition of Western Catholicism on a people who were devoted to an ancient and valid tradition led to a schism of the Malabar Christians in 1653. In time, many of the Malabarites were led back to the Catholic tradition after being allowed to resume their traditional Chaldean rite.

Nearly 400,000 Christians, who had been in the schism, refused to return to the Catholic tradition, however, and these were known as members of the "New Party." When this "New Party" was denied its own hierarchy, it turned to the Syrian Jacobite Church, which provided it with the necessary ordaining prelates. And so, by default, a major portion of Christendom, which had been in union with Rome, was parted from the Catholic Church and found itself in heresy. Since 1653, the Malabar Jacobites have experienced growing confusion brought on both by internal intrigues and by the arrival of Anglican missionaries, who introduced yet another form of Christianity to the already complex situation. In recent times, efforts have been made to bring about reunion with Rome, and those who have returned, identify themselves as Malankara Catholics — to distinguish themselves from the Malabar Catholics of the Chaldean Rite.

Christianity at the Beginning of the 7th Century

The early Christian Church struggled for existence in an alien and hostile religious climate of paganism. The numerous religious persecutions which the early Christians suffered were intense, but under Constantine, the Roman Emperor, Christians were finally allowed religious freedom. By the beginning of the 7th century, Christianity extended from Rome eastward all the way to India. Almost without exception, the continued existence of early Christianity depended on the beneficence of political rulers, and thus it became strongly bound by political considerations. This was particularly true of Christians living in Persia, who felt they had to disassociate themselves from the western center of Christianity, Constantinople, since it was also the center of the Christian Roman Empire.

The early Church was faced with internal problems as well, and the one problem which caused the most permanent damage was that of heresy. Poor communications, personal interpretations of doctrine, and

political problems — all abetted the heresies of the Nestorians and Monophysites in breaking down the unity of Christianity. The Council of
Chalcedon, in 451, brought about several schisms in the Church, and
these would in time solidify those who had disagreed into heretical Eastern churches. Among such churches still existing today are the Nestorians and the Monophysites, which include the Armenian Church, the
Coptic Church, the Abyssinian (or Ethiopian) Church, the Syrian Jacobite Church, and the Malabar Jacobite Church.

Those who remained loyal to the Church, whether in Rome or in
Constantinople, were called "Orthodox." This meant that they professed
the sound, or correctly defined, Catholic doctrine promulgated by the
early Church Councils.

At the time of the Council of Chalcedon, the Catholic Church was
organized into five major administrative districts: the patriarchate in
Rome, to which most Western Catholics felt allegiance; the patriarchate
in Constantinople (sometimes called New Rome), which was created
when Constantine moved the religious and political center of the Roman
Empire to that city; and the three Orthodox patriarchates at Antioch,
Alexandria, and Jerusalem. The patriarchate at Jerusalem was created at
the Chalcedon Council in order to honor the Holy City.

Each patriarchate was autonomous in its local administration, and
each had its own forms of liturgical worship and administration of sacra-
ment, which we know today as "rites." All believed the Patriarch of
Rome to be the head of the Catholic Church in matters of doctrine, although certain matters of major importance were decided upon by all the
bishops at Councils, such as Chalcedon. In time the Orthodox Patriarchs
of Alexandria, Antioch, and Jerusalem became more and more dependent on the Patriarchate at Constantinople. Alexandria and Antioch lost
many of their followers to heretical churches and thus lost much of their
stature in the Church structure. Gradually, the three patriarchates adopted the liturgy (including the use of Greek) of Constantinople, known as
the Byzantine rite.

While the patriarchate of Constantinople was faced with the task of
controlling the spread of heretical churches and bringing back both Nestorians and Monophysites to Orthodoxy, the patriarchate of Rome was
expending its efforts on trying to unify the Western rites of the Church.
Both Rome and Constantinople professed the same religious creed. Nevertheless, friction between the two patriarchates became increasingly apparent, especially when each tried to extend its jurisdiction over disputed
territories including Greece, the Balkans, and Southern Italy.

Thus at the beginning of the 7th century, Christianity had already
experienced its first major defections among the Christians of the East
and the first faint signs of an even greater split. This would culminate
some four hundred years later in the Great Schism.

In 135, the entire area of the Roman province of Judea was closed to members of the Jewish faith. The Jews found themselves scattered throughout the Near East, bereft of their Temple, and persecuted for their religious beliefs. They were in an Empire pursuing pagan religious practices. Had the Jews thought of themselves solely as members of a state prior to the Diaspora, they might well have been absorbed into the cultures of the areas where they settled. Thus, they would have lost both their Jewish identity and their faith. This was not the case, however, for their faith in the *Torah* and their tradition of oral interpretation, the *Midrash,* formed a common bond linking together Jews wherever they settled. The rabbis, or teachers, continued to meet together secretly to avoid persecution. At these meetings they discussed the *Torah* and its application to the new, and often unpleasant, situations in which the Jews found themselves. The most outstanding of these rabbis was Jochanan ben Zakkai, who had fled Jerusalem during the siege and settled in the town of Jabneh on the Mediterranean where he opened a center for discussion and learning.

Hadrian, the Roman Emperor who had allowed ben Zakkai to leave Jerusalem, realized only after its destruction that a center of learning such as the one at Jabneh was a threat to internal security. He was also aware of the small, but growing, threat of the Christians, and in an effort to suppress any rebellion, he instituted severe persecutions against both the Jews and the Christians. This forced many rabbis and scholars attending the school at Jabneh to flee to northern Palestine where they formed a new center. This was actually an underground movement, however, and was constantly forced to move from place to place in order to avoid identification. Similar schools developed outside of Palestine. All focused on the meaning of the *Torah* to the Jews in the Diaspora.

The Mishnah

Three factors in Jewish religious history — the discussions held by small groups of Jews during the Babylonian Exile, the work of the interpreters of the *Torah* in the Temple in Jerusalem, and the schools which developed after the destruction of Jerusalem — had led to the development of a large body of oral teaching on the practice of Judaism and the interpretation of the laws of the *Torah.* Until this time, there had been no written compilation of such teachings, for it was feared that such a document might become more important in the minds of the Jews than the *Torah* itself.

About 200, a rabbi named Judah Hanasi took it upon himself to collect as much of the oral law as possible, to compile it into segments, and to publish it. He hoped that by doing this the law would be clarified, and the continual reassessment of the meaning of the *Torah* carried on by rabbis and scholars would cease. The collection filled six volumes, which he called the *Mishnah,* or Repetition. In the volumes were contained over four thousand legal decisions that had been made stemming from 613 laws of the *Torah*. And, although meant to be used primarily as a text-book, the *Mishnah* soon became an additional code of law for the Jews rather than a clarifying interpretation of the *Torah* which Judah Hanasi had first envisaged.

The continual concern of Jews over the interpretation of Jewish law became, in a very real way, an insulation or protection for the Jews of the Diaspora. Citizens of Rome or Athens would place the laws of those cities in a position of primary importance, but Jews and Christians were not necessarily considered citizens. The Jewish religious law, therefore, became of primary importance to the Jews not only because it pertained to religious practices, but also because it applied to most aspects of every-day life. It provided one of the more advanced notions of personal moral-ity existing at that time, for before that law all Jews were equal. This manner of thinking resulted in Jews considering themselves as Jews living in Egypt or the Roman Empire, rather than as Egyptian Jews or Roman Jews.

The laws of the *Torah* and the *Mishnah* served to bind the Diaspora Jews together and provide a Jewish consciousness, but this wall of laws was not able to keep out the influences of the cultures in the midst of which the Jews dwelled. They were deeply affected by the humanistic and scientific knowledge of other peoples, just as they had been earlier in-fluenced by Greek philosophy. In the areas of morality and worship, however, the Jews worked studiously to avoid the pitfalls of polytheism and the growing influence of Christianity.

Babylonia and the Talmud

In the middle of the 4th century, the Roman Emperor Constantine was converted to the belief that Christianity should be allowed religious freedom, and shortly thereafter it became the official religion of the Roman Empire. As had happened during the Greek domination of Pales-tine, the imposition of a state religion led to extremely harsh laws and repressive action against all who did not practice Christianity. While Pal-estine was still a part of the Roman Empire, Babylonia had come under Persian rule. Many Palestinian Jews, seeking to avoid further persecu-tions by the Romans, fled back to the country where their forefathers had once lived in exile.

The Jews who had remained in Babylonia after the Exile ended had lived in relative peace and had advanced both culturally and economi-cally. Even though the Temple had been reestablished in Jerusalem after the Exile, the rabbis in Babylonia carried on their own discussions of the law of the *Torah* by applying it, as the now dispersed Jews were doing, to the situation in which they found themselves, namely living outside the center of Jewish religious faith. The discussions in Babylonia had led to the establishment of *yeshibot,* or academies, where all who were interest-ed in studying the law were welcome. There were no formal classes at each *yeshivah*. Rather, all who wished to learn gathered in one large lecture hall where open discussions were held. The fundamental subjects discussed were the writings of the Old Testament, the *Mishnah,* and important statements made earlier by teachers of Jewish law. Thus, the Jews of Palestine, who after the destruction of Jerusalem had been forced to move their centers of learning from place to place, now encountered established centers of learning where their faith could be discussed openly.

For three hundred years (from approximately 300 to 600) this form of learning went on with only minor interruptions. The rabbis, however, recognized the religious intolerance of the pagan faith of the Persians. Fearing they might lose their right to discussions in the academies and possibly be unable to remember all the details and decisions which had been made, the rabbis set about the task of writing down what had been learned. The final product of this scholarship was called the *Gemara,* or Supplement. Though it had been developed in part in Palestine, the Palestinian *Gemara* was not so sophisticated a piece of scholarship as the one developed in Babylonia. Little of the Palestinian tradition actually survived. When completed, the Babylonian work filled sixty-three volumes.

The *Gemara,* which was actually begun around 400 and completed about 600, is rather like an encyclopedia of many discussions on Jewish law and custom. It included not only a great portion of the *Mishnah* and the discussions of it which had taken place in the academies, but it also contained fables, legends, and proverbs that had been handed down through generations of Jews. In written form it became known as the *Talmud,* or Learning, and today it is still considered one of the most important expositions of Jewish thought in existence. Generally speaking for the Jews of the Diaspora, the centuries which followed the destruction of Jerusalem were years filled with scholarship leading to the strong codification of Jewish law.

Islam

Just as Judaism traces its beginnings to Abraham, and Christianity to Jesus, so too the third major monotheistic religion with roots in the Middle East traces its origins to a single man. Islam's birth in the Arabian desert in the seventh century came about through the teachings and actions of the Prophet Muhammad.

In studying Islam and the Prophet Muhammad, it is well to keep in mind several factors. First and perhaps most important is the fact that much more is known about the personal history of the man Muhammad than of either Abraham or Jesus. Sometimes students of Islam have allowed incidents in Muhammad's personal life, such as his multiple marriages, cloud their perspective of his theological message. There is a need to be objective and to view both the religion and the man in the historical and cultural contexts which prevailed in the Arabia of his time.

Another factor to keep in mind is that Islam, as taught by the Prophet, did not represent a drastic departure from other religious practices carried on in the Arabian peninsula. Though most Arabs practiced a rather primitive polytheistic form of worship, many had been exposed to Judaism and to Christianity either from travel or from Jews and Christians living in Arabia. Muhammad incorporated both the prophets of the Old Testament and Jesus of the New Testament into Islam. Certain pagan customs were slightly altered and also accepted as part of the Muslim's worship. Islam, therefore, though it brought a new message to the world of religion did not neglect the validity of other religious traditions.

Finally, Islam presented to the people of the seventh century a religion which, while positive in nature, was also notable for its simplicity. While Judaism's *Torah* presented 613 proscriptions, Islam presented the Five Pillars of Faith by which Muslims should abide. Islam presented no theological tangles, such as the Christians' disputes about two natures of Christ. Islam's theology can be summed up in one sentence: "There is no god but God, and Muhammad is the Prophet of God." And so, though Islam was first spread by the sword, in time its simplicity drew converts to it. Today there are almost five hundred million Muslims scattered throughout the world.

Arabia in the 6th Century

At the time of Muhammad's birth, the Arabian peninsula was geographically much as it is today. Composed mostly of desert land, there were few places in the Arabian peninsula where life could be supported. Semi-settled communities clustered around oases and attempted to cultivate crops and raise herds. Such settlements were usually made up of people who had at one time roamed the desert seeking pasturage for their herds of goats, but who had tired of the insecure life of the nomad and had sought refuge in the more settled existence of the farmer. Those who had settled down to an agrarian life still risked attack by other nomadic tribes, however, and oases were often plundered by enemies.

Because of its inhospitable terrain, the Arabian peninsula was not involved in the conflict which raged between the Persian and Roman Empires. Small communities of both Christians and Jews had found religious freedom in the desert land and had settled both in the north and in the west along the Red Sea. The Red Sea separated the peninsula from Egypt, the Sudan, and Ethiopia, and the Arabians had profited little from the mighty civilizations which flourished along the Nile River.

Yet the Arabians were not entirely isolated from the other cultures of the time. The peninsula was crisscrossed with trade routes which allowed camel caravans to bring the spices of India and the myrrh of Yemen north to the countries of the Mediterranean. Cities had sprung up along these trade routes, the most notable of which were Mecca and Medina in the west, Basrah in the east near the Persian Gulf, and Tabuk in the north.

Mecca was perhaps the most important of these cities not only because it was located midway between Yemen and the Mediterranean, but also because the *Kaaba* was located there. This fact made Mecca the religious center of the peninsula. The *Kaaba* was an ancient shrine, supposedly built by Abraham. In appearance, it was a cube and contained the Black Stone, an object venerated by the Arabians. By the seventh century, it also contained numerous primitive idols, representing various gods. While the Arabians still practiced animism and gave homage to the gods and spirits which they believed existed in stones and trees, it was around the *Kaaba* that the more formalized religious practices devolved. During the final month of the Arabian year, people would come to Mecca and gather to perform certain rites, including walking counterclockwise around the *Kaaba* and kissing the stone.

Generally, life in the Arabian peninsula at the beginning of the seventh century was still quite primitive. Lack of cultivable land meant that many tribes survived either as nomads or by raiding more settled communities or caravans. Those who did not raid the caravans often extorted money from them by allowing them to pass unmolested through the territories which the nomads controlled.

In retrospect, it would appear that the Arabian peninsula was a most unlikely area for the implantation of a monotheistic religion. Its peoples were widely scattered and led rather perilous existences. Organized religion centered on Mecca which was located in the western, rather than the central, part of the peninsula. Yet, in less than a century, the entire area would profess a belief in Islam, and the Muslim call to prayer would be heeded by almost all who lived in Arabia.

Muhammad and His Early Life

The exact date of Muhammad's birth is not known, but many historians agree that it was probably sometime in the year 570. His parents belonged to the Banu Hashim branch of one of the most powerful tribes in Mecca, the Quraish. While the Quraish was a leading tribe, the Hashim branch was not particularly wealthy, and by the standards of the day, Muhammad's parents were poor. His father died without ever hav-

Islam's holiest shrine, the Kaaba, in Mecca. Muslims face it five times a day and pray.

ing seen his son, and six years later his mother died. He was left an orphan dependent on the charity of other members of the Hashim family. For two years Muhammad was the ward of his grandfather, Abd al Muttalib, who was patriarch of the Hashim. When his grandfather died, responsibility for the Hashim passed to Muhammad's uncle, Abu Talib, who took the young boy into his own family. Abu Talib was a trader, and it is likely that the young Muhammad accompanied him on trips to Syria.

As a young boy growing up in Mecca, Muhammad must have participated in the religious activities which revolved around the *Kaaba*. For the Hashim, this shrine had particular significance, for Abd al Muttalib was responsible for the care of the holy well of Zemzem, which even today figures prominently in Islam. The well is believed to be the one where Ishmael, the son of Abraham by the slave girl Hagar, was saved from dying of thirst. Pilgrims who came to the *Kaaba* to worship often took water from the well back to their relatives. Muhammad's grandfather was responsible for apportioning this holy water.

Poverty prevented Muhammad from establishing himself as a trader. However, at the age of twenty-five he was hired as an agent for a caravan being sent to Syria by a wealthy widow, named Khadijah. Some stories relate that Khadijah was testing Muhammad by placing him in charge of the caravan; others relate that Muhammad's uncle suggested that he offer his services as agent to Khadijah because the family needed money. Whichever is true, it appears that Muhammad did his job well, for upon his return from Syria, Khadijah proposed matrimony. Muhammad accepted the offer of the widow who was fifteen years older than he, and they lived together for the next twenty-five years.

During the following fifteen years, Muhammad probably continued to engage in commerce using the money of his wealthy wife. She bore him six children, two boys who died in infancy and four girls all of whom lived to maturity. Little else is known about this period of Muhammad's life. Perhaps it was during this period that he learned more about the traditions and beliefs of Christianity and Judaism. He must, however, have been experiencing grave doubts about the religious practices of the *Kaaba* and the idolatry which was prevalent among his fellow Meccans. Possibly he discussed these doubts with Khadijah's cousin, Waraqah, who had converted to Christianity. Almost certainly he discussed them with Khadijah.

The Call to Prophecy

By the time Muhammad reached forty, he had begun to leave Mecca at various intervals and spend periods of time in contemplation on Mount Hira. He had at this time already experienced peculiar dreams, which he did not quite understand. Contemplating alone on Mount Hira, however, seemed to bring him peace. One night while alone on Mount Hira during the month of Ramadan, Muhammad experienced his first revelation. He had withdrawn to a cave and suddenly heard a voice commanding him, "Recite." He became aware of a figure which later he identified as the Angel Gabriel. He answered the figure by asking what it was he should recite. The figure answered: "Recite in the name of Thy Lord who created . . . Created man from a clot. Recite: for Thy Lord is most gracious who taught with the pen . . . Taught man what he knows not" (*Qur'an* 96:1-5).

The command to recite, as Muhammad interpreted it, meant far more than it might appear. Muhammad was not merely to repeat what he had heard, but rather to commit it to memory as he was being used as the instrument, by which God was transmitting to the world his final and complete revelation. This command, and all those which Muhammad subsequently heard, were committed to memory both by himself, and later by his followers. In time they would all be written down to be shared by other men, and the completed book of revelations became known as the *Qur'an*.

Muhammad was shaken by this experience and he returned to Mecca and told Khadijah of the vision. His wife reassured him that God would protect him for he was a just man. Shortly thereafter Muhammad experienced a second revelation. This time the bearer of the message was identified immediately by Muhammad as the Angel Gabriel. He told Muhammad that he was to be the prophet of Allah, and that he was to spread Allah's message. The message he was to teach was that Allah was one and unique and that worship should be given to him alone. Also, he was to warn the Meccans and all who would listen that each man was faced with a final Day of Judgement, when he would have to give an accounting of his life before Allah. All of this was gradually clarified in other revelations over the next three years. During these years Muhammad spoke of this message only to family and friends.

The first person to convert to Islam was Khadijah. There is little doubt that she believed her husband was the messenger of Allah. She, too, had shared in the discussions with her Christian cousin, Waraqah, and she knew of the prophet Jesus. Khadijah's conversion was soon followed by others including those of Abu Bakr, a close friend, Ali, a cousin of Muhammad and later his son-in-law, Zaid, who had been freed from slavery by Muhammad, and two other friends, Talha and Usman. At the end of these first three years, however, the number of converts to Islam was no more than about thirty persons.

Muhammad's public preaching began sometime during the year 613. It is said that he went to the Mount of Safa near Mecca and proclaimed openly to all who would listen that Allah was One and that the Meccans should begin to lead righteous lives in anticipation of the day of final judgement. Muhammad's message seemed to be aimed particularly at the wealthy merchants and traders of Mecca whom he chided for their greed and for not aiding the poor, orphans, and widows.

Muhammad's warning to the rich struck a responsive note, because it reminded them of the responsibilities which they had shared in the not too distant past. Probably most of Mecca's citizens were only two or three generations removed from the nomadic life in the desert. The nomads generally banded together in clans along family lines. All members of a clan shared not only in the material rewards, such as booty from raiding more settled communities, but also in the responsibility for their fellow clansmen's welfare. There was a solidarity among members of a clan which welded them together and provided a primitive kind of social welfare. If a man died in a raid, his wife and children were taken in by other members of the family. With the growth of Mecca there came a breakdown of this code and of the solidarity which the various clans had experienced as nomads. This was especially true in the business community where merchants would often cross clan lines and band together with others against members of their own clan. Individuality was fast replacing the law of the desert, and those who suffered most from this breakdown were the aged, the widows and orphans, and the poor.

Muhammad felt the wealthy merchants should bear the responsibility of relieving the burdens of such people. The merchants rebelled at this idea for they could not see why they should share what they had accumulated on their own through wise investment. Thus, the message of Allah which Muhammad was seeking to spread threatened the nonbelievers economically. His message also threatened them politically in an indirect way. The wealthy controlled the city of Mecca, and though it had become a leading center of trade, the city had its share of those who were poor and those who lived on a moderate income. Muhammad's railing against the rich would certainly appeal to those who were not. There was a danger that he would make many converts among the disadvantaged, and if large numbers accepted his message, it would imply that he was a man of outstanding wisdom and prudence. Again, the merchants were not far removed from their tribal traditions. If large numbers of persons began to follow his teachings, there was the danger that he might acquire actual political power in Mecca.

Because Muhammad's preaching threatened the merchants of Mecca, they were the first to oppose him, but their opposition, at least in the beginning, was relatively mild. For the most part it consisted in derision and scorn, and it was directed at Muhammad by way of insults shouted at him when he attempted to speak or when he was walking in the streets. Gradually, however, as those who heard him began to understand that his message also threatened their religious beliefs by placing Allah in a supreme position and by disavowing the other gods of Mecca, the verbal abuse against Muhammad and his followers changed to physical abuse. Muhammad, himself, was spared the physical violence which was suffered by his followers. So long as his uncle Abu Talib lived,

Muhammad was assured that no real harm would come to him for he was under his uncle's protection. If he had been seriously injured or killed, it would have been Abu Talib's responsibility as head of the clan of Banu Hashim to avenge the act. Such vengeance would have precipitated a blood feud between the clans involved. Mecca had just seen a civil war of some forty years end, and no one wished to be responsible for another.

For his followers, however, there often was no such protection. Many of them were poor, slaves, or men without clans to which they could turn. Muhammad recognized that persecution could be endured only so long, so he advised some of his followers to migrate to what is today Ethiopia. This migration is believed to have taken place about 615.

The Banu Hashim Are Boycotted

At about the time that the migration to Ethiopia took place, opposition to Muhammad began to intensify primarily because of a certain Abu Jahl, a man of about Muhammad's age. At first, this opposition took the form of repression of members within his own clan who had converted to Islam. Later, however, it was directed at trying to break the traditional clan ties, which offered Muhammad protection. This was done by appealing to Abu Talib to stop his nephew from preaching or to withdraw his protection. Abu Talib was not moved by these protests, so Abu Jahl took steps to enforce an economic boycott of other clans against the Banu Hashim.

Abu Jahl managed to convince the other clans that they should boycott the Banu Hashim by refusing to trade with them or to allow any intermarriages between themselves and the members of the Hashim clan. How well the boycott worked is not exactly known, although the Hashim must have suffered from it. It lasted two years from 616 to 618. It was the events which followed the boycott, however, that ultimately led to Muhammad's decision to seek another place where he and his followers could live in peace.

Even the boycott did not dissuade people from listening to Muhammad's message, and it was during this time that one of the most important conversions to early Islam was made. One of the men who had been active in opposing Muhammad was 'Umar, an influential member of one of the lesser clans. His conversion is sometimes likened to that of St. Paul in that it was a sudden and dramatic one. 'Umar's sister and her husband had quietly converted to Islam, and when 'Umar learned of this, he attacked his sister and one of the blows drew blood. The sight of blood brought him to his senses and in a repentant mood he made it his task to listen to the *Qur'an,* the recitation of the revelations which had been made to Muhammad. He was so moved by the experience that he went to Muhammad and professed his belief in Islam. 'Umar, after Muhammad's death, became the second Caliph, or "successor" to the Prophet.

Abu Talib and Khadijah Die

The year 619 saw the two mainstays of Muhammad's life taken from him. His uncle, Abu Talib, who had never converted to Islam, but had protected Muhammad from the wrath of the Meccans, died. Shortly, thereafter, Muhammad's wife, Khadijah also passed away. Muhammad had lost not only the physical support he needed to remain safely in Mecca, but also the moral support and love of his wife. Muhammad had taken no other wife while Khadijah lived, even though Islam allowed a man to have up to four wives. In later life when Muhammad had taken on the responsibility of many other wives, he remembered Khadijah and paid her great tribute when speaking of her.

Shortly after Khadijah's death, Muhammad remarried. His bride had been an early convert to Islam and was now a widow. This second marriage was to be followed by several others, until Muhammad had married eight times. It is these marriages which form one of the largest stumbling blocks to Westerners when they study the life of Muhammad, for they question the integrity of a man who taught that no man should marry more women than he could support and none should marry more than four. Viewed in the context of the times and the struggles which Islam was facing, it is not difficult to accept Muhammad's multiple marriages. His second wife, Sawdah, was faced with the choice of either marrying outside the Islamic faith which might cause complications and further persecutions of the small group of believers or of remaining unmarried and thus dependent on the good will of others. To be a Muslim and to be dependent on others was indeed a precarious position for a young woman. It appears that many of his subsequent marriages took place for the same reason or because by marrying a certain woman he ensured that ties between his clan and other clans would be strengthened. For instance, soon after marrying Sawdah, Muhammad became betrothed to Ayesha, the daughter of his close friend, Abu Bakr.

Abu Talib was succeeded by his brother, Abu Lahab, as leader of the clan of Hashim. At first, as honor would dictate, Abu Lahab promised to protect Muhammad. Abu Jahl, however, had not given up hope of ridding Mecca of the influence of Muhammad, and he prevailed upon Abu Lahab to withdraw his protection of the Prophet. Since Islam's theology taught that no one who believed in multiple gods would be given Allah's protection after death, Abu Jahl insisted that Abu Lahab question Muhammad as to what place Abu Talib inhabited in the afterlife. Naturally, if Muhammed maintained his grandfather was in Paradise, he was denying both the revelations of Allah and his own role as Allah's messenger, since his grandfather had never heard Muhammad preach. If he assigned his grandfather a place in hell, however, he was insulting not only the memory of the man who had taken him in as a young boy, but also the clan. Muhammad chose to take the latter course and answered Abu

Lahab's question by saying that Abu Talib was in hell. Thus ended the protection of the clan of Hashim.

Knowing that without the protection of his clan, he and his followers would now be in great danger, Muhammad began to search for a place where they might enjoy religious freedom. He looked first to a small city called Ta'if, which was located about forty miles east of Mecca. Ta'if was on the north-south trade route from Yemen and had at one time been a rival of the city of Mecca. Now, however, it was under control of the larger city. Muhammad journeyed to Ta'if and entered into discussions with some of the leaders about the feasibility of immigrating

A Muslim Arab father reads to two of his sons from the Qur'an, the holy book of Islam.

to the city. It may be that he tried to convince them that with the support of the followers of Islam, Ta'if could break away from Mecca, but those who talked with him feared the Meccans far more than Muhammad had thought, and they not only refused his proposition, but made it quite clear by actually stoning him as he left the city.

It was during the following year (620), during the month of the annual pilgrimage to Mecca that Muhammad attempted to find another city where the Muslims could take refuge. At this time he met several men from the city of Yathrib, now known more commonly as Medina. They listened with interest to his teachings. They were already familiar with Judaism, because Medina's population included both pagan Arabs and Jews. There were at that time in Medina five different tribes. Two were Arab and these tribes had been carrying on a blood feud for some time; the remaining three tribes were all Jewish. Perhaps because of their previous exposure to Judaism, the men were well disposed to listen and to accept Muhammad's teaching. By the time they returned to Medina, they had converted to Islam.

The following year the group which returned to meet with Muhammad had grown to twelve. This time Muhammad entered into an agreement with them known as the First Pledge of Al Aqabah, whereby they agreed to accept him as prophet and abide by his teachings. They were accompanied on their return to Medina by a teacher, sent by Muhammad to help them in spreading Islam. Throughout the next year, they won several more converts to the faith. Enough converts were made so that in the year 622, when they once again met with Muhammad, they numbered seventy-five persons. All agreed at this meeting to support and protect Muhammad, if he would come to Medina. This he agreed to do. For Muhammad, the agreement meant a safe place for himself and his followers. For the Medinans, it meant the coming of a man who might help to weld the city together and rid it of the long feud between the two Arab tribes.

In the meantime, while the persecutions in Mecca continued, no agreement had been reached by the leaders of the tribes as to how to deal with Muhammad. Though all were unhappy at having him in the city, the merchants did not want him to leave for they feared he would gain support from others (as, in fact, he had already done with the Medinans). This, in the end, would jeopardize Mecca's leadership as a trade center. While the Meccans were pondering Muhammad's fate, he was urging his followers to leave the city quietly and to go to Medina. They began to leave Mecca in small groups and to make their way north.

In the months that followed, the clans of Mecca devised a plan to silence Muhammad. Members of the many clans of the tribe of Quraish banded together and pledged to support each other, should anyone try to revenge the death of Muhammad which had become their goal. Assassins were chosen from various clans, and it was decided that all would attack

Muhammad together, while he slept, so that all would be guilty of the
crime. Should the Banu Hashim try to revenge the death, they would find
themselves in conflict with almost the entire city. By the time the actual
attack took place, only Muhammad, Abu Bakr, and Ali remained in
Mecca. On the night that the assassination was to take place, the murder-
ers found Ali sleeping in Muhammad's bed. Muhammad and Abu Bakr
had managed to escape from the city and were making their way, not
north to Medina, but south to a secluded cave on Mount Thaur. The es-
capees were pursued by the angry Meccans, and the hunt which followed
was thorough and lengthy. They did not find Muhammad and Abu Bakr,
however, and eventually the two made their way through the desert to
Medina and safety.

The entire event of the Muslims and their leader migrating to
Medina has special significance in tradition, and it is referred to in its en-
tirety as the *Hegira,* or "flight." After the second agreement with the people of Medina, which took place in mid-July, the *Hegira* began. Thus July
15, 622, is considered the beginning of the Muslim era. All events in
Muslim history date from that day, and the Muslim calendar marks its
beginning from that date. The calendar is based on lunar months, which
result in a year approximately 354 days in length, rather than on movements of the sun which is the basis for the 364 days of the Gregorian calendar, which the West accepts.

Medina — City of the Prophet

Medina was located near an oasis surrounded by several *wadis,* or
stream beds, which were dry except during the infrequent rainfalls. Because of its topography and because of the numerous tribes and the en-
mity felt between them, the city of Medina was more like a series of settlements than like a contained city. Each tribe had its own series of defense
fortifications, should it be attacked by another tribe. Muhammad faced a
difficult decision when he entered the city after his flight from Mecca,
for he had to select a place to live. He settled the question rather diplo-
matically by saying that he would live on the spot where his camel came
to a stop. The animal ultimately stopped in a quarter of the city which
belonged to one of the two Arab tribes, the Khazraj, in the yard of two
orphaned Arabs. It was a propitious sign, since Muhammad's great-
grandmother came from the same tribe.

The first act of the prophet after settling on a place to live was to
erect a mosque where public worship could be celebrated. He attached to
the mosque apartments to house himself and his family. The mosque was
not only a place where Muslims could pray, but also a shelter for those
who needed help or a place to sleep for the night.

Though the Muslims do not set aside an entire day for religious
worship as do the Christians and Jews, it became a tradition while in
Medina to meet together at the mosque for prayers at noon on Friday.

While praying, they would face northwest in the direction of Jerusalem which Muhammad considered a sacred city. Muhammad had chosen Jerusalem as the direction *(qiblah)* of prayer even before the *Hegira* from Mecca. Jerusalem was chosen because of a vision he had had. This is referred to in the seventeenth *surah* (chapter) of the *Qur'an:* "Glory be to God who did take his servant for a journey by night from the Sacred Mosque *(Kaaba)* to the Farthest Mosque, the precincts of which we have blessed, that we might show him some of our signs." The Farthest Mosque, according to Islamic teaching, was located within the Temple of David in Jerusalem. In his vision, Muhammad traveled to the Temple, and from that site he is said to have ascended into heaven before returning to Mecca. This event is spoken of as the "Night of the Journey and the Ascension," and it was following this vision that Muhammad instituted the five daily prayers, or *salat,* of Islam and the *qiblah.*

Another consideration which Muhammad may have had in choosing Jerusalem as the *qiblah* is that Jerusalem was also sacred to both Christians and Jews. Muhammad referred to the followers of both faiths as the "People of the Book," and it is probable that he thought his largest number of converts in Medina would come from the three Jewish tribes which had settled there. Muhammad was also familiar with the tradition of prophets which existed in both religions. Even though the Jews did not accept Jesus as a prophet, Muhammad may have reasoned that once the Jews heard him preach, they would recognize that he had been chosen by the One God to be the final prophet who recited the true word of God, and many would then convert to Islam.

During his first few months in Medina, however, Muhammad did not direct his full attention to the conversion of the Jews. Rather, he set about to solidify those who had emigrated from Mecca to Medina. Those who had converted to Islam in Mecca faced some very real problems in Medina, especially the fact that none had a means of livelihood, since the land which could be cultivated was already inhabited. Some, it was true, had other skills which they could use to bring in money and food, but this then had to be redistributed to the less fortunate. Charity was one of the bases of Islam. The first step which Muhammad took was to issue what is called the Constitution of Medina. The purpose of the Constitution was to give the followers of Muhammad a sense of religious union. It was the base on which he was to build an *'umma,* or community, linked together not by tribal or blood lines, but by a belief in the teachings of Islam. Thus, the Constitution did not reject those who already inhabited Medina, but left open the possibility that they would convert at some future date. Also, it provided guidelines on how the emigrants were to relate to those who already lived in Medina whether they were Jews or pagans. This concept of Muslim brotherhood is still fundamental in Islam today.

Muhammad's most immediate problem, however, was neither proselytizing among the Jews nor gaining political stature in Medina, since he ranked at the time only as an equal to the heads of other clans within the city. Rather, his main objective was to prevent further economic stress for the city by providing for his followers. In attempting to solve this problem, Muhammad resorted to a tradition of the desert which had a long history: the *razzia.* The caravan route from Syria to Mecca passed within a hundred miles of Medina. Bedouin tribesmen long before the birth of Muhammad had engaged in attacks on caravans which passed along this route moving goods from Syria to Mecca. This was done to augment their own meager incomes. Such attacks were carried out in order to steal camels or other animals not properly protected by the caravan guards. The raid on the caravan was known as a *razzia.* When such an attack was carried out, there was seldom human blood shed, for the taking of human life was a serious matter, and it usually resulted in blood feuds between the tribes involved. The followers of Muhammad, unable to find land or occupations, which would provide adequate income for the entire community of "emigrants," began engaging in *razzias* shortly after reaching Medina. They did so to provide a source of income to the otherwise indigent community.

Initially, the Muslim emigrants probably felt justified in participating in *razzias,* because they had been forced to leave Mecca as a result of their religious convictions. They may have believed, therefore, that any act which weakened the Meccans was justifiable as a reprisal for the suffering which the "emigrants" had had to endure. It was an "eye for an eye" ideology which matched the rugged terrain and living conditions of the desert. Thus, it can be said that the newly arrived contingent from Mecca initially supported themselves by thievery, which had a long tradition among those who dwelt in the desert.

Gradually, however, the justification for such raids underwent a change. What had formerly been excused as a righting of past wrongs slowly began to be justified in terms of religious belief. The believers carried out such attacks against nonbelievers. The Muslims thought of themselves as the believers, who by engaging in *razzias,* were striving in both a material and a personal way to carry out Allah's will. If a *razzia* was successful against the Meccans, did not that furnish further proof that they were performing the will of Allah? Thus, what had been purely a practical aspect of the "emigrant's" lives began to take on religious significance. Just as the *razzia* underwent a change in significance, so too did the term which identified such raids change. The Arabic term for "striving" is *jihad,* which in its broader context may be translated as "striving in all ways to do God's will." Today, the term *jihad* is applied to what is called "a holy war," and taken in its broadest meaning, this too is striving to do God's will.

The first three of four attempts at *razzias,* on the part of the Medinan emigrants were failures, because they lacked adequate manpower and because of poor planning. The first such successful attack, however, stands as a landmark both in Muslim tradition and as a break from tribal mores. This took place in January 624. Muhammad sent eight men to a place called Nakhlah, which was located on the caravan route from the south between the two cities of Mecca and Ta'if. He sent the men with sealed instructions which they were to open two days after they left Medina. When the men opened the letter they learned that Muhammad wished them to attack a caravan which was returning from Yemen to Mecca. Now this in itself was not unusual, but the men were instructed to attack the caravan during the holy month of pilgrimage. There was an honored tradition that caravans were not to be attacked during that month to ensure the safety of those going to Mecca to worship. Since this was true, the caravan was not heavily guarded and could be easily taken by a small force. Two of the eight men separated from the attackers before reaching the caravan, and when they later returned to Medina, they insisted they had lost a camel and in going to retrieve it, had lost their party.

The caravan was captured by the remaining six men and in the fight, one man guarding the caravan, was killed, one escaped, and two were taken prisoner. This broke the tradition not only of attacking caravans during the holy month, but also of shedding blood. The people of Mecca, already angry at Muhammad's escape from their plot to kill him, were further aroused by this plundering of their caravan, and it would be only a matter of time before they sought revenge. It is not completely clear how the people of Medina reacted to this violation of the holy month. It is likely that many disagreed with the action either publicly or privately, and it is certain that many feared a reprisal by the Meccans. As if in answer to those who questioned his right to instigate such an attack, Muhammad some time after the attack had a revelation wherein Allah spoke to him: "They will question you (Muhammad) with regard to warfare in the sacred month; say: Warfare therein is a serious matter, but to turn from the way of God and to disbelieve in him and in the sacred temple and to drive his people from it is more serious with God, and infidelity is more serious than killing" (Qur'an, surah 2:214). This could be interpreted as condemning the Meccans for having refused to allow Muhammad's followers to observe the holy month and the pilgrimage to Mecca, which for Muhammad was a far greater violation of honor than participating in razzias during that holy time.

The Battle of Badr

Muhammad now looked to other caravans making their way across the desert to Mecca. In March 624, he learned that a caravan of over one thousand camels was heading for Mecca from Syria. He enlisted about 300 men and left Medina in the hope of ambushing the caravan as it passed west of the city. The leader of the caravan, Abu Sufian, became suspicious at some point, and caused the caravan to be detoured further west along the Red Sea. At the same time, Mecca had learned of Muhammad's plan to raid the caravan which was one in which almost all the merchants had a stake. The traders took instant action and almost a thousand men rode out of the city to defend the caravan — certainly with the thought that they would teach Muhammad a lesson for his recent attack on the caravan near Ta'if. The men of Mecca were led by Abu Jahl, the man most responsible for Muhammad's departure from that city. It was soon learned that the caravan, by taking the detour towards the sea, had escaped Muhammad and his men. Many of those who rode out with Abu Jahl after learning the caravan was safe, wished to return to Mecca. There was now no reason to fight, except in revenge for the man who had been killed at Nakhlah, and one of the merchants offered to pay blood money for the guard's death. Abu Jahl, however, prevailed on the men to stay with him, and they proceeded to the area where Muhammad's force was camped.

Muhammad learned of this and decided that rather than retreat to Medina, he would stand and fight. A captured water carrier of the Meccans had told him of the size of the force, and though it seemed unbelievable that such a large force had left Mecca, he decided on a battle plan which would give him a definite advantage no matter how large the Meccan force. He ordered all the wells in the area blocked up with the exception of the one closest to Mecca and here he stationed his men. The tactic was an excellent one, since water is the greatest need of man in the desert. Muhammad's men had been refreshed by the well. Abu Jahl's men had been without water for some time, however, and were less prepared to fight. The battle which took place at the wells of Badr was a decisive victory for Muhammad. Approximately 130 Meccans were either killed or captured, while Muhammad's forces lost only fourteen men. And besides the military victory, there was a large amount of booty which the Medinans captured. They returned to Medina rejoicing.

But Muhammad had won more than a military victory. He had won a victory for Allah and for Islam. For three hundred men to rout almost the entire male population of Mecca was a miracle. Only with the aid of Allah could such a victory have been won. The battle at Badr, probably more than any one incident, convinced those in Medina who had been wavering in their convictions concerning Islam, that it was indeed the true religion. The "emigrants" from Mecca were now joined by more and more converts from Medina. The newcomers were classified as "helpers," and Muhammad's position as religious leader and also as political leader of Medina was considerably strengthened.

But even as Muhammad was solidifying his position among the pagan Arabs in Medina, he was encountering more and more opposition from the Jews. As he preached to them, they grew more vehement in their denial of him and of Islam. They had, of course, memorized the *Torah* and took issue with Muhammad's interpretation of it. They rejected entirely the proposition that Jesus was a prophet and that Muhammad was the last in a line of prophets extending back to Moses. "The People of the Book," whom Muhammad had hoped would be his first converts, rejected him just at a point when he had gained a position of leadership within Medina.

There were, as had been pointed out, three tribes of Jews living in Medina. These included the Banu Kainuka, the Banu Nadir, and the Banu Karaiza. All were aware of Muhammad's teachings and probably knew that the Muslims faced Jerusalem when at prayer. Muhammad's first act of rejection of the entire Jewish community was to change the direction of prayer (qiblah) from Jerusalem to Mecca. Also, it appears that Muhammad had required the Muslims in Medina to observe the Jewish holy day, the Day of Atonement, during which all fasted. Following the change of qiblah, Muhammad changed the requirement of fasting on the Day of Atonement to fasting throughout the holy month of Ramadan. These changes, however, did not seem to have much effect on the Jews in Medina. They continued to reject Muhammad's message. It was probably during this period that Muhammad decided to reject the Jews by reinterpreting the role which Abraham played in Islamic tradition. He was aware of the Jewish belief that Yahweh had promised to give the true religion to the seed of Abraham. The Jews based their claim of being the Chosen People on the fact that they could trace their heritage back to Abraham's son, Isaac. Abraham, however, had first sired Ishmael by a slave girl, Hagar. Isaac was not born to Sarah, Abraham's wife, until some time later. The Arabs trace their heritage to Ishmael. Was it not possible, therefore, that the true religion of God had been passed down from Ishmael rather than from Isaac? After all, Abraham himself was not a Jew. It was to his descendant, Moses, that God had revealed the traditional basis of the Jewish faith.

So direct descendance from Abraham was claimed. The religious ceremonies at the Kaaba were steeped in a tradition of Abraham, and the fact that his son, Ishmael, was saved from dying of thirst by drinking from the well of Zemzem, added to the tradition. With this shift, it was also possible for Muhammad to revise his attitude and actions towards the Jews.

The first tribe to feel Muhammad's ire was the Banu Kainuka. It is probable that Muhammad felt hostile to this tribe not only because they rejected his religious message, but also because they sided with certain other elements in Medina in feeling that continuing raids on Meccan caravans were potentially dangerous, since they would result in increased warfare between Mecca and Medina. Such an attitude was politically unfavorable to Muhammad and his tenuous leadership in the city. When a minor incident took place in the marketplace of Medina, Muhammad used it as an excuse to lay siege to the Banu Kainuka settlement. The siege lasted about two weeks and finally the Jewish tribe accepted Muhammad's offer to let them leave Medina and seek a less hostile place to live. They migrated from Medina in the spring of 624 and eventually settled in Syria.

Mecca's Revenge

Even as Muhammad was becoming more and more powerful in Medina, the Meccans had neither forgotten nor forgiven their defeat at Badr. Their chance for revenge came the following year, when a force of some 3,000 men marched on Medina. Not all of the force was made up of men from Mecca, however. Many represented other tribes from the surrounding area who had fallen victim to the continued *razzias* carried on by the Muslims. The force advanced on the city without any opposition and made camp near a small hill, called Uhud. They then allowed their animals to wander into a field of corn which was just about ready to be harvested and which was within sight of the Medinans. They hoped that the sight of the field being destroyed would spur the Muslims into attacking since to fight them in the city with its numerous fortifications would have been foolish.

At first Muhammad refused to act, but finally, under pressure from some of the younger men, a plan was made to attack. Early in the battle, the Muslims had a decided advantage and were succeeding in turning back the invaders, but confusion developed. The Meccans routed the Muslims who had to withdraw from the battle area, but they did not exploit this advantage. They withdrew and began making their way back to Mecca. The battle was not really a decisive victory for the invading force, but all felt that enough Muslims had been killed or injured to revenge their earlier defeat at Badr.

For Muhammad, however, the battle had presented both political and religious problems. Many of those who had aided in the fighting were "helpers" or converts from Medina. Would their deaths alienate the pagan or newly converted Medinans? Would possible converts reject Islam for fear that they would be drawn into future battles? Did this mean that the victory at Badr had been accidental, or did it mean that Allah was no longer willing to show favor to the Muslims?

Muhammad dealt with the situation again through revelation which later appeared in the *Qur'an*. The battle at Uhud has been a test of the believers' steadfastness to Islam. If they could accept these losses and still go on to defend Islam, they would in the future be as victorious as they had been at Badr. His followers accepted this explanation, and although there were many in Mecca who disbelieved and whom Muhammad had begun to call hypocrites, those who had converted remained faithful to Islam.

In the tense period which followed the battle of Uhud, all who did not follow the teaching of Muhammad were suspect, most especially the

Jews who it was feared might intrigue with the Meccans against the Muslims. Muhammad, well aware of this danger, instigated another siege this time against the Jewish tribe of the Banu Nadir. It did not last long and as in the case of the Banu Kainuka, the Banu Nadir were soon convinced that it was in their best interests to leave Medina. Unlike the earlier exodus, the Banu Nadir were allowed to take many of their possessions, and they left Medina in a proud procession, making their way north to the settlement of Khaibar.

The Final Victory

Throughout the year 626, Muhammad and his followers participated in several expeditions both for the purpose of gaining booty and of bringing bedouin and more settled tribes into the fold of Islam. Probably more important than either of these considerations, however, was that such expeditions, if successful, dissuaded desert tribesmen from aligning themselves with Mecca against the Muslims. In the meanwhile, the merchants of Mecca were busy raising yet another army to attack Muhammad.

The force that finally made its way to Medina in March 627 numbered almost 10,000 men, including not only the men of Mecca, but also members of other clans which had alliances with Mecca. Evidently, Muhammad was sufficiently warned in advance of the force's arrival, for he made preparations to defend Medina which included digging a ditch around the city in those places that were particularly vulnerable to attack by cavalry. The idea of the ditch may have come from a Persian convert to Islam, since this type of defense was used in the Persian Empire at that time but was unknown in the Arabian peninsula. The idea of the trench was to slow or even stop Meccans attacking on horseback, while those who were defending Medina were in position beyond the trench and could pelt the oncoming horsemen with arrows. The strategy worked exceedingly well, for the Meccans had neither expected it nor knew how to deal with such a barrier. They would attack, reach the trench, and then be repulsed by the arrows of the Muslims. Though superior in numbers, it appears the Meccans did not want to attack the city on foot, for they probably did not want to meet the Muslims in hand-to-hand combat. Followers of Islam were notoriously brave in close combat — probably because they were assured entry into Paradise should they be killed fighting for the cause of Islam.

The Meccans remained outside Medina for two weeks, but their morale quickly weakened and by mid-April, they had begun their retreat to Mecca. Though only nine men were reportedly killed in the campaign, it was an obvious victory for Muhammad, for he had now proven himself to be more astute militarily than his enemies.

One further act by Muhammad solidified his position as unquestioned leader of the Medinan community. Prior to and during the siege, the remaining Jewish tribe in Medina, the Banu Karaiza, had vacillated between aiding Muhammad in his fight and forsaking him in the event that the Meccans should win. It was not so much that they had actually participated in acts of provocation, though there were rumours that they had considered attacking Muhammad from the rear during a particularly difficult assault by the Meccans. Rather, it was their failure to take a stand which made Muhammad wary. He felt that they could no longer be trusted and that as long as they remained in Medina, they would represent an internal threat to his position of leadership. Shortly after the Meccans had departed, therefore, Muhammad instituted a siege against the Karaiza which lasted for three weeks. Finally, the Karaiza capitulated and totally surrendered to Muhammad. Influential members of the Arab tribe of Aus, who had formerly had an alliance with the Jewish tribe, intervened and asked that clemency be used in dealing with them. Muhammad agreed but only insofar as to promise that one of the Aus tribesmen would be chosen to decide the fate of the Karaiza. He then selected an Aus chief, who had been severely wounded in the Battle of the Ditch and who had heard the rumours concerning the near-treachery which the Karaiza were charged with. The Aus chieftain offered a swift and dreadful verdict — all of the men of the tribe were to be executed and all of the women and children were to be sold into slavery. This was perhaps a not uncommon verdict in times of total war, and it has been practiced in the name of religious conviction since, but the decision would leave a festering wound which has still not healed between Judaism and Islam.

Muhammad's Position in Medina

By now it may appear that Muhammad's life and the revelations he received concerning Islam and the will of Allah seem to fall into two distinct categories. The initial fundamental concepts of the Oneness of God, the belief in an afterlife, and the need for practicing charity towards one's fellowman all date back to Muhammad's early prophecy in Mecca. And the less fundamental but at least as practically important concepts of political, military, and legal actions which Muhammad put forth after the *Hegira* to Medina.

It may be difficult to accept some of the teachings put forth in Medina, such as the revelation after the fact, but Muhammad was not merely formulating a religion to be used by many on only formal occasions or one day a week. He was in the still primitive conditions which surrounded life in the desert revealing Allah's will that Islam be more practical — it was to be a way of life governing all of men's actions whether moral, social, or political. If a Muslim was faithful to his faith, he was also a good citizen, a good tribesman, and a good Arab. The *Qur'anic* teachings provided help not only for man's soul, but also for his body's material well-being.

Through the victory over the Meccans at the Battle of the Ditch and the subsequent massacre of the Jews, Muhammad had become the undisputed leader of Medina. In the five years that would follow until his death in 632, he would further clarify his teachings as they were revealed to him by Allah, and he would foster the spread of Islam throughout all of Arabia.

With his position in Medina secure, Muhammad set about making alliances with the bedouin tribes which lived in the area surrounding Mecca, for it was Mecca that was Muhammad's real goal. It contained the *Kaaba,* the sanctuary of Allah, and it represented the single largest stumbling block to the spread of Islam. If the inhabitants of Mecca could be converted, if the very people who had most strongly rejected Muhammad's teachings could be made to see the truth, then there would be evidence that it was the true faith, and there would be no stopping its spread throughout the rest of Arabia.

In 628, Muhammad, perhaps in an effort to test his strength among the tribes with which he had become allied and also the climate which existed in Mecca towards him, set off from Medina in an effort to make the annual pilgrimage to the *Kaaba.* He was denied entrance to the city, but the leaders of Mecca did reach an agreement with him known as the Treaty of Al Hudaibiyyah after a series of diplomatic exchanges carried on, mostly by messenger. The treaty granted Muhammad the right to proselytize among the bedouin tribes. This was a major concession, for it meant that those who accepted Islam would no longer be expected to honor former alliances with the Meccans. The treaty also made provisions for Muhammad to make the pilgrimage to Mecca the following year and for his being allowed to remain in the city three days during which time the Quraish would withdraw from the city. Finally, Muhammad agreed to honor a ten-year truce with the Quraish, during which time there would be no reprisals by Muhammad against the city of Mecca, should any of the followers of Islam living in Medina wish to recant and return to Mecca. On the other hand, Muhammad agreed that he would return to Mecca any person who was under age and who had not received parental consent to convert to Islam, should such persons try to come to Medina.

The treaty proved to be a turning point in the history of Islam, for it acted to solidify the treaties Muhammad had made with the tribes in the area surrounding Mecca. Often these treaties had been entered into by the bedouin either under duress or by force. Leaders of the tribes were wary of making any move to ally with Muhammad, for most had previously entered into similar agreements with the Quraish. They were fearful of Muhammad's growing strength, but they were also worried that the Quraish, who still represented the most powerful force in the area, would take revenge since most of the treaties were still in force. The truce between Muhammad and the Quraish meant that the tribes, which had made commitments to Muhammad, could now publicly honor them. Many now declared openly their allegiance to Muhammad and to Islam. Thus, Mecca was slowly surrounded with believers.

Shortly after returning from Mecca, Muhammad perpetrated an attack on Khaibar, the city to which he had exiled the Jewish tribe of Banu Nadir. The citizens of Khaibar, rankling under their exile and the loss of their land, had attempted to turn Arab tribes against Muhammad. Though the Jews of Khaibar had prepared for the attack, Muhammad's attack was successful, and there was much booty taken from the Jews. But, more significant was the manner in which Muhammad chose to deal with the Jews of Khaibar on a long-term basis. It laid the foundation for future dealings with Christians and Jews alike as the Islamic Empire spread out of Arabia. In order to ensure that there would be little money, with which to bribe Arab tribes into rebelling against Muhammad, he instituted a system whereby the Jews would continue to cultivate their lands, but at harvest time they would hand over one-half of their produce to the Muslims as a tax. In the future neither Christians nor Jews would be forced to convert to Islam, and all would be allowed to live in relative peace as long as they met their obligations by paying this exceedingly high tax.

The following year, Muhammad made the pilgrimage to Mecca which had been promised by the Treaty of Al Hudaibiyyah. The treaty had provided that members of the tribe of Quraish would leave the city and allow Muhammad and his followers to worship in peace. It is evident, however, that Muhammad hoped not only to worship at the *Kaaba,* but also to learn what the general feeling in Mecca was towards him at the time. His uncle, Abu Lahab, who had been responsible for his flight from Mecca had died, and leadership in the clan of Hashim had passed to yet another uncle, Al Abbas. Muhammad talked with his uncle while in Mecca, and, as he had done frequently before, he agreed to marry the sister of Al Abbas' wife, thereby forming a strong link with the clan which had formerly disowned him.

Muhammad left Mecca after the three days which had been allowed him and returned to Medina. What was in his mind on this return trip can only be conjectured, but it is probable that he was already making plans to subdue Mecca once and for all and to bring it under the sway of Islam.

Victory at Mecca

Mecca had long been Muhammad's goal. There are indications that this is so as early as the first year of the *Hegira,* when he changed the *qiblah* from Jerusalem to Mecca. This was strengthened later, when he fostered more fully the doctrine that Islam was the true religion promised to Abraham and passed on to the Arabs through Abraham's son, Ishmael. The long tradition linking Abraham to Mecca made it the focal point for the religious practices of Islam. Muhammad must surely have taken into account the importance which Mecca held in the religious practices of the pagans. It was now towards the pagans that attention was turned in the matter of proselytizing. To incorporate Mecca into the Muslim tradition would make conversions easier.

Preparations for mounting an attack on Mecca began in 629. The number of men who left Medina on January 1, 630, may not have been unusually large, since Muhammad had taken great pains to keep his goal secret. But, by the time the force reached the territory surrounding Mecca, over 10,000 men had been enlisted from the tribes which held allegiance to Muhammad. The actual capitulation of the Meccans was, therefore, somewhat anticlimatic. Leaders of two of the leading clans of Mecca rode out of the city before Muhammad entered it and, after promising they would submit to his will, were granted amnesty. The following day his men marched into Mecca from four directions. Though there was some bloodshed, the city was soon captured with a total of only thirty dead — twenty-four Meccans, four of the Meccans' allies, and two Muslims. The remaining clans of the city who had not already submitted to Muhammad now did so, and Mecca at last came under Muslim rule.

Muhammad's actions following the victory give us an interesting insight into the man. Eight years before, the merchants of Mecca had forced him to flee the city after plotting to kill him. For years these same men had harassed him and his followers and, with one exception, had refused to allow them to enter the city to participate in religious rites as the *Kaaba*. Yet Muhammad, instead of forcing these men to emigrate from the city or punishing them by death or torture, granted the citizens of Mecca a general pardon. There were a few exceptions to this amnesty. Men like Abu Jahl's son, Ikrimah, who had participated in unpardonable acts of treason, were ordered executed, but even many of these were eventually pardoned and allowed to remain in Mecca.

One of Muhammad's first acts after securing the city was to go directly to the *Kaaba*. He touched the sacred Black Stone once and then rode around the *Kaaba* itself. Dismounting from his camel he asked for the key to the sanctuary, opened the door, and entered. Once inside the sanctuary, Muhammad set about destroying the images of the 360 idols which it contained. This done, he came out and addressed those who had followed him to the *Kaaba*. His message was simple: paganism was dead. This meant that blood feuds must cease, worship of only Allah was to be allowed, debts and obligations of the pagans were cancelled, and from this time forward the men of Mecca must live by the precepts of Islam.

Though the Arabian peninsula in 630 could not really be thought of as a nation or state, since there were still numerous tribes which had not allied themselves with Muhammad, the seeds for the future Islamic state had been sown. The basis of this future was Islam, and while it was fundamentally a religion, it also had political and economic aspects which made it an integral way of life. Politically it acted to link together tribes which for centuries had acted independently of each other. The two areas where interdependent action took place were when formal allegiances took place among tribes, or when a blood feud arose between tribes over the death of a tribesman.

The formal allegiances which took place among tribes and Muhammad broke down the tribal consciousness somewhat. If each owed allegiance to Muhammad, then it followed that all were somehow interconnected. This interconnection was founded in the religion which all professed. With the accepting of Islam came obligations of acting with charity and justice towards others. It would be many years before all traces of the tribal mentality disappeared among the Arabians who accepted Islam, but the die had been cast.

The economic aspects of Islam were more easily discernible. Before the victory in Mecca, *razzias* had sustained the Muslims. Now, however, as tribes made treaties with Muhammad each brought with them gifts which added considerably to the wealth of the Muslim community. Since charity and the idea of caring for those who had little had always been a fundamental belief of Islam, no member of the community suffered, and the wealth was shared proportionately. Yet the spread of Islam would be threatened if expeditions were halted entirely, and Muhammad was looking towards the north and the crumbling Persian empire as a fertile field in which to proselytize.

Thus the *razzia* was replaced by *jihad.* The Muslims were carrying God's word to the nonbelievers, and thus they fulfilled a religious obligation. *Jihad* has come to mean "holy war" in our day and has been used recently more to mean defending the word of Allah, rather than spreading it.

At the time of his death in 632, Muhammad had certainly solidified his strength in central Arabia. It is likely too that in southern Arabia and in Yemen there were those who professed Islam. It was to the north that he looked for further expansion, and though in his own day he was not to see the fantastic spread of Islam out of the peninsular region, he had accomplished the amazing feat of supplanting paganism with Islam and of unifying the many diverse tribes of the central region.

The Pilgrimages of Farewell

Muhammad had not remained in Mecca as one might assume he would have done after working so long to subdue it. Rather he returned to Medina and from there carried on the business of directing expeditions, making treaties, and guiding his growing empire. In the spring of 632, however, Muhammad led a pilgrimage to Mecca which was to be the model for the religious practice of *hajj,* or greater pilgrimage. The rites practiced on this pilgrimage incorporated some of the practices which had formerly been used in pagan worship. The structure for the Fifth Pillar of Islam was finalized with Muhammad's *hajj.* Future pilgrims to Mecca would follow closely the form of worship he had practiced in 632, and unlike various forms of Christian worship which have modified since Christ's time, the *hajj* would remain the same. All Muslims who can are supposed to make the *hajj* once in their lives.

Muhammad returned from Mecca towards the end of March, and his health slowly began to deteriorate until at last on June 8, 632, he died — worn out by his long battle to spread the faith of Islam. The passing of the Prophet appears to have been rather unexpected, as he had made no arrangements for the succession of leadership. His death, therefore, caused confusion and not a little uncertainty among the Muslims. A meeting of those closest to Muhammad was held and it was decided that the successor, or Caliph, who would follow Muhammad as leader of the Muslims, should be Abu Bakr, his lifelong friend and one of his earliest converts. It was Abu Bakr who had observed the consternation of those praying in the mosque following the Prophet's death and had brought them together by observing in a speech to them: "If you worshiped Muhammad, he is indeed dead; but if you worship God, he is alive and can never die."

Abu Bakr and his successor Umar, another early convert, were responsible for keeping the Muslim world as it then existed together after Muhammad's death. Not only did they bind the Arabian peninsula together into a cohesive unit, but they also were responsible for the spread of Islam north into the Persian and Byzantine Empires through a series of *jihads,* unparalleled in their swiftness and their effectiveness.

After the Prophet's Death

At the time of Muhammad's death, Islam was already a well-developed faith. The next hundred years would see the new religion spread until it actually controlled all the territory from Spain to India. Muslim traders ventured as far north as Scandinavia. Jerusalem, Damascus, Alexandria — one by one they came under Islam's insignia, the sword and the crescent.

In the years to follow, Muslim theology would continue to develop, but it would always be faithful to the *Qur'an* and to the *Hadith,* sayings attributed to Muhammad. With the death of the Prophet, the faith would continue to spread as firmly anchored in the Five Pillars — belief in God and his Prophet, prayer, almsgiving, fasting, and pilgrimage to Mecca.

The years to come would see the constant interweaving of the three great monotheistic religions, Judaism, Christianity, and Islam.

STUDENT ACTIVITIES

A Short History of the Near East

Chapter I — Part 1

The Great Civilizations of the Ancient Middle East

1. Two methods of writing have been mentioned in the text: the Egyptian hieroglyphics and the Sumerian cuneiform. Do some research on how each developed, how modern man learned to read each, and what contributions each made to modern civilization. Display samples of each to the class using materials on which each might have been written.

2. Write some decrees on religion and human relations as Akhenaton and Moses might have written them. Discuss what the response of the early Egyptians and the Hebrews might have been to such decrees. See if you can find any information on the Code of Hammurabi.

3. Construct a model of the original Hebrew Temple in Jerusalem. Show what each section was used for and why. Find out what other religious structures were built on the site of the Temple, when they were built, and their importance to other religions.

4. Learn what you can concerning the building of the ancient city of Constantinople. Then discuss how the building of this city affected the Roman Empire.

The Conquest of Islam

1. Draw a map of the Islamic Empire as it existed in 750 A.D. Compare it with maps of other more ancient empires such as the Roman, Byzantine, and Persian empires.

2. Learn what the Five Pillars of Islam are. How do they compare with the Ten Commandments? Try to obtain the film "Pilgrimage to Mecca" and show it to the class.

3.   Obtain a copy of the Muslim holy book, the *Qu'ran,* and compare its writings with those of the Old and New Testaments.

The Crusades

1.   Give a report on the Crusades including how they began, how many took place, how they were financed, what happened to the city of Jerusalem during the Crusades, and the effect of the Crusades on the Holy Land. Were the Crusades successful? Why or why not?

The Ottoman Empire

1.   Have the class pretend it is the city of Beirut under Ottoman rule. Ask them to set up a *millet* form of government as it would have existed at that time.

2.   Have a mock trial between a Muslim and a Christian in the city of Beirut during the rule of the Ottoman Empire.

Western Influence in the Middle East

1.   Have a member of the class act as Ferdinand de Lesseps presenting his plan for the Suez Canal to Muhammad Ali. He must be prepared to explain what good it will do for Egypt, how it will be financed, and how the work will be done.

2.   Report on the special preparations made for the opening of the Suez Canal in 1869.

The Emergence of Nationalism

1.   Have a student report on the Dreyfus trial. Discuss anti-Semitism. Is the phrase "anti-Semitism" accurate? Why or why not? Under what conditions were Jews in Western Europe, Eastern Europe, and the Russian Pale living during the 1890's? Discuss the evolution of the ghetto.

2.   Have the class set up the first World Zionist Organization meeting with students representing Jewry from Eastern and Western Europe and Russia.

3.   Discuss the reasons why Arab nationalism was less organized than Zionism at the end of the nineteenth century.

4.   Find out how Syria, Lebanon, and Palestine were governed under Ottoman rule and what the boundaries of these areas were.

5.   Discuss why French and American Christian missionaries had such an impact on the Arab nationalist movement.

Chapter I — Part 2

1914 to May 14, 1948

World War I

1. Read the Hussein-McMahon correspondence (see *Documents on the Middle East*, edited by Ralph H. Magnus, published by American Enterprise Institute). Draw a map indicating the areas which were to become independent, those which would remain under French rule, and those areas which would be dominated by the British.

2. Read the Sykes-Picot Agreement (see *The Israel-Arab Reader,* edited by Walter Laqueur, published in paperback by Bantam Books). Draw a map indicating the areas which the French would control. Compare with Hussein-McMahon map and discuss.

The Balfour Declaration

1. Read the Balfour Declaration carefully. Consider how you might have written it had the responsibility been yours.

The Peace Talks at Versailles

1. Set up a mock Versailles Peace Conference and assume the positions of the major powers regarding the settlement of the Middle East problem. Have delegations representing: Great Britain, France, the United States, the Arabs, and the Zionists. Include discussion of the Hussein-McMahon correspondence, the Balfour Declaration, the Sykes-Picot Agreement, and the King-Crane Commission report.

The Mandates

1. Discuss the terms: *colony, trusteeship,* and *mandate.*

    Might a different form of governing in the Middle East after World War I been more effective? How? Why?

2. Discuss the French division of Syria. Give as many reasons as possible why the French divided Syria and Lebanon the way they did.

The Pre-War Years

1. Learn what you can about the al Husaini and the Nashashibi fami-

lies of Palestine. (See *A Palestine Entity?*, published by the Middle East Institute, Washington, D.C.)

Learn more about the role of the Grand Mufti of Jerusalem, Hajj Amin al Husaini, in the Palestine Arab Nationalist movement.

2. Build a model *kibbutz*. Explain why the *Haganah* was so important to settlers on the *kibbutzim* during the 1930's.

3. Look up the term "Revisionist Zionist party" in *The Book of Jewish Knowledge* by Nathan Ausubel. Discuss the goals of this party and how these goals differed from those of other Jewish settlers in Palestine.

The White Paper of 1939

1. Read the White Paper of 1939 (see *The Israel-Arab Reader*). Discuss why the British might have issued such a policy statement. Might the British have devised a policy which would have pleased both the Arabs and the Jews? Why or why not?

World War II

1. What were the *Irgun Zvai Leumi* and the *Stern Group?* Learn what you can of their activities during the war and report to the class.

One Final Try

1. Read the report of the Anglo-American Commission of Inquiry. Discuss the findings of that report. Do you think it was an accurate reflection of the situation in Palestine? Why or why not?

The United Nations and Palestine

1. Set up a mock United Nations session of the General Assembly to discuss the Palestine problem as it existed following World War II. Assume the roles of the major and minor powers which were member states of the United Nations at that time.

Have delegations representing the Arab and the Zionist points of view also.

Try to reach agreement on what the best plan of action would be in Palestine, e.g., partition, binational state, trusteeship, etc.

Have someone represent the Anglo-American Commission of Inquiry and present the Commission's report to the General Assembly. Debate that report.

2.   Hold a similar session placing the time as early September 1947. Have a delegation representing the United Nations Special Committee on Palestine. (See *The Israel-Arab Reader.*)

3.   Draw up a list starting with the Hussein-McMahon correspondence of all the various plans that were made for Palestine between 1915 and 1948. List what decision was made — binationalization, partition, etc. Show how the Arabs and the Jews stood on each plan.

Chapter I — Part 3

May 15, 1948 to November 22, 1967

The 1948 Arab-Israeli War

1.   Find out the statistics on the number of troops available to each country (Israel, Egypt, Jordan, Syria, Lebanon, Iraq, and Saudi Arabia) in the spring of 1948. Discuss why the Israelis were successful in defeating the Arab nations.

The Arab Refugees

1.   Hold a United Nations General Assembly debate setting the time as the spring of 1949. Have delegates representing the member nations, the Arab point of view, the Israeli point of view, and the view of the Palestinians who had been displaced and made refugees.

The object of the debate will be to find a just solution to the Arab refugee problem. Discuss what has been done to date (1949) for the refugees, what could be done, and possible consequences. Include in the debate a proposal calling for the establishment of a relief agency. Under whose auspices should the agency work, what should its focus be, and how will it be funded?

U.S. Interests in the Middle East

1.   Hold a debate in the class acting as the U. S. Congress. Discuss all the interests which the United States has in the Middle East. Try to formulate a policy which the United States might follow towards the various states of the Middle East in the early 1950's.

2.   Write the various oil companies asking for information on their

overseas work. Discuss how these companies have affected the lives
and economies of the various states of the Middle East.

The Egyptian Revolution

1. The Egyptian Revolution has just taken place. Have nine members
    of the class act as the Revolutionary Command Council. Egypt has
    had a monarchy since 1922 and has maintained a strong British pres-
    ence since 1883. It is the Revolutionary Command Council's task to
    set up a new form of government. They must take into account the
    internal problems which the country faces as well as the strong feel-
    ings against foreign domination which are prevalent throughout the
    Arab Middle East.

    What structures of government will be most effective? Who is to rule
    and how? What should be the priorities in nation-building — a
    sound economy, more schools, industrialization, seeking foreign aid,
    etc.?

Suez Crisis

1. A cease-fire has been called in the Suez Crisis, but French and Brit-
    ish troops are still in Port Said and Israeli troops are still in the Sinai.
    Hold a United Nations General Assembly meeting to discuss what
    measures must be taken to ensure free passage of Israeli ships
    through the Straits of Tiran. Negotiate for the presence of a United
    Nations Emergency Force in the area. Discuss other possible poli-
    cies which the United Nations could have adopted to bring peace to
    the area.

2. Report on the importance of the Aswan High Dam project. Take
    into account arable land, need for power, and population expansion
    in Egypt. Discuss possible alternatives as to how the dam might have
    been financed after the United States withdrew its support of the
    project.

Unsettling Events of 1958

1. Discuss the various reasons why the Arab states sought greater unity
    between 1958 and 1963. What various kinds of agreements could
    have been made to strengthen the Arab states? Why was Lebanon
    unwilling to enter into agreements aimed at greater Arab unity?

2. Learn how the Lebanese government is structured? Why would the
    Arab refugees living in Lebanon have threatened Lebanon's govern-
    ment had they been allowed to become citizens?

Attempts to Promote Arab Unity Fail

1.   Hold an Arab Summit meeting with the heads of state from members of the Arab League in attendance. President Nasser is attempting to bring about greater Arab unity. Have him state his position and give suggestions as to how greater Arab unity can be obtained in 1960.

     Have other Arab leaders refute or uphold Nasser's opinions. Take into account the differences felt by monarchies and revolutionary leaders. Take into account relationships with the West.

Palestinians Begin to Acquire a New Identity

1.   You are a young Palestinian refugee who has been living in a camp since 1948. It is now 1963. Tell us about life in the refugee camp. Tell us what you would like to do with your life. Tell us what you think is the best way to get out of the refugee camp and start a new life.

2.   It is 1965 and you have become a *fedayeen.*Tell us why you joined the *fedayeen.* What do you do? Is it helping you to achieve your goal? Are there other ways you might achieve the same goals? What are they?

Prelude to War

1.   Have two members of the class act as Nasser and as Secretary General U Thant. Have them discuss the withdrawal of United Nations Emergency Forces from the Sinai. What reasons does Nasser give for such a withdrawal? Can U Thant convince him this is an unwise move? What alternative actions might U Thant suggest?

2.   In Israel, tension is mounting. An emergency session of the Knesset is called. What do various members suggest should be Israel's course of action?

The Six-Day War

1.   The Six-Day War has just begun. Have one member of the class act as President Johnson and another member act as Soviet Premier Alexei Kosygin. The "hot line" between Washington and the Kremlin has been activated for the first time. What do these two major world leaders say to each other?

2.   Have members of the class act as members of the United Nations Security Council. The June War has begun and the Council has gone into emergency session. What transpires at this session?

A Cease-Fire but No Peace

1. Have members of the class represent administrative staff from the United Nations Relief and Works Agency and as staff of other welfare agencies designed to aid the refugees. The June War has ended and these people are meeting to discuss the problems caused by the June War. Consider the placement of the new refugees, the most immediate needs, funding, and loss of buildings, housing, and schools.

2. The United Nations General Assembly is meeting to discuss the annexation of Jerusalem by the Israelis. What is discussed in this meeting? Take a vote to see how member nations view this annexation.

Formula For Peace

1. The United Nations General Assembly and the Security Council have passed a great deal of time in discussing how peace can be brought to the Middle East. On November 22, 1967, the Security Council passes a resolution which it feels can provide a formula for peace.

    Have the class work out a peace plan based on this resolution taking into account the attitudes and the demands made by both the Arabs and the Israelis since 1948.

    Read the United Nations Charter and discuss the avenues for peaceful solution to conflict situations which it contains. Are they realistic? Can they be applied to the Middle East? Why or why not?

2. Hold Four-Power talks with students representing France, Britain, Russia, and the United States. The U.N. Special Mediator Gunnar Jarring should also be in attendance. The task of this meeting is to begin negotiations between the Arabs and the Israelis. You must work out a formula for talks which will be acceptable to both sides. Learn more about the Rhodes talks which were held after the 1948 war. Take into account the Palestinians.

3. On the basis of the decisions made by the Four Powers and the peace plan of the United Nations, hold negotiation talks between the Arabs and the Israelis. Decide on a timetable for the measures which must be taken to bring peace to the Middle East.

4. Discuss the Middle East today as it relates to the Western Powers and take into account the armaments race, foreign aid, lack of diplomatic relations, etc. What should the stance of the United States be towards the various countries of the Middle East in the future?

Chapter II

Country Profiles

1. Discuss why profiles of only certain countries in the Middle East were included in this section. Are there other profiles you would have included? If so, which ones? Write profiles on those countries using resource materials from your library.

2. Prepare a bibliography of books available in your school library and your local library which relate to the Middle East. Include all of the relevant volumes on geography, history, economics, religion, travel, and fiction. Prepare it so it may be used by other classes. Collect bibliographies already available on the Middle East and compare them to your bibliography. Are there books in these bibliographies which you think ought to be in your school or local library? Discuss the possibilities of having these books purchased with your school and local librarians.

3. What are the fundamental characteristics which Semitic peoples share? What are the differences?

   A. As a project learn more about Arabic and Hebrew. In what scripts are they written? How important are these languages in the Middle East today?

   B. Discuss the differences and the similarities between Judaism, Christianity, and Islam.

   C. Find out about as many Semitic tribes of ancient times as possible. Make an overlay map showing where these tribes lived, when they became important, and their contributions to mankind.

4. Build a topography map of the entire Middle East using clay, paper mache, or other suitable materials. Paint it to show elevations and

bodies of water. Discuss the importance of water to this region. How could more water be made available. What is necessary to make desert land arable? Which countries need more arable land? Which are capable of producing such land? Mark on the map those areas which might be reclaimed.

5.   Draw a map of the Middle East showing population centers. Include on the map the present population of each and the predicted population in 1975. Show the annual rate of increase in each country. Which countries can support the expected increase in population? What facilities (schools, hospitals, roads, airports, etc.) must be built or enlarged to meet future needs?

6.   Find maps showing where oil has been discovered in the Middle East. What has the development of the oil industry done for the countries in which it was found? What is the importance of this oil to the international community? How does the oil industry work in each country? What products besides crude oil and natural gas can be made from oil? What is Petromine? How would the development of Petromine affect the countries of the region?

7.   Which countries are considered "reactionary" and which are considered "revolutionary"? Why? Could other labels be applied to these countries? How have these labels affected the interrelationships of these countries to one another and to the nations of the West?

8.   What are some of the foods common to all countries of the Middle East? Which are common only to Israel? Which are common to only one Arab country? Do both the Jews and the Muslims have certain foods which they consider unclean? What are they? Why are they considered unclean?

   A.   Plan and if possible give a dinner as it would be given in an Orthodox Jewish home.

   B.   Plan and if possible give a meal as it would be given by Bedouin living in the desert.

   C.   Collect traditional Jewish and Arabic recipes and plan a meal at which both Muslims and Orthodox Jews could sit down to eat together using recipes from both cultures.

9.   Listen to Arab and Jewish records which feature traditional and

modern music from both cultures. Learn folk dances from each tradition and perform them in appropriate costumes.

10.   Plan a Middle Eastern Folk Festival which would display the art, architecture, writing (calligraphy) including both Hebrew and Arabic script, music, folk dancing, and artifacts from the countries of the area. Serve foods which are typical. Also have a Middle East bazaar and display items from the Arab countries and Israel. Learn if there are any people in your community from Middle Eastern countries and invite them to participate in the Folk Festival.

11.   Try to visit a synagogue, a mosque, and an Orthodox and an Eastern Rite church. If this is impossible, build models of each showing the parts of the building which are particularly important in worship. Discuss a typical worship service in each.

12.   Invite members of the local community who have lived or visited countries of the Middle East to talk with your class. If they have slides, ask them to show the slides to the class. In metropolitan areas, you may be able to locate diplomats who will speak to your class.

13.   Write to the various embassies of the countries studied and ask them to send you more information about their countries. Ask if they have films available which would give you a better knowledge of life in each country.

14.   Discuss the *kibbutzim* and their importance to life in Israel. How are they like communes in our own country? Would the concept of *kibbutzim* work in America? Divide your class into a typical *kibbutz* structure and during one class period conduct the class as though it were a *kibbutz* community.

15.   Find out about the currencies of the various countries of the Middle East. Try to collect an assorted sample of each and display these with their names, values, and the countries from which they come. Find out what the per capita income is for each country in the Middle East and show this with the display of money.

16.   Find out the various kinds of weights and measures used in the Middle Eastern countries. Make a display showing the differences in weights and measures and include a display of those used in the United States.

17. Find out more about the Bedouin. How do they live? Do they have customs which differ from more settled people? Divide the class and have each half represent a different tribe. Act out the meeting of the two tribes in the desert and the ceremonies which would take place.

18. Discuss the place of women in the modern Middle East. Take into account the differences between women in rural areas and urban areas. Discuss customs and dress among women and whether it has changed over the years.

19. Discuss the codes of ethics practiced by Jews, Christians, and Muslims. What are the differences? What are the similarities? What part does religion play in the lives of Middle Easterners?

Chapter III

Judaism, Christianity and Islam

Primitive Religion:

1. The transition from polytheism to monotheism took some time, for primitive man was unwilling to give up the protection of many gods for just one God. Divide the class into two groups and hold a debate. One section will represent primitive man and defend polytheism; while the other section will represent monotheism and defend the existence of only one God.

2. Judaism, Christianity, and Islam all arose in areas where the worship of many gods was prevalent. However, in each area polytheistic worship differed. Have three students research and report on how polytheism was practiced in each area, i.e., Egypt, Palestine, and Arabia.

3. Using books on ancient art and primitive religions, make a display of artifacts which resemble those images used by primitive man to represent gods in his religious practices.

Judaism:

1. Using a map of the ancient Middle East, trace the journeys of Abraham. Show the major powers and the areas in which lesser tribes existed. If possible, make an overlay transparency of the modern Middle East showing present boundary lines and modern states.

2. Using a map of the Sinai Desert, discuss the forty years which the Hebrews spent wandering in the desert (also refer to the *Book of Exodus* in the Old Testament). How did the Hebrews survive in the inhospitable desert? Why did they not enter the land of Canaan earlier? Why did they not return to Egypt?

3. Chapters 20 through 23 of *Exodus* include many laws given to the Hebrews by Yahweh. Read these chapters and discuss whether the laws would be appropriate today. Discuss also why they were appropriate in ancient times.

4.   Find pictures of Jerusalem as it existed at the time the Hebrews conquered it and made it their capital. Discuss why Jerusalem was chosen, and if possible find an account of how the city was taken. Compare pictures of Jerusalem today with those of ancient Jerusalem.

5.   The Temple in Jerusalem has always played a prominent role in Jewish tradition. Reconstruct a floor plan of the original Temple showing the major areas including where the Ark of the Covenant was kept, the areas for sacrifice, etc.

6.   The prophets played an interesting role in Hebrew life. Read some of the Prophetic Books of the Old Testament and discuss if and how the prophecies came true.

7.   Many holy days in the Jewish faith date back to the time of the Old Testament. Perhaps the most joyous of these is the Sukkoth or Feast of Tabernacles, while Rosh Hashanah and Yom Kippur are serious and solemn and in some respects like the Christian Lent. Have students report on the major Jewish holidays, their origins, and how they are observed.

8.   Jews do not proselytize as do Christians and Muslims. *Anyone* who wishes to join the Jewish faith and meets the requirements may join. Discuss why Jews do not seek converts to their faith.

Christianity

1.   Jesus is considered a prophet both in the Jewish and Islamic traditions. However, no writings of Jesus exist. Rather, we have the New Testament writings of others telling of Jesus' life. Discuss whether or not Jesus was, in fact, a prophet.

2.   John the Baptist is thought to have been an Essene. Research and report on the life-style of the Essenes including how they lived, why they chose that type of life, and how they were treated by their contemporaries. Compare the Essenes' life-style with that of today's counter-cultures.

3.   In the New Testament we find that Paul was responsible for the writing of many books which were written in the form of letters to various peoples throughout the Roman Empire. Using Damascus as a focal point, locate on a map of the Ancient Middle East the areas in which the peoples lived. Discuss how the various cultures of these peoples might have differed, and compare two of Paul's letters to see if he approached different peoples in different ways.

4.   Initially, the Apostles attempted to convert the Jews living in Palestine to Christianity. Why did they first attempt to convert the Jews? Were they successful? Why or why not?

5.   The Apostles also attempted to convert the Greeks and the Romans who practiced a more sophisticated polytheism than did the peoples of the Eastern Mediterranean. Through research find out the major gods in the Roman and Greek cultures and contrast them with the *baals* used in Canaan and the gods of Egypt.

6.   Many of the Christians who split away from the Church as it existed in Constantinople were later reunited with the Roman Catholic Church. These churches are now known as the Eastern Rite Catholic Churches. Report on the various Eastern Rites and also on the Orthodox Church. Discuss whether these Churches could be reunited into one Church.

7.   The Church of the Holy Sepulchre has meaning for all Christians as it stands on the place where Jesus was crucified. Through the years, however, contention over various parts of the Church has arisen among various sects of the Christian Church. Find out how the Church of the Holy Sepulchre is presently divided and administered. Discuss your findings.

Islam

1.   Islamic religious practices are based on the Five Pillars of Faith. Find out what these Five Pillars are, and compare them with the Ten Commandments of the Old Testament and Jesus' law of love as found in the New Testament.

2.   Non-Muslims may not as a rule travel to the holy city of Mecca. Why is this so? Some people who were non-Muslim have disguised themselves at various times in history and traveled to Mecca during the time of Pilgrimage. See if you can find a description of such a trip and report to the class.

3.   In many ways the pilgrimage to Mecca which Muslims make today has not changed from the days of Muhammad. Report to the class how the various elements of the pilgrimage are carried out and the significance of each.

4.   The idea of the extended family (responsibility for all who are related to you no matter how distantly) has played an important role in the conversion of the early Arabians to Islam. Discuss why this might be so.

5.   All mosques are basically the same. Find information on the structure of the Muslim mosque and draw a floor plan showing how various parts of the mosque are used in worship. Also discuss the importance of the mosque for use as a place to study, a refuge, and a place for worship.

6.   Obtain a copy of the *Qur'an* and read a *Surah* aloud in class. Discuss similarities between the thoughts presented in the *Qur'an* and those found in the Old and New Testaments. Discuss the dissimilarities.

7.   Islam, too, has a penitential season similar to the Jewish Rosh Hashanah and the Christian Lent. Find out how the Muslims observe their penitential season known as Rammadan, and compare it to the Jewish and Christian holy seasons.

Comparative Religion

1.   Have three members of the class represent a Jew, a Christian, and a Muslim. Have each present a short speech explaining how his religion worships the one true God and why members of the class should choose to belong to the religion he represents. Allow time for questions.

2.   Invite a representative of the Jewish faith, the Orthodox faith, one of the Eastern Rite Churches, and a member of the Muslim faith to speak to your class about their religious practices.

3.   If possible, attend a religious service at a synagogue, mosque, Orthodox or Eastern Rite church.

4.   Discuss if and how members of the three major monotheistic faiths could gain a better understanding of each other and whether through better understanding peace could be reached in the Middle East.

5.   Using the Old Testament, the New Testament, and the *Qur'an,* find passages which show similar beliefs and passages which show divergent beliefs among the three faiths.

6.   Reproduce a map showing the spread of Judaism, Christianity, and Islam through the eleventh century. Discuss why Islam never spread to central Europe.

7.   At present there is much tension in the Middle East over the various shrines and Holy Places. Find out which ones are being disputed and discuss possible ways that tension could be lessened.

ANNOTATED BIBLIOGRAPHY

Chapter I — Part 1

Ancient Times to 1914

ANCIENT MIDDLE EAST

Breasted, James Henry. *The Conquest of Civilization.* New York: Harper & Brothers, rev. ed., 1954. 609 pp.

Casson, Lionel. *Ancient Egypt.* New York: Time-Life Books (Great Ages of Man Series), 1965. 192 pp.

Dimont, Max I. *Jews, God and History.* New York: Simon & Schuster, Inc., 1962. 463 pp.

Kramer, Samuel N. *Cradle of Civilization.* New York: Time-Life Books (Great Ages of Man Series), 1967. 183 pp.

Muller, Herbert J. *The Loom of History.* New York: New American Library, 1961. 495 pp.

Woolley, Sir Leonard. *The Beginnings of Civilization.* New York: New American Library, 1965. 636 pp.

CONQUEST OF ISLAM

Andrae, Tor. *Mohammed: The Man and His Faith.* New York: Harper & Row, 1960. 194 pp.

Azzam, Abd-al-Rahman. *The Eternal Message of Muhammad.* New York: Devin-Adair Co., 1964. 297 pp.

Gabrieli, Francesco. *Muhammad and the Conquests of Islam.* New York: McGraw Hill Book Co., 1968. 249 pp.

Stewart, Desmond. *Early Islam.* New York: Time-Life Books (Great Ages of Man Series), 1967. 192 pp.

Watt, W. Montgomery. *Muhammad: Prophet and Statesman.* London: Oxford University Press, 1961. 250 pp.

THE CRUSADES

Atiya, Aziz S. *Crusade, Commerce and Culture.* Bloomington, Indiana: Indiana University Press, 1963, 280 pp.

Duggan, Alfred. *The Story of the Crusades.* New York: Doubleday & Co., 1966. 240 pp.

Lamb, Harold. *The Crusades.* New York: Doubleday & Co., 1960. 594 pp.

Runciman, Steven. *A History of the Crusades.* New York: Harper & Row, 1965. Three volumes.

THE OTTOMAN EMPIRE

Davison, Roderic H. *Turkey.* Englewood Cliffs, N.J.: Prentice Hall, 1968. 181 pp.

Lewis, Bernard. *The Emergence of Modern Turkey.* New York: Oxford University Press, 1968. 544 pp.

Vuchinich, Wayne S. *The Ottoman Empire: Its Record and Legacy.* Princeton: D. Van Nostrand Co., 1965. 191 pp.

WESTERN INFLUENCES IN THE MIDDLE EAST PRIOR TO WORLD WAR I

Batal, James. *Assignment: Near East.* New York: Friendship Press, 1950. 118 pp.

Finnie, David N. *Pioneers East: The Early American Experience in the Middle East.* Cambridge, Mass.: Harvard University Press, 1967. 333 pp.

Kinross, Lord (Patrick Balfour). *Between Two Seas: The Creation of the Suez Canal.* New York: William Morrow & Co., 1969. 306 pp.

Sharabi, Hisham. *The Arab Intellectuals and the West: The Formative Years, 1875-1914.* Baltimore: Johns Hopkins Press, 1970. 176 pp.

Tibawi, A. L. *British Interest in Palestine, 1800-1901.* London: Oxford University Press, 1961. 280 pp.

——————————— . *American Interests in Syria, 1800-1901: A Study of Educational, Literary and Religious Work.* London and New York: Oxford University Press, 1966. 333 pp.

Wright, L. C. *United States Policy Toward Egypt, 1830-1914.* New York: Exposition Press, 1969. 247 pp.

EMERGENCE OF NATIONALISM

Antonius, George. *The Arab Awakening.* New York: G. P. Putnam's Sons, 1965. 471 pp.

Binder, Leonard. *The Ideological Revolution in the Middle East.* New York: John Wiley & Sons, Inc., 1964. 287 pp.

Hourani, Albert. *Arabic Thought in the Liberal Age,* 1798-1939. New York: Oxford University Press, 1962. 403 pp.

Litvinoff, Barnt. *To the House of Their Fathers: A History of Zionism.* New York: Frederick A. Praeger, 1966. 311 pp.

Sharabi, Hisham B. *Nationalism and Revolution in the Arab World.* Princeton, N.J.: D. Van Nostrand Co., 1966. 176 pp.

Weizmann, Chaim. *Trial and Error.* New York: Schocken Books, Inc., 1966. 493 pp.

GENERAL HISTORIES

Hitti, Philip K. *The Arabs.* New York: Henry Regnery Co., 1960. 274 pp.

Hodgkin, E. C. *The Arabs.* New York: Oxford University Press, 1966. 120 pp.

Lewis, Bernard. *The Arabs in History.* New York: Harper & Row, 1960. 224 pp.

Nutting, Anthony. *The Arabs.* New York: Clarkson N. Potter, Inc., 1964. 416 pp.

GEOGRAPHY

Cressey, George. *Crossroads: Land and Life in Southwest Asia.* New York: J. B. Lippincott, 1962. 592 pp.

Kingsbury, Robert C. and Norman J. G. Pounds. *An Atlas of Middle Eastern Affairs.* New York: Frederick A Praeger, 1964. 117 pp.

Chapter I — Part 2
1914 to May 14, 1948

Begin, Menachem. *The Revolt — Story of the Irgun.* New York: Henry Schuman, 1951. 386 pp.

Crum, Bartley C. *Behind the Silken Curtain.* New York: Simon & Schuster, Inc., 1947. 297 pp. (Anglo-American Committee of Inquiry on Palestine, 1946)

De Novo, John A. *American Interests and Policies in the Middle East, 1900-1939.* Minneapolis: University of Minnesota, 1963. 447 pp.

Feis, Herbert. *The Birth of Israel: The Tousled Diplomatic Bed.* New York: W. W. Norton & Co., 1969. 90 pp.

Frank, Jerold. *The Deed.* New York: Simon & Schuster, 1963. 307 pp. (The assassination of Lord Moyne, November 1944)

Glubb, Sir John Bagot. *A Soldier with the Arabs.* New York: Harper & Brothers, 1957. 458 pp. (Glubb Pasha's memoirs as Commander of Jordan's Arab Legion from 1939 to 1956)

Hadawi, Sami. *Bitter Harvest: Palestine 1914-1967.* New York: New World Press, 1967. 355 pp.

Howard, Harry N. *The King-Crane Commission: An American Inquiry in the Middle East.* Beirut: Khayats, 1963. 369 pp. (Study of the Commission's findings in Syria and Palestine following World War I)

Kimche, Jon and David. *A Clash of Destinies.* New York: Frederick A. Praeger, 1960. 287 pp.

——————— . *The Secret Roads: The Illegal Migration of a People, 1938-1948.* New York: Farrar, Straus & Cudahy. 1955. 223 pp. (Story of the illegal entry of Jews into Palestine)

Longrigg, Stephen. *Oil in the Middle East: Its Discovery and Development.* New York: Oxford University Press, 1968. 3rd ed. 519 pp.

Mardun, Munya. *Haganah.* New York: New American Library, 1964. 295 pp. (Story of the *Haganah* which after 1948 became the Israel Defense Forces)

Monroe, Elizabeth. *Britain's Moment in the Middle East, 1914-1956.* Baltimore: Johns Hopkins Press, 1963. 254 pp.

Sachar, Howard M. *The Emergence of the Middle East, 1914-1924.* New York: Alfred A. Knopf, 1969. 518 pp.

Stein, Leonard. *The Balfour Declaration.* New York: Simon & Schuster, Inc., 1961. 681 pp.

Sykes, Christopher. *Crossroads to Israel: From Balfour to Bevin.* New York and Cleveland: The World Publishing Co., 1966. 404 pp.

Truman, Harry S. *Years of Trial and Hope. Memoirs — Vol. II.* New York: Doubleday & Co., 1956.

Williams, Ann. *Britain and France in the Middle East and North Africa, 1914-1967.* New York: St. Martin's Press, 1968.

Chapter I — Part 3

May 15, 1948 to November 22, 1967

Bell, J. Bowyer. *The Long War: Israel and the Arabs Since 1946.* Englewood Cliffs, N.J.: Prentice Hall, Inc., 1969. 467 pp.

Burns, Lt. Gen. E.L.M. *Between Arab and Israeli.* New York: Ivan Obolensky, Inc., 1963. 336 pp. (The author was Chief of Staff of the United Nations Truce Supervision Organization during 1954-1957 and this book recounts events which took place along the Arab-Israeli Armistice Demarcation Lines at that time)

Campbell, John C. *Defense of the Middle East: Problems of American Policy.* New York: Frederick A. Praeger, 1961. 400 pp. (Development of U.S. policy in the Middle East vis-à-vis Soviet penetration of the area)

Davis, John. *The Evasive Peace: A Study of the Zionist/Arab Problem.* London: John Murray, 1968. 124 pp. (Written by the former Commissioner General of the United Nations Works and Relief Agency for Palestine, this work focuses primarily on the Arab refugee problem)

Dayan, Moshe. *Diary of the Sinai Campaign.* New York: Harper & Row, 1966. 236 pp. (The 1956 Suez Crisis)

Ellis, Harry B. *Challenge in the Middle East: Communist Influence and American Policy.* New York: The Ronald Press, 1960. 238 pp. (Explores Communist influence in the Middle East during the late 1950's)

——————— . *Heritage of the Desert.* New York: The Ronald Press, 1956. 300 pp. (Modern history of the Middle East)

Hurewitz, J. C. *Middle East Politics: The Military Dimension.* New York: Frederick A. Praeger, 1969. 553 pp.

Hutchison, Elmo. *Violent Truce*. New York: Devin Adair Co., 1956. 199 pp. (Observations of events along the Israel-Jordan Armistice Demarcation lines between 1951 and 1955 by a military observer for the United Nations Truce Supervision Organization)

Kerr, Malcolm. *The Arab Cold War: A Study of Ideology in Politics*. New York: Oxford University Press, 1967. 169 pp. (Discusses attempts at bringing about Arab unity between 1958 and 1963)

Kraines, Oscar. *Government and Politics in Israel*. Boston: Houghton Mifflin Co., 1961. 246 pp.

Laqueur, Walter Z. *The Struggle for the Middle East: The Soviet Union and the Middle East, 1958-1968*. New York: Macmillan & Co., 1969.

Lenczowski, George. *United States Interests in the Middle East*. Washington, D. C.: American Enterprise Institute for Public Policy Research, 1968. 132 pp. (Covers the political-strategic, economic and cultural interests in the United States in the Middle East)

Love, Kennett. *Suez: The Twice-Fought War*. New York: McGraw Hill Book Co., 1969. 767 pp. (Recounts in great detail events leading up to the invasion of Suez and the Suez Crisis of 1956)

Nasser, Gamal Abdel. *The Philosophy of the Revolution*. Washington, D.C.: Public Affairs Press, 1955. 102 pp. (Nasser's thoughts on the Egyptian Revolution of 1952)

Nutting, Anthony. *No End of a Lesson*. New York: Clarkson N. Potter, Inc., 1967. 194 pp. (Another look at the Suez Crisis of 1956 by the former Minister of State for Foreign Affairs in Britain)

O'Ballance, Edgar. *The Arab-Israeli War 1948*. London: Faber & Faber, 1956. 220 pp.

Peretz, Don. *Israel and the Palestine Arabs*. Washington, D.C.: Middle East Institute, 1958. 264 pp.

Polk, William R. *The United States and the Arab World*. Cambridge, Mass.: Harvard University Press, 1969 rev. ed. 350 pp.

Safran, Nadav. *From War to War: The Arab-Israeli Confrontation 1948-1967*. New York: Pegasus, 1969. 464 pp.

Stevens, Georgiana G. *Jordan River Partition*. Stanford, Calif.: Stanford University Press, 1965. 90 pp. (An important book for understanding the ongoing dispute over available water for use in agriculture)

Stock, Ernest. *Israel on the Road to Sinai, 1949-1956, with a Sequel on the Six-Day War, 1967.* Ithaca, N.Y.: Cornell University Press, 1967. 284 pp.

von Horn, Maj. Gen. Carl. *Soldiering for Peace.* New York: David McKay Co., 1967. 402 pp. (One section of this book is devoted to peace-keeping in the Middle East between March 1958 and July 1960)

REFERENCE BOOKS

Laqueur, Walter (ed.) *The Israel-Arab Reader: A Documentary History of the Middle East Conflict.* New York: Citadel Press, Inc., 1968. 371 pp. (A compilation of documents, statements, and speeches dating from 1882 to 1967)

Magnus, Ralph H. (ed.) *Documents on the Middle East.* Washington, D.C.: American Foreign Enterprise Institute for Public Policy Research, 1969. 232 pp. (Purpose of this collection of documents is to illustrate the development of United States policies in the Middle East)

The Middle East and North Africa, 1972-1973. 19th ed. London: Europa Press, 1972. 931 pp. (Covers both general topics and individual countries of the Middle East. Excellent reference)

The Middle East: Tricontinental Hub. Washington, D. C.: Government Printing Office, 1968. (A compilation of bibliographic materials on both magazine articles and books, background notes from the State Department on the countries of the Middle East, individual maps, and information on sources of similar materials)

Select Chronology and Background Documents Relating to the Middle East. Washington, D.C.: Government Printing Office, 1969. 287 pp. (Printed for use by the Committee on Foreign Relations of the U.S. Senate, this publication includes an excellent chronology of events which took place between 1946 and 1969 relating to the Middle East)

BOOKS RELATING TO THE MIDDLE EAST CONFLICT
1967 to Present

Avnery, Uri. *Israel Without Zionists: A Plea for Peace in the Middle East.* New York: Macmillan Co., 1968. 215 pp.

Dodd, Peter, and Halim Barakat. *River Without Bridges: A Study of the Exodus of the 1967 Palestinian Arab Refugees.* Beirut: The Institute for Palestine Studies, 1969. 66 pp.

Forrest, A. C. *The Unholy Land.* Old Greenwich, Conn.: Devon-Adair Co., 1972. 178 pp.

Furlonge, Sir Geoffrey. *Palestine Is My Country: The Story of Musa Alami.* New York: Frederick A. Praeger, 1969. 256 pp.

Howe, Irving, and Carl Gershman. *Israel, the Arabs and the Middle East.* New York: Bantam Books, 1972. 440 pp.

Israel Ministry of Foreign Affairs. *Jerusalem: Issues and Perspectives.* Jerusalem: Israel Government Information Division, 1972. 28 pp.

Jiryis, Sabri. *The Arabs in Israel.* Beirut: The Institute for Palestine Studies, 1968. 180 pp.

Khadduri, Majdia D. (ed.) *The Arab-Israeli Impasse.* Washington, D.C.: Robert B. Luce, Inc., 1968. 221 pp.

Khouri, Fred J. *The Arab-Israeli Dilemma.* Syracuse, N. Y.: Syracuse University Press. 1968. 436 pp.

Landau, Julian J. *Israel and the Arabs.* Jerusalem: Israel Communications, 1971. 216 pp.

Peretz, Don, Evan M. Wilson and Richard J. Ward. *A Palestine Entity?* Washington, D.C.: Middle East Institute, 1970. 119 pp.

Pfaff, Richard H. *Jerusalem: Keystone of an Arab-Israeli Settlement.* Washington, D.C.: American Enterprise Institute for Public Policy Research, 1969. 56 pp.

Search for Peace in the Middle East. Philadelphia, Pa.: The American Friends Service Committee, 1970. 75 pp.

Shalem, Diane, and Giora Shamis. *Jerusalem.* Jerusalem: Municipality of Jerusalem, 1971. 119 pp.

Sharabi, Hisham. *Palestine and Israel: The Lethal Dilemma.* New York: Pegasus, 1969. 224 pp.

_____. *Palestine Guerrillas: Their Credibility and Effectiveness.* Washington, D.C.: The Center for Strategic and International Studies, Georgetown University, 1970. 56 pp.

Taylor, Alan R., and Richard N. Tetlie. *Palestine: A Search for Truth.* Washington: Public Affairs Press, 1970. 284 pp.

Wilson, Evan M. *Jerusalem: Key to Peace.* Washington, D.C.: Middle East Institute, 1970. 176 pp.

SELECTED BIBLIOGRAPHY

Chapter II

Country Profiles

EGYPTIAN ARAB REPUBLIC

Ayrout, Henry Habib. *The Egyptian Peasant.* Boston: Beacon Press, 2nd ed. 1967. 167 pp.

Cremeans, Charles D. *The Arabs and the World: Nasser's Arab Nationalist Policy.* New York: Frederick A. Praeger, 1963. 338 pp.

Little, Tom. *Modern Egypt.* New York: Frederick A. Praeger, 1967. 276 pp.

Mahmoud, Zaki Naguib. *The Land and People of Egypt.* Philadelphia: J. B. Lippincott Co., 1959. 127 pp.

Wilber, Donald A. (ed.) *The United Arab Republic — Egypt: Its People, Its Society, Its Culture.* New York: Taplinger Publishing Co. (Human Relations Area Files Press), 1969. 395 pp.

IRAQ

Birdwood, Christopher, *Nuri as-Said: A Study of Arab Leadership.* London: Oxford University Press, 1960. 306 pp.

Fernea, Elizabeth. *Guests of the Sheik.* Garden City, N. Y.: Doubleday & Co., 1965. 333 pp.

Harris, George L. *Iraq: Its People, Its Society, Its Culture.* New York: Taplinger Publishing Co. (Human Relations Area Files Press), 1958. 350 pp.

Thesiger, Wilfred. *The Marsh Arabs.* London: Longmans, Green & Co., 1964. 242 pp.

ISRAEL

Ben-Gurion, David. *Israel: Years of Challenge.* New York: Holt, Rinehart & Winston, 1963. 240 pp.

Bermant, Chaim. *Israel.* New York: Walker & Co., 1967. 224 pp.

Fein, Leonard J. *Israel: Politics and People.* Boston: Little, Brown & Co., 1968. 338 pp.

Israel Today: A Profile. New York: Foreign Policy Association, 1965. 95 pp.

St. John, Robert and the Editors of *Life. Israel.* New York: Time-Life Books (Life World Library Series) rev. ed. 1965. 160 pp.

JORDAN

Harris, George L. *Jordan: Its People, Its Society, Its Culture.* New York: Taplinger Publishing Co. (Human Relations Area Files Press), 1958. 246 pp.

Hussein, H. M. King. *Uneasy Lies the Head.* New York: Bernard Geis Associates, 1962. 306 pp.

Copeland, Paul W. *The Land and People of Jordan.* Philadelphia: J. B. Lippincott Co., 1965. 160 pp.

Sanger, Richard H. *Where the Jordan Flows.* Washington, D. C.: Middle East Institute, 1963. 397 pp.

KUWAIT

Freeth, Zahra. *Kuwait Was My Home.* London: George Allen & Unwin, 1956. 164 pp.

Hewins, Ralph. *A Golden Dream: The Miracle of Kuwait.* London: W. H. Allen, 1963. 317 pp.

Marlowe, John. *The Persian Gulf in the Twentieth Century.* New York: Frederick A. Praeger, 1962. 280 pp.

LEBANON

Hitti, Philip K. *History of Lebanon from the Earliest Times to the Present.* New York: The Macmillan Co., 1957. 584 pp.

Hourani, Albert H. *Syria and Lebanon.* New York: Oxford Press, 1946. 402 pp.

Salibi, K. S. *The Modern History of Lebanon.* New York: Frederick A. Praeger, 1965. 272 pp.

Winder, Viola H. *The Land and People of Lebanon.* Philadelphia: J. B. Lippincott Co., 1965. 160 pp.

LIBYAN ARAB REPUBLIC

Brown, Leon Carl (ed.) *State and Society in Independent North Africa.* Washington, D. C.: Middle East Institute, 1966. 332 pp.

Copeland, Paul W. *The Land and People of Libya.* Philadelphia: J. B. Lippincott Co., 1967. 158 pp.

Khadduri, Majid. *Modern Libya: A Study in Political Development.* Baltimore: Johns Hopkins Press, 1963. 404 pp.

Wright, John. *Libya.* New York: Frederick A. Praeger, 1969. 304 pp.

SAUDI ARABIA

Asad, Muhammad. *The Road to Mecca.* New York: Simon & Schuster, 1954. 400 pp.

Harris, George L. *Saudi Arabia: Its People, Its Society, Its Culture.* New Haven: Human Relations Area Files Press, 1959. 367 pp.

Howarth, David. *The Desert King: Ibn Sa'ud.* New York: McGraw-Hill, 1964. 307 pp.

Morris, James. *The Hashemite Kings.* New York: Pantheon Books, Inc., 1959. 208 pp.

Thesiger, Wilfred. *Arabian Sands.* New York: E. P. Dutton & Co., 1959. 326 pp.

SUDAN

Collins, Robert O. and Robert L. Tignor. *Egypt and the Sudan.* Englewood Cliffs, N.J.: Prentice-Hall, 1967. 180 pp.

El Mahdi, Mandour. *A Short History of the Sudan.* New York: Oxford U. P., 1965. 154 pp.

Holt, P. M. *A Modern History of the Sudan.* New York: Grove Press, 1961. 241 pp.

Jackson, H. C. *Behind the Modern Sudan*. London: Macmillan & Co., 1955. 266 pp.

Moorhead, Alan. *The Blue Nile.* New York: Harper & Row, 1962. 241 pp.

Wingate, Ronald. *Wingate of the Sudan*. London: John Murray Ltd., 1955. 274 pp.

SYRIAN ARAB REPUBLIC

Copeland, Paul W. *The Land and People of Syria*. Philadelphia: J. B. Lippincott, 1964. 160 pp.

Hitti, Philip K. *Syria, A Short History*. New York: The Macmillan Co., 1959. 271 pp.

Seale, Patrick. *The Struggle for Syria: A Study of Post-War Arab Politics, 1945-1958*. New York: Oxford Press, 1965. 366 pp.

Ziadeh, Nicola. *Syria and Lebanon*. New York: Frederick A. Praeger, 1957. 312 pp.

Tibawi, A. L. *A Modern History of Syria Including Lebanon and Palestine*. New York: St. Martin's Press, 1970. 421 pp.

YEMEN

Bethmann, Erich W. *Yemen on the Threshold*. Washington, D. C.: American Friends of the Middle East, 1960. 78 pp.

Ingrams, Harold. *The Yemen: Imams, Rulers and Revolutions*. London: John Murray Ltd., 1963. 164 pp.

Macro, Eric. *Yemen and the Western World, 1571-1964*. New York: Frederick A. Praeger, 1967. 160 pp.

Schmidt, Dana Adams. *Yemen: The Unknown War*. New York: Holt, Rinehart & Winston, 1968. 316 pp.

Wenner, Manfred W. *Modern Yemen*. Baltimore: Johns Hopkins Press, 1967. 256 pp.

OTHER

Stewart, Desmond and the Editors of *Life*. *The Arab World*. New York: Time-Life Books (Life World Library Series), rev. ed. 1968. 160 pp.

SELECTED BIBLIOGRAPHY

Chapter III

Judaism, Christianity and Islam

General Reference

Aharoni, Yohanan and Michael Avi-Yonah. *The Macmillan Bible Atlas.* New York: The Macmillan Co., 1968. 264 pp.

Arberry, A. J. (ed.) *Religion in the Middle East.* New York: Cambridge University Press, 1969.
     Vol. I: *Judaism; Christianity.* 600 pp.
     Vol. II: *Islam: The Three Religions in Concord and Conflict.* 750 pp.

Hollis, Christopher and Ronald Brownrigg. *Holy Places: Jewish, Christian and Muslim Monuments in the Holy Land.* New York: Frederick A. Praeger, 1969. 224 pp.

Jurji, Edward J. *The Great Religions of the Modern World.* Princeton, N.J.: Princeton University Press, 1946. 387 pp.

Kramer, Samuel N. *Cradle of Civilization.* New York: Time, Inc. (Great Ages of Man Series), 1967. 182 pp.

McCasland, S. Vernon, Grace Carins and David Yu. *Religions of the World.* New York: Random House, 1969. 760 pp.

National Geographic Book Service. *Everyday Life in Bible Times.* Washington, D.C.: National Geographic, 1967.

Noss, John B. *Man's Religions* (4th ed.) New York: Macmillan Co., 1969. 598 pp.

Welles, Sam (ed.) *The World's Great Religions.* New York: Time Inc., 1957. 310 pp.

Primitive Religion

Albright, William F. *From the Stone Age to Christianity.* Garden City, N.Y.: Doubleday Anchor Books, 1956.

Brandon, S.G.F. *Religion in Ancient History,* New York: Charles Scribner's Sons, 1969. 411 pp.

James, E. O. *Ancient Gods.* New York: G. P. Putnam's Sons, 1960. 359 pp.

——————— . *Prehistoric Religion.* New York: Frederick A. Praeger, 1957. 300 pp.

Smart, Ninian. *The Religious Experience of Mankind.* Charles Scribner's Sons, 1969. 576 pp.

Judaism

Albright, William F. *Yahweh and the Gods of Canaan.* New York: Doubleday & Co., 1968. 290 pp.

Ausubel, Nathan. *The Book of Jewish Knowledge.* New York: Crown Publishers, Inc., 1964. 560 pp. (Encyclopedic resource book)

Bernstein, Philip S. *What the Jews Believe.* New York: Farrar, Straus & Young, 1950. 100 pp.

Dimont, Max I. *Jews, God and History.* New York: Simon & Schuster, Inc., 1962. 463 pp.

Fast, Howard. *The Jews.* New York: Dial Press, Inc., 1968. 334 pp.

Finkelstein, Louis (ed.) *The Jews: Their History, Culture and Religion.* (Two vols.) New York: Harper & Brothers, 1949.

Frost, Stanley Brice. *Patriarchs & Prophets.* Montreal: McGill University Press, 1963. 232 pp.

Josephus. *The Jewish War.* Baltimore: Penguin Books, 1959.

Schauss, Hayyim. *The Jewish Festivals.* New York: Union of American Hebrew Congregations, 1961. 319 pp.

Stack, Hagen. *Living Personalities of the Old Testament.* New York: Harper & Row, 1964. 147 pp.

Christianity

Attwater, Donald. *The Christian Churches of the East.* (Two vols.) Milwaukee: The Bruce Publishing Co., 1961.

Badeau, John S. *The Lands Between.* New York: Friendship Press, 1958. 138 pp.

Benz, Ernest. *The Eastern Orthodox Church: Its Thought and Life.* Garden City, N.Y.: Doubleday & Co., 1963. 230 pp.

Cowie, Leonard W. *The March of the Cross.* New York: McGraw-Hill, 1962. 214 pp.

Daniel-Rops, Henri. *Daily Life in the Time of Jesus.* New York: Hawthorn Books, 1962. 500 pp.

Schmemann, Alexander. *Historical Road to Eastern Orthodoxy.* New York: Holt, Rinehart & Winston, 1963. 342 pp.

Islam

Andrae, Tor. *Mohammed: The Man and His Faith.* New York: Harper & Row, 1960. 194 pp.

Guillaume, Alfred. *Islam.* Baltimore: Pelican Books, 1968. 210 pp.

Payne, Robert. *The Holy Sword.* New York: Harper & Brothers, 1959. 335 pp.

Pickthall, Mohammed Marmaduke. *The Meaning of the Glorious Koran.* New York: New American Library, 1955. 464 pp.

Stewart, Desmond. *Early Islam.* New York: Time Inc., (Great Ages of Man Series), 1967. 192 pp.

Watt, W. Montgomery. *Muhammad: Prophet and Statesman.* London: Oxford University Press, 1961. 250 pp.

Wilson, J. Christy. *Introducing Islam.* New York: Friendship Press, 1954. 64 pp.